C

THE BASICS

Critical Theory: The Basics brings clarity to a topic that is confusingly bandied about with various meanings today in popular and academic culture.

First defined by Max Horkheimer in the 1930s, "critical theory" now extends far beyond its original German context around the Frankfurt School and the emergence of Nazism. We now often speak of critical theories of race, gender, anti-colonialism, and so forth. This book introduces especially the core program of the first-generation of the Frankfurt School (including Horkheimer, Theodor W. Adorno, Erich Fromm, and Herbert Marcuse), and shows how this program remains crucial to understanding the problems, ideologies, and systems of the modern world, including capitalism, racism, sexism, and the enduring problems of colonialism. It explores basic questions like:

- What is critical theory?
- What can critical theory be? What *should* it be?
- Why and how does critical theory remain vital to understanding the contemporary world, including notions of self, society, politics, art, religion, culture, race, gender, and class?

With suggestions for further reading, this book is an ideal starting point for anyone seeking an accessible but robust introduction to the richness and complexity of this tradition and to its continuing importance today.

Martin Shuster is Professor of Philosophy and the Isaac Swift Distinguished Professor of Jewish Studies at the University of North Carolina at Charlotte. In addition to many journal articles, public essays, and edited volumes, he is the author of *Autonomy after Auschwitz: Adorno, German Idealism, and Modernity* (2014), *New Television: The Aesthetics and Politics of a Genre* (2017), and *How to Measure a World? A Philosophy of Judaism* (2021).

The Basics Series

The Basics is a highly successful series of accessible guidebooks which provide an overview of the fundamental principles of a subject area in a jargon-free and undaunting format.

Intended for students approaching a subject for the first time, the books both introduce the essentials of a subject and provide an ideal springboard for further study. With over 50 titles spanning subjects from artificial intelligence (AI) to women's studies, *The Basics* are an ideal starting point for students seeking to understand a subject area.

Each text comes with recommendations for further study and gradually introduces the complexities and nuances within a subject.

For a full list of titles in this series, please visit www.routledge.com/The-Basics/book-series/B

CRITICAL THEORY

THE BASICS

Martin Shuster

Routledge
Taylor & Francis Group

NEW YORK AND LONDON

First published 2024
by Routledge
605 Third Avenue, New York, NY 10158

and by Routledge
4 Park Square, Milton Park, Abingdon, Oxon, OX14 4RN

Routledge is an imprint of the Taylor & Francis Group, an informa business

Library of Congress Cataloging-in-Publication Data
Names: Shuster, Martin, author.
Title: Critical theory: the basics / Martin Shuster.
Description: New York, NY : Routledge, 2024. |
Series: The basics; vol. 210 | Includes bibliographical references and index |
Identifiers: LCCN 2023047578 | ISBN 9781032061559 (hardback) |
ISBN 9781032061566 (paperback) | ISBN 9781003200963 (ebook)
Subjects: LCSH: Critical theory.
Classification: LCC HM480 .S58 2024 | DDC 142—dc23/eng/20231019
LC record available at https://lccn.loc.gov/202304757

ISBN: 978-1-032-06155-9 (hbk)
ISBN: 978-1-032-06156-6 (pbk)
ISBN: 978-1-003-20096-3 (ebk)

DOI: 10.4324/9781003200963

Typeset in Bembo
by codeMantra

For my mother

CONTENTS

ACKNOWLEDGMENTS

Exactly 180 years ago, in September of 1843, Karl Marx wrote a letter to Arnold Ruge, a fellow philosopher and political actor. That letter has now become quite famous, for in it Marx writes that, "if we have no business with the construction of the future or with organizing it for all time, there can still be no doubt about the task confronting us at present: the ruthless criticism of the existing order, ruthless in that it will shrink neither from its own discoveries, nor from conflict with the powers that be." I do not know of a more compact or more inspiring understanding of the impulses behind and the tasks of criticism. I regularly thought about this quote while writing this book; I also frequently found myself drawn to a particular soundtrack—Fugazi's lyrics, "to surge and refine, to rage and define—ourselves against your line," oftentimes accompanied these thoughts and my work. I take it that both together urge that our present is no different than earlier times: there is still work to be pursued, criticism to be had, authorities to be called into question, paths to be trod.

This is one way to understand why Max Horkheimer would claim in "Traditional and Critical Theory," that the very "future of humanity depends on the existence today of the critical attitude." I don't take this as hyperbole. Horkheimer notes that this critical attitude, that critical theory, "of course contains within it elements from traditional theories and from our declining culture generally." This isn't an unimportant addition: if we know how the world works, then we must realize that planetary collapse or destruction remains a standing, if not increasing, possibility. This too has been on my mind, especially as war, systemic ills, natural disasters, and financial crises mount. With these later thoughts, though, Katie Stelmanis's simple lyrics continue to resonate with me and animated other portions of writing: "there's only one way: future politics."

So much for my process (think of these paragraphs as a sort of epigraph, made necessary by the ways in which certain presses now avoid epigraphs for legal reasons). What follows, then, are the various notes of thanks that I owe. My fear in writing the acknowl-edgments is always that I have forgotten someone; if I have, please know it is unintentional.

I am especially grateful to Espen Hammer, Owen Hulatt, Ada Jaarsma, Kathy Kiloh, and Henry Pickford for reading earlier versions of this manuscript and offering so many helpful and encouraging comments on it. This would be a far, far worse book without their comments and I am very grateful to them. I am also grateful to Marc Stratton and Andy Beck at Routledge, especially the latter's editorial guidance on this project. Thank you also to Gareth Vaughan for copyediting.

I am equally grateful to friends and colleagues with whom I have discussed things that ended up here or with whom I have corre-sponded, whether specifically regarding the Frankfurt School or with regard to critical theory more generally, whether in theory or in practice. In this vein, I'm grateful to John Abromeit, Asaf Anger-mann, Jen Bess, Emily Billo, Donald Bloxham, Kent Brintnall, Julie Chernov, Jazmine Contreras, John Cox, Julia Kolchinsky Dasbach, James Dator, Seble Dawit, Evan Dawley, Hent de Vries, Tarek Dika, John Drabinski, Ann Duncan, Rick Elmore, Irline François, William Freeman, Samir Gandesha, Daniela Ginsburg, Gordon Hull, Nyasha Grayman-Simpson, Ailish Hopper, Alex Host, Tam-sin Kimoto, Reuben Krauson, Sandra Laugier, Jenny Lenkowski, Iain Macdonald, Joanne Maguire, Paola Marrati, Flo Martin, April Oettinger, Trevor Pearce, Kathryn Reklis, Amy Roza, William Sherman, Ian Shifrin, Tina Shull, Oshrat Silberbusch, Lissa Skitolsky, Shannon Sullivan, Joyce Tsai, Agnieszka Tuszynska, Joe Weiss, and Rick Werner.

Writing this book was not easy because in the middle of writing I moved to a new city and started a new job at the University of North Carolina at Charlotte. The fabulous colleagues I've met here have been incredibly warm and I'm grateful to my entire department and to UNCC for such a lively, kind, and supportive environment. I am also grateful to the various classes I've taught throughout the years on topics related to critical theory. I have been lucky to have incredible students—teaching them critical theory has been a privilege, and I have learned an immense amount from doing so.

Finally, I am grateful to my immediate and extended family who also sometimes served as an unknowing springboard for some of these ideas, but mostly who just provided the entire large, beautiful frame around which such projects make sense.

This book is dedicated to my mother, Raisa "Lyalya" Shuster, who died entirely too young. While my mother was not "trained" as a critical theorist, she certainly embodied for and instilled in me many of its most fundamental impulses, including especially a sensitivity to needless suffering, a drive for justice, and a love (albeit one tempered by critical distance) of human endeavors like art, society, and religion. In addition to being a talented, wise, and remarkable person in her own right, she was most remarkable to me for being my mother, and her loss continues to be a wound in my world. May her memory always be for a blessing.

INTRODUCTION
Suffering

1. WHY CRITICAL THEORY?

It is 2023. Across the globe, every 20 seconds, a child dies from a preventable disease. Almost 3 billion women do not have the same life and job choices as men. Most of the world's population lives on around $5.50 a day. A little over 20 billionaires own as much wealth as half of the people in the world.

These problems are not exclusive to certain regions. For example, the United States is one of the wealthiest countries in the entire history of the world. Yet roughly nine million children are at risk for hunger.

These problems have to do with how we have organized ourselves—politically, economically, and socially. *Things could be different.* If these statistics gall you, stick in your craw, somehow shake you to your very being, then you are entering the standpoint of critical theory. It may be that such a standpoint, as one of the architects of this theoretical tradition once suggested, is central to "the future of humanity."

Invoking the future of humanity may perhaps not be the best way to start a book (the stakes are so high that almost anything that follows will likely fall short of them). Yet it nonetheless may also be true.

You perhaps picked this book up for different reasons. You may be curious about critical theory. You may already know something about the so-called Frankfurt School, a school of social theory and philosophy established in Frankfurt, Germany, associated with the Institute for Social Research (established in 1923—exactly 100

DOI: 10.4324/9781003200963-1

years ago of this writing). The Institute continues its operation, but the approach it introduced—critical theory—extends far beyond its confines, and now often means many different things to many different people. You may thereby even be interested in the current United States context, where invocations of "critical race theory" continue to rage as certain teaching methods and books are attacked or even banned in certain states.

This book operates with these contexts in mind, and with the assumption that even 100 years later, critical theory remains important and relevant. Despite all our technological sophistication, we live in grim times, with the possibility of almost complete planetary destruction by no means unimaginable. The Frankfurt School felt like they lived in a similar time, with one of the directors of the Institute once describing their work in a letter to a colleague as "destined to being passed on through the night that is approaching: a kind of message in a bottle."

2. WHAT THIS BOOK IS

The book that follows is written for the novice with the aim of presenting an understanding of critical theory as inspired by the Frankfurt School. The bottle is waiting; let's open it. At the same time, our moment requires its own critical theory, and so for this reason, I do not merely reconstruct the positions of the various members of the Frankfurt School, choosing instead sometimes to modify or extend their thinking in ways that strike me as fruitful. It is for this reason that I generally use "critical theory" to denote both the explicit positions I attribute to the Frankfurt School as much as positions that may be inspired by, derived from, or related to theirs; it is this way of proceeding that allows me to draw connections throughout to other traditions of critical theory. There are now many good introductions to and histories of the Frankfurt School, and this book does not aim to replace those. Read those books. They give more context and even frame many of the issues differently. For example, most books proceed historically, tracing the development of the Frankfurt School over time. This book proceeds conceptually, presenting a reconstructed core program of critical theory that remains crucial and compelling. I use the term "a reconstructed core program" intentionally to highlight that what's termed the Frankfurt School has had dozens of members and has now existed for a hundred years. There are conflicting views to be mined from the Frankfurt School. Sometimes members changed their views over time or disagreed with each other. For example, one of the first members of the Institute for Social Research, Erich Fromm (1900–1980), writes to the philosopher Raya Dunayevskaya (1910–1987) in 1976, years after he had split from the Institute, that he sees critical theory as a sort of "hoax" created so that they could speak of "critical theory in order not to say Marx's theory." I will have more to say about this but suffice it to say right now that I do not agree with Fromm. (Fromm's 1939 split from the Institute, discussed more in Chapter 2, was not amicable, nor was the relationship between the Frankfurt School and Marx so straightforward, as I will shortly elaborate.)

Scholars speak of "generations" of the Frankfurt School, acknowledging that the concerns of its members shifted in response to developments within the Institute and within the world. This is the first lesson of critical theory: it is a program that must perpetually be pursued anew. It shifts as the world shifts. At the same time, especially when one looks to the so-called first-generation of the Frankfurt School, there are certain common aims. Much of this book is oriented around explaining those aims so that they can be marshaled, renewed, repurposed. These aims remain pressing, and they equally continue to be marginalized within contemporary society (if not also philosophy). For this reason, unless specified, references throughout this book to "the Frankfurt School" are always to the first-generation of the Frankfurt School. No doubt there have been many subsequent developments in Frankfurt School critical theory, especially in the work of members like Jürgen Habermas, Axel Honneth, and Rainer Forst. I do not pursue these developments in the detail that they would require. While I will say a little more about why in subsequent chapters, I note here only that these developments have a different enough character as to largely require their own introductory texts. The nature of this difference can be glossed in many ways, but a unifying feature may be a shying away from the radicalism of the first-generation and its largely oppositional if not pessimistic relationship to the entire contemporary social, economic, and political order. Such a shift away from radicalism has led to an increasing formalism and institutionalism in subsequent generations, to a noticeable acceptance of contemporary liberalism, and to a concomitant decreasing interest in aesthetics. In *The Domestication of Critical Theory* (2016), the political theorist Michael Thompson goes so far as to claim that subsequent generations have "domesticated" critical theory. More pertinent in the present context, though, is philosopher Max Pensky's suggestion in "Third generation critical theory" (1998) that subsequent developments have run against a core aim of the first-generation of the Frankfurt School, which was "to be envisioned as an interdisciplinary cooperative enterprise, in which an interlocking constellation of various theoretical-critical interventions in modern culture would coalesce to form a basis for organized oppositional political action." In short, neither the theoretical nor the practical methods were entirely fixed but rather as Pensky puts it, "critical theory was to liquidate the tradition of theory *within* theory itself." What subsequent developments in Frankfurt School critical theory (and critical theory more generally) reveal above all, though, is an established tradition, one whose aims have in fact either paradoxically never been achieved (first-generation) or allegedly may be unachievable and must be tweaked (subsequent generations). Perhaps there is something to be said, then, for returning to this first generation of critical theory, especially in the present context, not somehow now finally to establish the tradition "properly," but, given the state of the world, to recover and repurpose where necessary its radical aims in the current moment, and perhaps thereby even to refashion any understanding of such a "tradition of theory within theory itself."

3. SUBJECTIVITY, NORMATIVITY, AND SECOND NATURE

One way to see how the Frankfurt School could animate such related but distinct approaches over time would be to stress that at a very high altitude, the Frankfurt School participates in one of the oldest impulses of Western philosophy: it examines the relationship between humans and their world. To bring this thought into focus, note that humans are a distinct kind of object in the world. We are an object that is capable of thinking, capable of reflecting on itself as an object that can think. It is thereby in fact not entirely appropriate to refer to ourselves as objects. Philosophers now use the term "subject" to register this significance. In antiquity, though, for example in the thought of Aristotle (384–322 BCE), the notion of a subject captured the material substratum underlying something: it was that to which predicates were applied (in the *Metaphysics*, Aristotle uses the remarkable phrase: "that of which the other things are said, but which is itself not further said of any other thing"). Think of the idea of "subject matter," where what we're talking about is captured exactly through the application of predicates. This apple is green, firm, crunchy, sweet, and so forth. Such a notion of subject fit with a world where things were taken to be there by purposeful design. Humans were one more feature of an orderly and rational world, themselves capable of discovering its order by means of their rational capacities. In politics, a political subject evinced the same formal relationship: someone was *subjected* to kingship, oftentimes divinely ordained.

Such premodern notions, though, barely fit our contemporary notion of a subject. With modernity, the notion of a subject underwent change. As the philosopher Susan Neiman argues in *Evil in Modern Thought* (2002), the brutal Lisbon earthquake of 1755 generated the "birth pangs of a sadder but wiser era that has learned to live on its own." No longer did the world evince purposeful design. Scientific innovation since then has only raised more forcefully the question of how much of this world must be understood as humanly constituted (think now even of the alleged rise of an Anthropocene era where humans affect the planet on a geological scale). Where we once saw design, we now generally just see an opportunity for greater human intervention. In modern Western thought, this shift was accelerated by philosophers like René Descartes (1596–1650) and Jean-Jacques Rousseau (1712–1778). By the middle of the 17th century, Descartes stressed the radical independence of the human mind from nature. While in the middle of the 18th century, Rousseau argued—in a way that would be pivotal especially for the German philosophical traditions that inspire the Frankfurt School—that there are moral and political implications to such independence. Such independence rests not on some fact about the world but rather on the fact that humans are the sorts of creatures that can raise questions about whether particular facts *ought* to be a certain way. Philosophers term such questions normative ones: what ought to be done, what ought to be believed, what ought to be hoped for, and so forth (the philosopher Wilfrid Sellars [1912–1989] wrote in "Truth and 'Correspondence'" [1962] that such questions are "fraught with ought").

Such questions are normative because to answer them we refer to a norm: you ought to do this because of that. And such questions are ubiquitous: What ought to be done after I have been harmed by you? What ought to be believed after seeing this commercial? After watching this film? How ought I assess your claims of love towards me? Ought police be able to do that? How ought we see this country's past? What ought I do with my time? Contemporary society everywhere suggests that such normative questions can simply be answered by discovering the facts: just think of the number of popular articles about what "neuroscience" tells us about this or that, as if it is mere *natural* facts that explain what we ought to believe or do. But this is just another means of maintaining the status quo, as if the way things stand is the way they ought to stand (because, say, they have allegedly evolved to be this way, or because biologically or neurologically they just are). While there are of course basic physical facts about what it means to be human (that we need to breathe, to sleep, to eat, that we age and will die, and so forth), such facts can be—and are—actualized in a great variety of ways. As the philosopher Robert Pippin notes, this is especially true when I am deliberating from *my own* perspective, for when I decide what *I* ought to believe or what *I* ought to do, no one except me can settle or determine matters for me (I may in fact ignore or deny any fact, any reason, any claim, any suggestion you say I ought to believe or take seriously). As Pippin puts it in "Natural and Normative" (2009), "I cannot simply stand by, waiting to see what my highly and complexly evolved neurobiological system will do. The system doesn't make the decision, I do—and for reasons that I find compelling, or that, at least, outweigh countervailing considerations."

In philosophy, "subject" thereby now refers to a capacity for self-consciousness, a capacity that has an irreducibly normative, and thereby a moral and political, dimension. We trade in reasons, and we may assess whether the reasons are sound or unsound, compelling or uncompelling, and why. Human judgment by means of norms is key. Such a picture of things is quite different from earlier approaches in philosophy, where it was allegedly just a matter of discovering features of a world. For example, questions about the relationship between evil and nature were often mediated by a story about the fact that nature evinced some sort of design. This tradition received a powerful expression by the philosopher G.W. Leibniz (1646–1716) who in his eponymously titled *Theodicy* (1710), coined the notion of "theodicy" as denoting the potential vindication of the goodness of God in the face of the existence of evil in nature. Although not the first to do so in the history of philosophy, Leibniz rigorously and powerfully argued that evil in nature is part of a broader divine plan. God in fact creates the best of all possible worlds, and the presence of evil in it is required for the world to be the best. Just a little more goodness or a little less evil would make the world no longer the best over the entire course of its existence. Although Voltaire (1694–1778) quickly mocked it in *Candide* (1730) by asking that "if this is the best of all possible worlds, what are the others," Leibniz's claim is difficult to dispute given his assumptions about ultimate reality, since to do so seems to require knowledge of the course of this world in its entirety. Note, though, that even so a normative question can still be raised about such a view. For example, the writer Fyodor Dostoevsky (1821–1881) asks in *The Brothers Karamazov* (1880), whether God can be justified in having created the world in the first place. Perhaps, if the world involves the suffering of even one innocent child, then it ought never to have been created (indeed such a question may even be asked even if God were to address us directly; not even omnipotence can settle such a normative question unless we take omnipotence to be important to doing so).

Normative questions, including how they may or may not be answered, animate strands of critical theory, past and present. Theodor W. Adorno (1903–1969), one of the most prominent members of the Frankfurt School, wrote in *Negative Dialectics* (1966), that "the earthquake of Lisbon sufficed to cure Voltaire of the theodicy of Leibniz," but "the visible disaster of the first nature was insignificant in comparison with the second, social one." Adorno's invocation of "second nature" here hearkens to the fact that our social world oftentimes appears to us as entirely natural, as if the way things are is the way they must be. On such a view, we think of world as a sort of brute fact (we frequently even say: "it is what it is"). Things appear natural, immutable, inevitable. The philosopher G.W.F. Hegel (1770–1831) used the term "second nature" to account for how the humanly constructed world around us often appears natural to us, as if it apparently can't be changed (an idea that the Frankfurt School inherits). Many features of human organization have appeared natural throughout history, from the alleged irrationality of women to the inferiority of so-called "savages." Such features appeared natural and unchangeable until they didn't; until they weren't. As the author Ursula Le Guin (1929–2018) put it, even "the divine right of kings" once seemed "inescapable," but in fact "any human power can be resisted and changed by human beings." Governments, customs, laws, practices, habits, and so forth are humanly made and maintained. Humans organize their world (as the punk band Bad Religion puts it: "you are the government"). Whether things ought to be a certain way is a normative question that can always be raised. And such a question can be raised at any moment, in any context.

Adorno delivered an early address called "The Idea of Natural History" (1931), where he argued that we must rethink our very notions of both history and nature, since the former can oftentimes appear natural, the latter as historical. The two in fact perpetually mediate one another, standing in tension, one incapable of being thought without the other. In his later lectures *History and Freedom* (1964/1965), Adorno develops the thought as follows: humans reach a point where "the laws of nature [are] capable of being abrogated." He explains his meaning with the image that even "the blind *continuation* of eating and being eaten" can be jettisoned once humans have "achieved self-consciousness." In other words, once humans are capable of reflective—normative—thought, then even allegedly basic activities like survival and procreation can be repudiated and rejected (as, for example, in various streams of antinatalism, or, in a quite different register, certain understandings of Christian sacrifice). Second nature is then the locus for a range of questions, especially to the extent that historical developments may appear natural as easily as nature itself may appear as historical. About the former, just think of the way in which certain sexual or dietary practices are claimed as "most" natural (e.g., "Paleo" diets). About the latter, think of how even the notion of a natural resource is determined by market forces, or how the idea of a natural space may be determined by the contingent boundaries of what is or is not a park or a reserve. Adorno urges philosophical investigation exactly into the point at which nature and history meet.

4. CRITICAL THEORY, NEEDLESS SUFFERING, AND IDEOLOGY

Needless suffering is exactly one such prominent nexus between nature and history. Such suffering suggests, at the very least, that it ought not to exist. Just think of a pain you experience—part of the pain seems to be a demand that it go away. Things could be different. Things *ought to be* different. To bring this point into focus, note that the Frankfurt School's approach emerged from the crucible of two world wars. The destruction and suffering these wars produced is almost unimaginable, with deaths between them equaling more than 120 million people. The writer Jonathan Littell calculates in a remarkable passage in his historical novel *The Kindly Ones* (2006) that in a four-year period, from 1941 to 1945, "we have an average of 572,043 dead per month, 131,410 dead per week, 18,722 dead per day, 782 dead per hour, and 13.04 dead per minute, every minute of every hour of every day of every week of every month of every year." The brutalities unleashed—total war, mass starvation, chemical and nuclear warfare, genocide—continue to haunt us. The scope of suffering involved cannot be limited merely to death toll numbers. As the Soviet dissident Aleksandr Solzhenitsyn (1918–2008) suggested in another context, death is only one aspect of such suffering, so much so that, "when we count up the millions of those who died ... we forget to multiply them by two or three." Equally, such atrocities are not unrelated to earlier European atrocities perpetrated under the banner of colonialism in the Americas, Asia, and Africa. The thinker and politician Aimé Césaire (1913–2008) claimed in *Discourse on Colonialism* (1950) that such earlier horrors have generally been overlooked exactly because they were directed "only to non-European peoples." There are direct lines, for example, from the brutal conditions of the Shark Island concentration camp in Germany's African colonies to the brutal conditions of later Nazi camps. There are here then also potential connections already from the context of the Frankfurt School to the context of other kinds of critical theory (e.g., anti-colonial theory, critical theories of race and gender, and so forth).

Critical theory starts with the claim that needless suffering ought not to exist. That such suffering is produced in a systemic way because of the way that we have organized ourselves is the motor that drives critical theory. Phenomena like colonialism, imperialism, and Nazism are not demonic instantiations of pure evil; they are rather human possibilities, actualized by human subjects acting for a great variety of reasons. And crucially these possibilities could have been avoided: humans could have organized themselves differently. That such kinds of suffering continue to exist makes critical theory still relevant. We still can organize ourselves differently. There are, for example, currently 32 million refugees in the world. These are people who have no home, who have been displaced because of the way the world is organized. These numbers are extreme: 32 million people is a greater number than the populations of more than 185 countries. In a relatively short time, this number of refugees will double, then it will triple. Adorno strikes a related moral tone in "Late Capitalism or Industrial Society?" (1968), when he notes that "the fact that the extended arm of mankind can reach distant, empty planets but is incapable of establishing a permanent peace on earth makes visible the absurd goal towards which the social dialectic is moving." If we acknowledge that certain systemic problems exist only because humans have organized—made—their world a certain way, then we must also acknowledge that the world could be such that these problems didn't exist. Such a normative claim is part and parcel of the approach of critical theory. *Things could be different.* In short, we can mitigate such suffering. Yet we do not. The reasons why may involve a variety of factors: we may not agree on what to do, we may not agree about or even acknowledge the suffering, we may think we are doing something when we are not, or we may not even know what to do (just to name a few). Some kinds of ignorance may be accidental, but others may be structural. Emerging here is a notion of ideology: we may have false or problematic beliefs about what's going on around us and/or about what's possible. Such beliefs may be generated, intentionally or unintentionally, by the structures of society and the sorts of relations of domination present around us (and it is not by accident that in *The Idea of a Critical Theory* [1981], the philosopher Raymond Geuss located ideology as the great thematic concern of the critical theory of the Frankfurt School).

Needless suffering is involved with the question of ideology, especially around the relationship between nature and history. To see this, note that not all forms of suffering are alike. Neither are all kinds of suffering humanly created. That every human being dies, for example, is a biological fact, one that may cause suffering. So does the fact that human beings die from accidents. Such cases may be mitigated or minimized (say, by living well into old age or by making accidents less likely). They cannot (yet?) be abolished. People also die because other people kill them (out of malice or rage or love or countless other reasons). Perhaps such kinds of suffering are unavoidable when humans live amidst other humans. What's central for critical theory, though, is the fact that a great many people die in *avoidable* ways. They die because some kinds of suffering are structurally and/or systemically produced. Such suffering is presented as necessary or natural when it is in fact contingent and socially modifiable. People die because they are born in certain areas or to certain classes, religions, races, genders, or without certain abilities. They die because their lives are not valued as much as other lives. As the philosopher Judith Butler points out in *Precarious Life* (2004), they die because certain lives do "not even qualify as 'grievable.'" For example, it is still common in the United States media to refer to the Iraq War (2003–2011) as a mere "misstep" even though it was a gruesome war that led to immense Iraqi casualties, rested on faulty evidence, and continues to produce suffering. Such language reveals the kinds of value the American media imputes to the lives of Iraqis. Such examples can be multiplied (many marginalized lives fall into a similar category of being hardly considered). Relatedly, but speaking more generally, the first-generation of Frankfurt School theorists frequently pointed out that humans possess the capacity to feed everyone on the planet. Yet people still starve, and food is in fact wasted by the tons.

When we focus on needless suffering, we also recognize the possibility of changing or ending the systems that produce such suffering. Adorno takes up a thought of the philosopher Friedrich Nietzsche (1844–1900), summing things up with the idea that:

"woe says go." Such an impulse raises the most significant questions of critical theory:

- What are these systemic structures? How do we discover and assess them?
- How do we conceive a world without them? What are the alternatives?
- What do we need to do in order to do away with such systemic ills? How do we actualize these alternatives?

Critical theory, thereby, already always concerns itself equally with theory as much as practice. An influence here is the philosopher Karl Marx (1818–1883) who claimed in "Theses on Feuerbach" (1845) that "philosophers have hitherto only interpreted the world in various ways, the point is to change it." And equally, there is emerging here a sort of positive project revolving around the sort of freedom or maturity required to pursue critical theory, which is difficult and requires some expertise or training (all of this must also still be detailed—at the very least, though, note that needless suffering suggests freedom from such suffering).

5. THE FRANKFURT SCHOOL AND MARX

The invocation of Marx may make certain readers (especially in the United States), suspicious or uncomfortable. It is worth reflecting on this discomfort or suspicion. One possibility is that such uneasiness is guided by a justifiable moral outrage at the brutality of regimes like the Soviet Union or Cambodia, who claimed to be communist (and claimed to be inspired by Marx). Another possibility, however, is that this apprehension reflects a desire to avoid critically assessing the ills of capitalism (an assessment Marx was deeply interested in). We may share the former moral outrage while rejecting the latter willed ignorance. The Frankfurt School believed all systemic forms of brutality require critique.

Still, the Frankfurt School's relationship to Marx and Marxism merits commentary. The first director of the Frankfurt School, Carl Grünberg (1861–1940), was a committed Marxist who understood Marx's analysis of political economy generally in non-philosophical, social scientific terms. Similarly, the earliest members of the

Institute were all steeped in Marx's thought, registered excitement about the possibility of revolution, and oftentimes had some involvement with working class parties in Germany. Grünberg, however, only served as director for five years, leaving after suffering a stroke. When Max Horkheimer (1895–1973) took over as director in 1930, the Institute began to pivot, becoming far less traditional and heterodox in its orientation. Horkheimer and the prominent first-generation of the Institute certainly incorporated Marx's analyses of capitalism and modern society, but they were by no means traditional Marxists. By the time of the deadly sham Moscow Purge Trials (1936–1938), the Frankfurt School had no illusions about the Soviet Union. They rejected and criticized regimes like the Soviet Union and other totalitarian projects because such regimes produced their own share of needless suffering (some explicit critique can be found in first-generation member Herbert Marcuse's [1898–1979] *Soviet Marxism* [1958], although there they are also couched in relation to developments in the West, seen part of a bigger human tapestry). After Grünberg's departure, the Frankfurt School also generally rejected doctrinal forms of Marxism and the politics of Marxist parties. Such approaches were rejected because of how they tended towards dogmatism. Historical circumstances require critical analysis, not party sloganeering. Nonetheless, Marx himself remained a constant influence. Horkheimer once described the position they pursued in a letter as accepting "some theoretical aspects of the Marx oeuvre," but with the caveat that "there can't be any talk of us somehow having philosophically ascribed to the so-called Marxist tradition."

Especially after fleeing to the United States, the Frankfurt School, rather than focusing on the brutality of regimes like the Soviet Union, focused on the Western liberal societies of which they were a part. They were especially concerned with the ways in which such societies, with all their advances, could at the same time co-exist with repression and inhumanity (their native country, Germany, claimed to be "the land of poets and thinkers" even as it also pursued antisemitism, colonialism, imperialism, and Nazism). Such concerns emerged in part because of their biographical circumstances, but in part they flowed from a basic normative commitment: while the brutality of such societies is oftentimes overlooked or avoided by these societies, it ought to be acknowledged.

To bring this into even sharper focus, some historical points are in order. The great majority of the early members of the Frankfurt School were Jewish. The Institute for Social Research was founded in Frankfurt, Germany in 1923, where it was affiliated with the city's university. It was founded through the efforts of Felix Weil (1898–1975), the son of Jewish millionaire, Hermann Weil (1868–1927), who at one point was the largest grain trader in the world. Felix Weil, like many of his generation, became enamored with Marx's thought as a means for responding to the needless suffering he perceived in the world. Weil aimed to establish an institute that could be responsive to such suffering, something he felt was missing from the German university. One of the first research programs of the Institute was into the politics of German workers, who the Institute concluded, despite their leftist leanings, would not resist the coming tide of authoritarianism. In 1930, thereby, the Institute developed plans for a move to Switzerland. When the Nazis came to power in 1933, the Institute moved to Geneva. In 1934, the Institute again moved to the United States, where it was associated with Columbia University. Some members of the Institute like Marcuse and Franz Neumann (1900–1954) then aided the war effort, working for years at the Office of Strategic Services (a precursor to the Central Intelligence Agency—it was this work that likely formed the basis for Marcuse's aforementioned book, *Soviet Marxism*). After the war, the Institute returned to Frankfurt, reopening in 1951. Some of the Institute's members returned to Germany while others stayed in the United States or split their time between the two. While there may be a tendency to see these contexts— Europe and its ills and the United States and its ills—as somehow radically distinct, the transatlantic existence of the Institute testifies to the fact that there are important commonalities.

6. THE FRANKFURT SCHOOL, MARX, AND THE UNITED STATES

Alexis de Tocqueville (1805–1859), a relative contemporary of Marx, may be useful for situating these commonalities. A French aristocrat who traveled to the United States in 1831 initially to study its prisons, Tocqueville ended up writing a broader reflection titled *Democracy in America* (1835). In it, he notes that: "American society, if I may put it this way, is like a painting that is democratic on the surface but from time to time allows the old aristocratic colors to peep through." Close to two hundred years ago, then, Tocqueville already noted how American society was wrought by contradiction. The United States is a land of freedom and equality, yet it was built on chattel slavery, patriarchy, and genocide, each of which continue to have effects in the present.

To register the full force of this point, note that as an explicit federal law, women were given the right to vote only in 1919 (on the state side, things were no better—Wyoming, the first state to grant women the right, did so only in 1869). Racial restrictions on voting were explicitly prohibited at the federal level only in 1965 (responding to implicit restrictions at the state level in the form of poll taxes, literacy tests, or outright violence). Barriers to voting continue to exist—for example, voting in the USA is not a national holiday, so it must be juggled always with work (and strong correlations between race and poverty continue to persist in the USA). In short, contradictions continue to be a part of the American social fabric (not unrelated here is Tocqueville's observation that US prisons offer "the spectacle of the most complete despotism," a claim just as apt now as it was then, as books like Michelle Alexander's *The New Jim Crow* [2010] illustrate). In relocating to the United States, the Frankfurt School, just like Tocqueville, was struck by contradiction. For this reason, Marx remained a central figure for them and ought to remain for us: his analyses of capitalism can be harnessed, developed, and built upon to understand these contradictions in the context of the United States.

Considering how Marx tends to be viewed in the United States is in fact one way to bring out both the particular American features of such contradictions in addition to their global character. To see this, let's make explicit what's been suggested already: the United States began as a racial state (a state whose institutions were organized by race). This is so much the case that when Nazi Germany sought to codify its own racial laws in the early 1930s, they explicitly researched and referred to Jim Crow laws in the United States. James Whitman's book, *Hitler's American Model* (2017) documents this story in detail. Whitman remarkably shows, for example, how the example of United States policy was championed by the most radical Nazis in Germany exactly to undermine the more temperate suggestions of Nazi moderates (as odd as such a moniker may sound).

This racial history also directly informs how Marxism is viewed in the United States. For example, as already noted, problems around race did not simply disappear in the United States with the abolition of slavery. They instead moved to different contexts. In response to the subversion of Reconstruction and the emergence of Jim Crow laws, Black Americans pushed and fought for political rights. Other American communities, responding explicitly to the rise of monopolistic forms of capitalism also pushed and fought for political rights. Unsurprisingly, there was potential (and oftentimes actual) overlap between these struggles. A deep, structured, mass alliance between them could threaten the status quo, making each movement more effective than in isolation.

Undermining such a possibility became important to those opposed to these causes. Strategies emerged for doing so (e.g., "divide and conqueror," a phenomenon Marx already diagnosed in "The Eighteenth Brumaire of Louis Bonaparte" [1852]). To bring this into focus, note how capitalism is a global phenomenon. Unrest around the monopolistic (and brutal) tendencies of capitalism were not exclusive to the United States. Many states, especially as they navigated industrialization, were in turmoil, often threatened by war or revolution. And revolutionary impulses were frequently inspired by Marxist analyses of capitalism. The United States saw bombings by insurrectionists and anarchists, widespread strikes, and racial conflict due to a regressive status quo (think here, for example, of the Haymarket affair, Mary G. Harris Jones, the Palmer raids, or the Battle of Virden, just to name some signposts). The general tenor was no different in Europe, but it was compounded by European imperialism, which multiplied the consequences and stakes of these dynamics. As World War I ravaged Europe, a general climate of fear and nationalism emerged. The Russian Revolution only compounded these issues. Radicalism appeared as a standing threat.

The racial history of the USA affected how these issues played out within its borders. One way to avoid acknowledging internal problems is to reframe them instead as external problems of the kind described above. Genuine problems—racial violence and exclusion, economic inequality, and sexual oppression—could be reframed and dismissed as outside agitation by globalist radicals. For example, Black political struggle, a justifiable response to everyday Black life in the United States, might be seen instead as external agitation by foreign elements. Within Congress such arguments were sometimes made explicitly: Blacks in the USA were alleged to be content unless otherwise incited by foreign forces. Accompanying such racism was often antisemitism: Blacks were perceived as simply incapable of organizing themselves, requiring the allegedly more intelligent Jew to do the organizing. Prominent lawyer Madison Grant (1865–1937), for example, lamented in his popular *The Passing of the Great Race* (1916), how "the man of the old stock" was being destroyed by the Jews (his book is also another instance of American influence traveling to Germany rather than the other way around—Hitler adored Grant, even writing a fan letter to him thanking him for what Hitler called his "bible").

Such an approach winds its way through American politics to the present day. To avoid soberly confronting domestic conditions of suffering, the origins of those conditions are imputed instead to external factors. Domestic political responses are thereby undermined. This is one way to trace a line from the Red Scares (1917–1920; 1947–1957) to the Democratic Party's response to the election of Trump (2016). Domestic ills allegedly originate from foreign involvement in American politics. What's lost is the extent to which any foreign involvement could only be successful if there already exist problems that could be aggravated (this is exactly to acknowledge that sometimes there were and can be foreign operatives involved, but their involvement merely adds fuel to a fire, it does not start it).

The relationship of Americans with the thought of Marx is motivated by this historical context. Radical thought has frequently been demonized as foreign interference rather than seen as a plausible response to domestic problems (an approach that reached its apex in the Cold War). It also means that an avoidance of any serious engagement with Marx's thought may be a feature of the United States's general avoidance of its own history, especially around slavery. In the *Poverty of Philosophy* (1846), Marx already understood that slavery was "an economic category of paramount importance." He noted that slavery was "as much the pivot upon which our present-day industrialism turns as are machinery, credit, etc.

Without slavery there would be no cotton, without cotton there would be no modern industry." He stresses that it is slavery which has "created world trade, and world trade is the necessary condition for large-scale machine industry." Scholars since Marx have only deepened this insight. Marx's thought thereby cannot be ignored, for it is central to any analysis of capitalism as much as to an understanding of the United States. For example, without some understanding of a critique of capitalism, the thought of Martin Luther King, Jr. (1929–1968) is entirely sanitized, his radical political commitments erased, so that, as the historian Jacquelyn Down Hall puts it in "The Long Civil Rights Movement and the Political Uses of the Past" (2005), King's "speeches retain their majesty yet lose their political bite." King after all stressed in "A Testament of Hope" (1968) that "the black revolution is much more than a struggle for the rights of Negroes. It is forcing America to face all its interrelated flaws—racism, poverty, militarism, and materialism. It is exposing evils that are rooted deeply in the whole structure of our society … radical reconstruction of society is the real issue." There are here deep resonances between such American currents and the critical theory of the Frankfurt School (a link explored in Chapter 5).

While more work is required here to draw out points of analogy and disanalogy between these contexts, and despite the fact that the Frankfurt School were mostly Jews forced to flee to the USA from Europe due to the Nazi genocide, there arises here the possibility of seeing many of the central works of the first-generation of the Frankfurt School as in fact "American" texts, in their own way addressed to the United States context (a point taken up in different ways by contemporary scholars of the School like Claus Offe and Shannon Mariotti). The Frankfurt School may be yet another site for thinking about the general American avoidance of Marx and of its own American history (this would be again to stress the importance of notions of ideology and second nature).

Viewing the Frankfurt School in this way is to situate them as both critics and champions of the United States, akin to others in the American tradition like, for example, Martin Luther King, Jr. and James Baldwin (1924–1987). This point orients Adorno's "Kultur and Culture" (1958), a lecture he gave in Germany almost a decade after his return to the country. While the lecture does not shy away from critiquing the United States, it is also highly effusive about elements of American society. For example, an image that Adorno thinks is symbolic of the United States is "the way in which every American child can devour an ice cream cone and thereby at any moment find a fulfillment of childhood bliss." He claims this "is truly a part of the fulfilled utopia." Ever stressing nuance, though, Adorno is careful to make clear that his assessment should not be taken to mean that "everything has its positive and its negative sides." Instead, his sober analysis is meant to be an example, where "what we should [always] try to overcome, here and there, is actually nothing else than our becoming hardened against critical thought." The idea is not to draw out platitudes, but rather to pursue a critical analysis that responds to concrete particulars.

In this vein, let me note that critical theory requires discussion and analysis of problems both in general terms and in terms of particular social and political contexts. As the reader may be surmising, an aim of this book is to show that critical theory remains philosophically, socially, and politically relevant to the multitude of sites of needless suffering that confront us, globally and locally. Oftentimes, though, exactly as someone also situated in a particular context, I pursue examples from within my own most immediate social and political context of the United States. I take it as given, however, that these examples and the problems they suggest have analogous or related examples across the globe. The aim of critical theory is to sharpen the tools we have to track such problems, such needless suffering. My hope is that this book will thereby be of use to others in other contexts.

7. THE FRANKFURT SCHOOL ON HISTORY

Critical theory requires understanding the historical record so as to be able to better situate the critique being pursued. The American President Ronald Reagan (1911–2004) once claimed that, "today is better than yesterday, and tomorrow will be better than today." Liberals decry the Reagan presidency, yet it is striking that they also often echo such sentiments (nor are strands of allegedly critical Marxism immune, as when they conceive of history as a sort of mechanical process leading to revolution). The Frankfurt School rejected such views of history. They did not, however, adopt its opposite: the view of pessimism (this is in fact so much the case that when wondering about what view to take of America, Adorno ultimately concludes in *Towards a New Manifesto* [1956] that we must "believe that things can come out right in the end").

Central to the Frankfurt School on this point was the thought of Walter Benjamin (1892–1940), a sometime associate of the Frankfurt School. In attempting to escape the Nazis, Benjamin likely committed suicide trying to evade capture in Portbou on the Spanish/French border. His death had a profound effect on the members of the Frankfurt School. Before his death, he was able to give his last work to the philosopher Hannah Arendt (1906–1975) who preserved it as she fled Europe, eventually delivering it to the reconstituted Institute in New York. Titled "On the Concept of History" (1940), the text is a profound reflection on how history has been and may yet be conceptualized. Benjamin claims in it that "there is no document of civilization which is not at the same time a document of barbarism." Progress—or even worse, what is glorified as progress—rests on (needless) suffering. The catastrophe of World War II was thereby not a surprise to Benjamin, so much so that in the same text he claims that "the current amazement that the things we are experiencing are 'still' possible" is neither "philosophical," nor "the beginning of knowledge." What such claims instead reveal, Benjamin thought, was the utter failure of the view of history that underwrites them.

Benjamin's point remains applicable because the view of history he criticizes remains dominant. For example, the psychologist Steven Pinker has risen to recent prominence arguing in *The Better Angels of Our Nature* (2011) that today's humans live "in the most peaceable era in our species' existence." Such a claim rests on a too limited understanding of violence and a too narrow view of history (points taken up throughout this book). Perhaps direct warfare and physical violence have decreased (although recent events in Ukraine or the Sudan or Gaza might suggest or presage otherwise, as do even the radically different ways in which Western media covers them). Or perhaps violence has become harder to see, as, for example, in the transfer of violence from urban centers to prison peripheries in the United States. Or perhaps violence has simply taken on new forms, as in the sort of psychological or existential violence that quite different theorists of modernity highlight—think here of everything from Henry Thoreau's (1817–1862) "lives of quiet desperation" to Max Weber's (1864–1920) "iron cage" to Michel Foucault's (1926–1984) notion of how modern societies discipline individuals to pursue predetermined and increasingly homogeneous ends. The Frankfurt School's invocations of "internal despotism" (Marcuse), "socially necessary illusion" (Adorno), or simply "general, systematically engineered brainwashing" (Horkheimer) capture analogous themes. Perhaps violence now begins at home, so to speak (as the band Gang of Four sings: perhaps it begins when we fill our "head with culture").

Benjamin notes how our general view of history is always constructed from the perspective of those who dominated and were victorious. In "On the Concept of History," he notes that our historical record is constructed as a "a tool of the ruling classes." The winners determine how history is written and to what ends (and Benjamin astutely but depressingly notes that "this enemy has never ceased to be victorious"). The practice of history is itself normative, open to critical inquiry and dispute. As Benjamin argues, doing history is not merely capturing the past "the way it really was," as the historian Leopold van Ranke (1795–1866) once claimed. The past is already always polyvalent, disputed, and disputable, even at the source. Nowadays historians acknowledge this point by pursuing history from the perspective of various marginalized groups, so that the same event may look quite different from the perspective of different groups. For example, when Columbus lands in the Americas in 1492, is what has occurred a discovery or an invasion (or a repetition)? Answering that question will affect not only how you see that event, but also how you see subsequent events *and* prior ones. Of course, there are potential distinctions to be made here around the construction of different narratives (biased accounts of the historical record are different from entirely invented ones, especially in the political realm, and each of these need to be confronted differently).

Yet Benjamin pushes for an even more fundamental reorientation around the practice of history. Oftentimes, history is conceived as a sort of detective story, where clues are pursued to develop a picture of the past (a point made in different ways in the works of scholars like Carlo Ginzburg, Thomas Howard, and Hayden White [1928–2018]). It may be said that Benjamin puts stress on a different aspect of detective work: the pursuit of justice in the face of a crime.

Here the analogy between the historian and the detective begins to break down. The historian's access to the past is such that the crime scene is always already staged: it is history's winners, the powerful, the dominant, who have passed down the historical record. Yet always we can ask: what—who—is left out? We increasingly train our gaze to see more of history's vanquished, but many still do not appear, and in fact never will. We may know they existed, but we know little or nothing about them. Think, for example, of the history of the Carthaginians. When Rome destroyed Carthage in 146 BCE, in addition to its people, it also destroyed almost all Carthaginian texts. Think about how different Carthaginian (and Western) history would look if those texts were available (to register this point, just imagine what the history of the Indigenous people of the Americas would be if it was told *entirely*—as opposed to mostly entirely—from the sources of the settlers). Despite advances in archaeology, the Carthaginians will always be largely seen through Roman eyes. This is the case across many times and places. In "On the Concept of History," Benjamin remarks that, "whoever has emerged victorious in the thousand struggles traversing history up to the present day has his share in the triumphs of those now ruling over those now ruled." He advises us to "take only a highly critical view of the inventory of spoils displayed by the victors before the vanquished," noting that in fact it is "this inventory" that "is called culture." An alternative approach to history would be, in Benjamin's words, "dedicated to the memory of the anonymous."

Such an approach is at best a heuristic device, a conceit, a guide—it is incapable of ever being fully actualized (this is why Benjamin, for example, registers the possibility of any full realization of such an approach in generally religious or theological terms). The philosopher Stanley Cavell (1926–2018) wrote in *Must We Mean What We Say?* (1958), that "history will not go away, except through our perfect acknowledgment of it (in particular, our acknowledgment that it is not past)." In the context of the present discussion this means above all acknowledging that the present is propped up by a history of needless suffering in the past. Such suffering, though, is not entirely past, for domination continues. While the actors may have shifted (or not), a relationship between victor and vanquished continues to be operative. The Frankfurt School invites us to pursue a quite deep inquiry into the conditions of contemporary suffering and oppression, acknowledging how it may be maintained, even if inadvertently, as a byproduct of structures not explicitly aimed at domination. Such a deep inquiry equally allows, if not suggests, that perhaps a proper understanding of needless suffering and oppression requires an analysis of many interconnected systems (which if taken individually may even appear innocuous) and across many differing disciplines and modalities. Furthermore, such kinds of needless suffering will still require analysis even if Pinker turns out to be right about contemporary conditions (although I remain skeptical on this point).

Horkheimer, the prominent second director of the Institute for Social Research, articulates the Frankfurt School's assessment of their present when he claims in notes from the late 1920s that, "most people are born into a prison-house." Adorno echoes the thought when he writes in *Minima Moralia* (1951) that "there is no right life in one that is false." Although these words were written in far closer proximity to the Nazi genocide than our historical moment, the conditions that gave rise to that genocide have not disappeared. This is apparent on the international stage, where calls of "Never Again" rang hollow in the face of genocides in Cambodia, Rwanda, Bosnia, or ring hollow against present genocidal currents in Yemen, Sudan, or Myanmar. And it is apparent domestically here in the United States, where Nazis march in Charlottesville chanting slogans like "Blood and Soil" and "Jews Will Not Replace Us," while racist and paramilitary groups continue to multiply, themselves echoes from the Vietnam war, a continuing legacy, that like a boomerang, brings the violence developed and unleashed there back home (a point developed in Kathleen Belew's *Bring the War Home* [2018]). Adorno understood such features of the modern world already when he claimed in "The Meaning of Working Through the Past" (1959) that he considered "the survival of National Socialism *within* democracy to be potentially more menacing than the survival of fascist tendencies *against* democracy."

8. GENOCIDE, CAPITALISM, AND THE GLOBAL ORDER

While the Nazi genocide is incredible in its scope and scale, it is also by no means singular in the context of the historical record that

precedes and follows it. As noted already, prior to the Nazi genocide, slavery, colonialism, antisemitism, and religious annihilation
each educated the modern perspective into systematically seeing
categories of humans as disposable or eliminable. The historian
Mark Levene argues in *Genocide in the Age of the Nation State* (2005)
that genocide cannot be understood as a "systemic dysfunction,"
and so "cannot be simply or solely dismissed as the aberrant or devi-
ant behavior of rogue, revolutionary, or 'totalitarian' regimes or for
that matter ones with particular, one might say peculiar, types of
political culture or social and ethnic configuration." Rather than an
anomaly, Levene stresses again in *The Crisis of Genocide* (2013) that
genocide is instead "integral to a 'mainstream' historical trajectory
of development towards a single, global, political economy composed of nation states." The Frankfurt School agrees. Adorno wrote
in *Negative Dialectics* (1966), for example, that "genocide is the absolute integration, which is prepared anywhere human beings are
made the same, 'polished off' as the German military would say,
until they are literally erased." As Levene notes, such integration
occurs at the national and international level under the banner of
capitalism and the nation-state order. While features of this story
will be detailed and deepened in the pages that follow, some facets
of the basic picture can be brought into focus now.

In the "Economic and Philosophic Manuscripts" (1844), Marx
details how the capitalist form of life increasingly commodifies all
facets of human existence. Such commodification affects how
humans see themselves, how they see their world, and how they see
even other humans and species. When everything is potentially a
commodity, the value of all things turns on the market. This is
apparent in phenomena like how highly specialized workers come
increasingly to be alienated from their work to how human beings
may even explicitly sell their bodies or body parts. Because value
comes to be entirely indexed to the market and its profits, human
life becomes homogeneous and qualitatively poorer. As Adorno
notes in "Free Time" (1969), even "free" leisure time functions to
"regenerate labor power." Human beings increasingly appear made
for capitalism rather than the other way around (leading to Marx's
famous phrase, often invoked by the Frankfurt School, that humans
are increasingly "appendages of the machine"). The horizon of
what constitutes a human world is irrevocably changed, a point that
is detailed in the pages that follow.

These changes in human subjectivity are underwritten by profound shifts in material conditions. On one hand, capitalism offers great advances over prior systems of human organization. It introduces many new and useful productive capacities, and undoubtedly drastically improves human life in countless ways. First-time readers of Marx are in fact frequently surprised by how effusive he is about the capitalist mode of production. On the other hand, there is also a dark underbelly. Engels and Marx invoke in *The Communist Manifesto* (1848) the image of a "sorcerer who is no longer able to control the powers of the nether world whom he has called up by his spells."

Almost two centuries after Marx, after countless labor reforms and struggles, the world continues to revolve around harmful and brutal labor practices. This is not to deny advances since Marx, but rather to acknowledge, especially from a global point of view, that human productive activity continues to degrade the world, causing irrevocable damage to humans and to other species. Whether it is forced labor, deforestation, pollution, species extinction, toxicity, destruction, or "just" continuing or increasing conflict, human relations across the globe continue to be defined by such phenomena. The child laborer in a Congolese cobalt mine, the American graduate student with a laptop, the brutalized employee in a Chinese factory, and the executive in Cupertino are all connected and mutually implicated. The philosopher Judith Lichtenberg captures the ubiquity of potential harms around us in a memorable passage in "Negative duties, positive duties, and the 'new harms'" (2010):

> Turn off the lights. Use compact fluorescent bulbs (even if they produce an ugly glare). Drive a small, fuel-efficient car. Drive less. Take public transportation. Don't fly unless you really need to (no more trips to international conferences, no more exotic vacations). Turn down the thermostat in winter. Turn off the air-conditioning in summer. Make sure your appliances are energy-efficient. Take cooler showers. Eat local (except sometimes; find out when). Don't eat factory-farmed meat; leaving aside harm to animals, producing it is not energy efficient. Don't buy Chilean sea bass, or salmon, or … (fill in the blank, depending on which sea food is overfished at any given time). Don't drink bottled water—the energy costs of producing and transporting it are wasteful (leaving aside that only 14 percent of bottles are recycled). Don't use plastic bags (not paper bags either!). Recycle. Compost. Don't use chemical fertilizers on your lawn; better still, get rid of your lawn. In this new world in which we find

ourselves, "each bite we eat, each item we discard, each e-mail message we send, and each purchase we make entails a conversion of fossil-fuel carbon to carbon dioxide," with possible deleterious consequences for others and for the globe. Apart from the environmental consequences of our actions, which disproportionately affect poor people, other kinds of harms also loom. Don't buy clothing made in sweatshops. (Find out which those are.) Was your oriental rug knotted by eight-year-olds? (Find out.) Do you own stock in a company that exploits its workers? (Find out.) Is the coltan in your cell phone fueling wars in the Congo?

Capitalism is the dominant global system and it rears its head in even the most ubiquitous and omnipresent features of modern human life. Indeed, it seems to require "transnational governance structures" in the words of Nancy Fraser in *Cannibal Canibalism* (2022). These structures, as Fraser notes, exploit some and expropriate from others; there is no outside to the generalized system. It exerts a coercive pull upon every human being on the planet. To the extent that capitalism is fundamentally a system of competition, one where some must win and some must lose, tension or conflict perpetually haunt it. Access to resources; a competitive model of nation-states at various levels of development, power, and need; a historical legacy of colonialism and imperialism and their continuing effects; the threat of nuclear holocaust and/or environmental collapse; outright theft and violence from racialized or marginalized populations; and a perpetual drive for profit underwrite the benefits of the system.

This global state system, exactly because of the capitalist framework that binds it together, is, in Mark Levene's words one of "almost perpetual crisis." Levene is not alone in his estimation. For example, the political scientist A. Dirk Moses writes in "Genocide and Modernity" (2008) that "it is the modernizing process, rather than modernity per se, that forces insecure states to catch up to the core, often liberal, states in the system." Moses sees the rise of the current global order as intimately linked to genocide, for "the imperative to establish sovereign autonomy collided with reality as the leaders of ethnically heterogeneous states mobilized their demographic and natural resources to survive in the competitive environment. The rise of the West, then, led to unprecedented state-driven modernization that often destroyed domestic obstacles, like ethnic or national minorities." This basic idea—that the rise of modern capitalism is equally bound up with the rise of an array of needless suffering, including even genocide—is echoed by other scholars like the historian Donald Bloxham and the sociologist Michael Mann; the idea can be teased out from Marx and the Frankfurt School.

9. CRISIS AND CAPITALISM

Central to Marx's account was the idea that the capitalist system involved antagonism, contradiction, shock, and crisis. On one hand, Marx described what he termed "primitive accumulation," a process where public lands, holdings, and resources were (forcibly and violently) seized by capitalists and harnessed as the initial capital available for profit. Equally meant to explain the seizure of common natural resources for the creation of a landless working class (say, the rural countryside) as much as the enslavement or subjection of humans (say, slavery or colonialism), Marx understood the results as always involving destruction and suffering. As he writes in *Capital* (1867):

> The discovery of gold and silver in America, the extirpation, enslavement and entombment in mines of the Indigenous population of that continent, the beginnings of the conquest and plunder of India, the conversion of Africa into a preserve for the commercial hunt of blackskins, all things which characterize the dawn of the era of capitalist production. These idyllic proceedings are the chief moments of primitive accumulation.

On the other hand, as the philosopher Rosa Luxemburg (1871–1919) noted in *The Accumulation of Capital* (1913), "capital cannot accumulate without the aid of non-capitalist organisations." Luxemburg's point is that the drive for profit is operative equally with demand as much as supply. The system leads to perpetual expansion, especially into new territories (on the demand side, profits would be lost without expansion since more is produced than can be bought domestically; on the supply side, profit maximization forces expansion abroad for more resources, in the form of raw materials as much as human labor). There is a circuit here: the colonized sites of resource extraction are also the expanded markets for goods; and these are ongoing processes, now increasingly occurring nationally as much as internationally. Formerly common—public— lands and resources continue to be privatized in the United States and elsewhere (for example, note the shrinking realm of public goods and spaces in the United States, or recall the way in which the public resources of the former Soviet Union were divvied up amongst the mafia and oligarchs during its collapse). These processes do not proceed without conflict or suffering. As Marx astutely observed in *Capital*: "capital comes dripping from head to toe, from every pore, with blood and dirt."

Such national and international effects are underwritten by a central feature of the entire capitalist economic system, namely its continual production of economic crisis. This feature of Marx's account is often misunderstood or ignored, even by sympathetic readers. This was not the case, however, for Henryk Grossman (1881–1950), one of the early members of the Frankfurt School. Grossman, a student of Carl Grünberg (1861–1940), the first director of the Institute, was an economist and historian. His work focused on Marx's theory of crisis, and in fact his *The Law of Accumulation and the Breakdown of the Capitalist System* (1929) was one of the first publications of the Institute for Social Research.

Grossman stresses how the theory of crisis is one of Marx's deepest insights. Because it is a system driven by profit, there is in capitalism a constant struggle between capitalist and worker. Increased profits require that capitalists pay as little for labor as possible. There is a limit, however, to how low wages can go. For example, the labor force requires enough compensation to reproduce—sustain, but also literally reproduce—itself. Equally, a laborer can only work so many hours in a day. Capitalists thereby can only decrease the cost of labor so much and must pursue technological innovation to increase the productivity of labor. For example, the invention of a machine that aids the hand may double or triple what's produced. Marx then draws a distinction between constant capital (the various technological means of production and the raw materials required) and variable capital (the labor force required for production). Surplus value is the market value of commodities beyond these two kinds of capital. Surplus value drives profit. For example, if the costs of a commodity that sells for $50 includes $10 of labor and $20 of technology, then the surplus value that the capitalist can gain in profit is $20. Because this capitalist is in competition with other capitalists, he must push for greater surplus value. The capitalist can either reduce labor costs or increase productivity through technological innovation. The latter, however, always has a cost: technological investment increases constant capital costs.

This point about constant capital costs and technological innovation is crucial to Marx's account. Marx notes that the general *rate* of profit will *always* fall over time because of this. Any technological innovation always leads to an increase in capital costs. Such increases guarantee that, given enough time, capitalists will always experience a decline in the rate of profit. As Marx puts it in the unfinished third volume of *Capital* (1894): "the progressive tendency for the general rate of profit to fall is thus simply the expression, peculiar to the capitalist mode of production, of the progressive development of the social productivity of labor."

Exactly the defining feature of the capitalist system—profit—leads to the threat of constant crisis in that system. When the rate of profit falls, a decrease in investment follows (less profit leads to less desire for investment). A decrease in investment and a falling rate of profit lead to a decrease in employed labor (the work force is reduced to reduce costs and increase profits again). Less employed labor leads eventually to a decrease in the demand for goods (labor has less income to spend on goods). This leads to more cuts, less spending, and crisis. With crisis, though, the rate of profit again rises (labor becomes cheap because many firms have closed and unemployment is high), which allows for more investment and accumulation, which only sets the cycle of crisis into motion again. Such crises can, in turn, be connected back to the violent geopolitical contexts noted above.

The Frankfurt School took seriously this insight of Marx's. In *The Law of Accumulation and the Breakdown of the Capitalist System,* Grossman highlighted it as "decisively important" for any understanding of capitalism. In 1936 and 1937, the falling rate of profit was the topic of discussion of internal seminars at the Institute for Social Research, and even as late as 1962, in the lecture on "Marx and the Basic Concepts of Sociological Theory," Adorno stresses the crisis character of capitalism, noting it as "the essence of dialectics," where capitalists themselves create "a dynamic which turns against themselves," thereby instantiating conditions where there is a "continuously increasing threat to the system itself." The Frankfurt School increasingly recognizes how elements of such crisis are quite varied, involving more domains than just the economic.

Such a stress on crisis runs counter to current trends in the Western understanding of itself, especially in the economic realm, where crisis is seen as an anomaly from the norm rather than a standing feature of the system. In this vein, the work of economists like Anwar Shaikh, Michael Roberts, and Murray Smith may be a fruitful contemporary supplement to the work of the Frankfurt School for any understanding of crisis in the contemporary world. (Roberts, for example, argues that the rate of profit has fallen 27% from 1945–2021.) Equally, ordinary experience suggests the same, where, in a very short time, we have moved from the Global Financial Crisis (2007–2008) to the COVID-19 pandemic. Whatever one thinks about the origins, features, or ultimate lessons of these recent crises, it is indisputable that they had (and continue to have) pronounced effects that are of a systemic kind; equally they follow in a long list of such crises around the capitalist order in the modern period. (Just thinking of history going back to Marx's death, we may cite major events like Black Wednesday [1992], Black Monday [1987], the Energy Crisis [1979], the Great Depression [1929–1939], the Long Depression [1873–1896], and this is not even to mention the panoply of allegedly minor crises—they are minor only from their memorialization in historical records, not in the ways in which they have wreaked havoc on the lives of human beings.)

Of course, it is also the case, as the second-generation Frankfurt School member, Jürgen Habermas, notes in *Legitimation Crisis* (1973) (and as suggested above): the notion of crisis itself has become significantly more complex, requiring analyses that cannot be reduced solely to the economic sphere. To see why this might be the case, we need a more robust understanding of critique, the topic of the next chapter. But already it is my hope that the impetus for a complex, multidisciplinary, and bold program like that pursued by the Frankfurt School is at least starting to come into better focus.

SUGGESTED READING

MARX

Marx, Karl. *The Marx-Engels Reader.* 2nd ed. New York: Norton, 1978.

Thier, Hadas. *A People's Guide to Capitalism: An Introduction to Marxist Economics.* Chicago: Haymarket Books, 2018.

Wheen, Francis. *Karl Marx.* London: Fourth Estate, 2000.

While Marx's work is extensive, the reader is an excellent place to start with primary sources. The Thier book is a stellar introduction to Marx's analysis of capitalism.

INTRODUCTION TO/HISTORY OF THE FRANKFURT SCHOOL

Abromeit, John. *Max Horkheimer and the Foundations of the Frankfurt School.* Cambridge: Cambridge University Press, 2011.

Bronner, Stephen Eric. *Critical Theory: A Very Short Introduction.* Oxford: Oxford University Press, 2017.

Geuss, Raymond. *The Idea of a Critical Theory: Habermas and the Frankfurt School.* Cambridge: Cambridge University Press, 1981.

Held, David. *Introduction to Critical Theory: Horkheimer to Habermas.* Berkeley: University of California Press, 1980.

Jay, Martin. *The Dialectical Imagination: A History of the Frankfurt School and the Institute of Social Research 1923–1950.* Berkeley: University of California Press, 1973.

Wheatland, Thomas. *The Frankfurt School in Exile.* Wheatland: University of Minnesota Press, 2009.

Wiggershaus, Rolf. *The Frankfurt School: Its History, Theories, and Political Significance.* Translated by Michael Robertson. Cambridge: MIT Press, 1994.

HISTORICAL CONTEXT AND HISTORY (INCLUDING THE EMPIRICAL HISTORY OF GENOCIDES REFERENCED)

Arendt, Hannah. *The Origins of Totalitarianism.* London: André Deutsch, 1986.

Bloxham, Donald. *The Great Game of Genocide: Imperialism, Nationalism, and the Destruction of the Ottoman Armenians.* Oxford: Oxford University Press, 2005.

———. *The Final Solution: A Genocide.* Oxford: Oxford University Press, 2009.

———. *Genocide, the World Wars and the Unweaving of Europe.* Middlesex: Mitchell Vallentine & Company, 2008.

———. "Organized Mass Murder: Structure, Participation, and Motivation in Comparative Perspective." *Holocaust and Genocide Studies* 22, no. 2 (2008): 203–45.

Bloxham, Donald, and Tony Kushner. *The Holocaust: Critical Historical Approaches.* Manchester: Manchester University Press, 2005.

Césaire, Aimé. *Discourse on Colonialism.* Translated by Joan Pinkham. New York: Monthly Review Press, 2001.

Ginzburg, Carlo. *Clues, Myths, and the Historical Method.* Translated by John Tedeschi and Anne C. Tedeschi. Baltimore: Johns Hopkins University Press, 2013.

Howard, Thomas A. *Religion and the Rise of Historicism: W.M.L. De Wette, Jacob Burckhardt, and the Theological Origins of Nineteenth-Century Historical Consciousness.* Cambridge: Cambridge University Press, 2006.

Levene, Mark. *Genocide in the Age of the Nation State*. 4 vols. London: I.B. Tauris, 2005.

———. *The Crisis of Genocide*. 2 vols. Oxford: Oxford University Press, 2016.

———. "Why Is the Twentieth Century the Century of Genocide?" *Journal of World History* 11, no. 2 (2000): 305–36.

Mariotti, Shannon L. *Adorno and Democracy: The American Years*. Lexington: University Press of Kentucky, 2016.

Moses, A. Dirk, ed. *Empire, Colony, Genocide: Conquest, Occupation, and Subaltern Resistance in World History*. London: Berghahn Books, 2008.

Offe, Claus. *Reflections on America: Tocqueville, Weber and Adorno in the United States*. Translated by Patrick Camiller. London: Polity, 2005.

Veidlinger, Jeffrey. *In the Midst of Civilized Europe: The Pogroms of 1918–1921 and the Onset of the Holocaust*. New York: Metropolitan Books, 2021.

White, Hayden. *Metahistory: The Historical Imagination in Nineteenth-Century Europe*. Baltimore: Johns Hopkins University Press, 2014.

These are excellent overviews of the broad historical picture I am referencing throughout this chapter.

SOME CRITICAL THEORY REFERENCED

Benjamin, Walter. "On the Concept of History." In *Selected Writings*, edited by Howard Eiland and Michael W. Jennings, 4, 389–400. Cambridge: Harvard University Press, 2002.

Grossman, Henryk. *The Law of Accumulation and Breakdown of the Capitalist System, Being Also a Theory of Crisis*. Translated by Jarius Banaji and Rick Kuhn. Chicago: Haymarket Books, 2022.

Habermas, Jürgen. *Legitimation Crisis*. Translated by Thomas McCarthy. Cambridge: Beacon Press, 1975.

Horkheimer, Max. *Between Philosophy and Social Science*. Translated by G. Frederick Hunter, Matthew S. Kramer, and John Torpey. Cambridge: MIT Press, 1993.

———. *Critical Theory: Selected Essays*. New York: Seabury, 1972.

Horkheimer, Max, and Theodor W. Adorno. *Dialectic of Enlightenment, Philosophical Fragments*. Translated by Edmund Jephcott. Cultural Memory in the Present. Edited by Mieke Bal and Hent de Vries. Stanford: Stanford University Press, 2002.

The Horkheimer book has most of the essays cited in this volume (including the essential essay "Traditional and Critical Theory"), while the Grossman work is the aforementioned book on crisis.

CRITIQUE

1. STRATEGIES FOR CHANGE

Having a picture of contemporary capitalism in place brings two connected issues into focus. Note how difficult it is in fact to imagine an
alternative structural arrangement, one that does not produce needless suffering. This is why the philosopher Fredric Jameson once
wrote in "Future City" (2003) that "it is easier to imagine the end of
the world than to imagine the end of capitalism." This problem of
imaginative capacities is not a purely cognitive problem, but also a
problem of our sensibility (a point to which we'll return in the fourth
chapter of this book—it is also a way to register already why the
Frankfurt School was deeply interested in art and aesthetics). A focus
on capitalism equally brings into view a second set of issues that
revolve around questions of action. Were an alternative imagined and
proposed, it is not immediately obvious how such an alternative
could be achieved given the omnipresent nature of capitalism and its
effects, as ideology, on our subjectivity. Everyone is by now aware
that our desires can be manipulated by market forces (just in the USA
more than 285 billion was spent on advertising and marketing this
past year). Would we then even desire change if it was in sight and
possible? What's necessary is a change in our entire form of life. As
Marcuse often remarked, what's required is "qualitative" rather than
"quantitative" change.

Things are not, however, hopeless. In the classic programmatic
statement of critical theory, "Traditional and Critical Theory" (1937),
Horkheimer stresses that despite whatever difficulties confront historical change, it must always be kept in mind that capitalism, even in

DOI: 10.4324/9781003200963-2

this expansive sense, is a historical phenomenon. The social processes and institutions and beliefs that animate it are contingent. They depend on humans—on us—for their existence. They are not eternal. They can in fact, as Horkheimer stresses, "be changed." Things could be different. Change oftentimes follows criticism or critique, and this is the great theme of this chapter. How is critique to be pursued? Who gets to pursue critique? When? And to what end? To work our way into these issues, note that in response to the worries presented in this paragraph, the Frankfurt School initially pursues two distinct (but related) strategies.

What might be termed a "positive" strategy is pursued by Marcuse when he highlights how the various practices associated with capitalism undermine possibilities available to every human being to flourish *as* a human. Capitalism dehumanizes us. The argument here relies on Marx's "Economic and Philosophic Manuscripts." Although written in 1844, these were only published and available to scholars in 1930. Marcuse's "The Foundation of Historical Materialism" (1932) is a lengthy essay on these manuscripts. There he stresses that "the factual situation of capitalism is characterized not merely by economic or political crisis but by a catastrophe affecting the human essence." Marcuse highlights how the central concept for Marx in these manuscripts is human freedom. For Marx, the fundamental essence of a human being is the ability to transcend any given environment, to move beyond what is merely given and to affect and manipulate what's given into a humanly constituted environment. If this is true, then, a possible question arises about the extent to which such manipulation of the environment occurs in a free manner. It is easily understood that this was not the case for most parts of human history, where the environment would be manipulated for the interests of the few (monarchs, tyrants, oligarchs, conquerors, clerics, or whomever). Although democracy potentially promised the possibility of more genuine freedom, its prospects have since antiquity been marred by other ills like slavery, patriarchy, and religious exceptionalism. The modern world, Marx argues, is no different, and, in some ways, worse, because these systemic ills are now animated by the entire capitalist structure, which guarantees that manipulation occurs only for increased profit, and does so often in a hidden way (appearing unremarkable and entirely natural). Our possibilities for living a free human life are thereby undermined in modernity, regardless of any other advances. Marx's theory of alienation takes up this point: human beings, when embedded in the capitalist system, are incapable of feeling at home—what they do oftentimes feels foreign to them, because not fully or freely chosen.

Such an approach hearkens to Aristotle who argued that a good life could be specified for human beings when their essence was properly understood (Marx notably produced a translation of one of Aristotle's central works in 1840, just a short time before writing these 1844 manuscripts). Central to the view is a proposal about what it means to be human, deriving its normative force—what *ought* to be pursued—from an understanding of what is a good life for any member of the human species. On such a view, at a very high-altitude view, Marx's claim is that under capitalism humans are a deficient version of a human being. Like a plant without proper light or nutrients, humans may continue to live, but will do so malformed, sick. While Marcuse and Marx stress a notion of freedom as central, there are now contemporary approaches that pursue analogous arguments by focusing instead on delineating core human capabilities. Martha Nussbaum, a prominent contemporary proponent of such a view, even explicitly references Marx's 1844 manuscripts when she discusses the idea in "Capabilities as Fundamental Entitlements" (2007). On such a view, when core capabilities are incapable of being actualized, then human beings are being maltreated and deprived of something valuable.

Any prioritization of what it means to be human may, however, be met with skepticism. Perhaps there is no such thing as a human essence or nature. Perhaps there is no distinct notion of human flourishing nor a best human life. Perhaps being human is a thoroughly contingent prospect and human beings are capable of achieving satisfaction in a variety of ways (even the revised version of a capabilities approach is not entirely immune from such objections, as proponents like Amartya Sen and Martha Nussbaum argue exactly about whether particular capabilities need to be mapped out and made explicit). Some members of the Frankfurt School—most notably Horkheimer—explicitly reject any ahistorical notion of a human nature that already suggests particular (political) aims or goals. While there may be basic biological necessities, these can be satisfied through a range of social, economic, and political arrangements (even highly oppressive ones). Note, though, that any such denial of a human essence or a positive account of human flourishing does not thereby undermine the extent to which we may diagnose genuine sites of needless suffering.

Adorno pursues an analogous critique of the ills of capitalism but takes it only as suggesting what ought not to be. There is no positive picture of what human flourishing would look like. The claim is instead that we can only know for sure that *this* isn't it. Bodily pain may here be a sort of model. The experience of needless pain is enough reason to desire that it not exist. No alternative picture of what else must exist is necessary. Pain carries its own normative force: *this* ought not be (as noted earlier: "woe says go"). To claim that any particular needless pain ought not to exist does not require a picture of what ought to exist. What's required is only an understanding of the pain and what its cessation requires. The contemporary philosopher Fabian Freyenhagen notes that such an approach is still an approach inspired by Aristotle. Like the Aristotelian view above, it does present a view of what it means to be human, but only in a negative way. Any human ought not to experience such suffering. No concept of human flourishing or positive understanding of what it means to be human is necessary beyond this claim. Such an approach thereby prioritizes claims to and about needless suffering.

It is important to note that the suggestion is not that no pain ought to exist. Some pain is useful in teaching us how the world works or in unlocking access to particular achievements. Pain may sometimes be chosen. And some pain, like accidents or unrequited love, may be unavoidable. The target for analysis here is needless pain. Take the pains associated with torture, food insecurity, or oppression, for example. Equally, though, take the pains associated with regular, systemic, and normalized suffering, of the kind experienced daily by, say, exploited workers and/or those marginalized in oppressive ways due to race, gender, class, or ability. For a vivid example, think of Hurricane Katrina (2005). While humans cannot (yet?) control the weather, they can control how they prepare for and/or respond to weather events. There are better and worse ways of doing so. The worse ways produce more suffering, sometimes drastically so. In the case of Katrina, deadly engineering flaws in the levee flood protection system combined with massive failures at all levels of government led to death and suffering that could have been prevented with a better response in each area. Such examples can be multiplied in the contemporary global world (e.g., the unequal effects of climate catastrophe or the effects of the COVID-19 pandemic around patterns of global wealth distribution). Note also how so many different features of society may be worthy of examination: small- and large-scale socio-political organization, the apportioning of resources, beliefs about the world and about the role of suffering in it, media and cultural artifacts that reinforce certain beliefs, avoidable biases, and so forth. Think here, thus, for example, of the especially prominent American idea that hard work is all that separates someone from living in poverty from being Elon Musk (an ideological point with a long history unifying everything from Horatio Alger [1832–1899] to contemporary hip-hop to American television series to the American dream invoked by mainstream liberals and conservatives alike).

2. THE METHOD(S) AND DISCIPLINE(S) OF CRITICAL THEORY

This last point about what becomes salient raises a question about the precise object of inquiry for critical theory. Given the scope of what's coming into focus as of interest—roughly all the superfluous suffering that the modern world produces—it appears as if society in its entirety is of interest. As Horkheimer puts it in "Traditional and Critical Theory," critical theory has "society itself for its object." In a postscript, he stresses that unlike certain kinds of Marxist theory, critical theory will not restrict itself to economic analysis, for it is ultimately not just about "a change in certain property relations or on increased productivity in new forms of social collaboration." Critical theory is instead an analysis of "the nature and development of the society in which all these particular developments are taking place."

Such critique requires a thoroughgoing interdisciplinary approach. Social, economic, and political elements are intertwined with religious, artistic, and cultural ones, among others. This is why critical theory cannot be reduced to one kind of scholarly method, for the methods of inquiry may change across disciplines and topics of inquiry. Developments in one area may affect others. It is no longer simply the case—if it ever was—that changing material or economic conditions will straightaway affect psychological or cultural ones. To easily see the point of this last claim, just think of a phenomenon like colonialism. As philosophers like Frantz Fanon (1925–1961) and Albert Memmi (1920–2020) both noted in *The Wretched of the Earth* (1961) and *The Colonizer and the Colonized* (1957), respectively: achieving independence and doing away with colonial relations is no guarantee that the effects of such relations do not continue to affect subjects in the form of psychological disorders and/or racialized forms of thinking.

A feature of any such interdisciplinary approach is that critique in one area may in fact illuminate another area, contributing to a greater understanding in and of each. Such an approach is on display especially in Adorno's *Minima Moralia*. For example, Adorno diagnoses how fascist features may already animate quite ordinary and omnipresent features of society:

> Technology is making gestures precise and brutal, and with them men. It expels from movements all hesitation, deliberation, civility. It subjects them to the implacable, as it were ahistorical demands of objects. Thus the ability is lost, for example, to close a door quietly and discreetly, yet firmly. Those of cars and refrigerators have to be slammed, others have the tendency to snap shut by themselves, imposing on those entering the bad manners of not looking behind them. The new human type cannot be properly understood without awareness of what he is continuously exposed to from the world of things about him, even in his most secret innervations. ... And which driver is not tempted, merely by the power of his engine, to wipe out the vermin of the street, pedestrians, children and cyclists? The movements machines demand of their users already have the violent, hard-hitting, unresting jerkiness of Fascist maltreatment.
>
> The taboo on talking shop and the inability to talk to each other are in reality the same thing. Because everything is business, the latter is unmentionable like rope in a hanged man's home. Behind the pseudo-democratic dismantling of ceremony, of old-fashioned courtesy, of the useless conversation suspects, not even unjustly, of being idle gossip, behind the seeming clarification and transparency of human relations that no longer admit anything undefined naked brutality is ushered in. The direct statement without divagations, hesitations, or reflections, that gives the other the facts full in the face, already has the form and timbre of the command issued under Fascism by the dumb to the silent.

Adorno's point is not that there is some causal relationship between such moments and fascism: the argument is not that these features of the world cause fascism. The idea instead is that such moments are micro (his word is "micrological") "prefigurations" of or versions of or features related to macro phenomena. What Adorno is highlighting is that everything matters: the objects and institutions around us may inculcate in us certain values or sensibilities even as we are unaware that they are doing so (a point even more obvious since Adorno's time as the addictive and depressive qualities of our phones and social media are now well documented).

3. NEEDLESS SUFFERING, BROADER CONTEXT, AND METHOD(S)

The following example may be useful for thinking about the broader point. Think of a court room and note how the norms that animate it also express certain values. This is most obvious in an extreme example like when the court room is structured around, say, trial by combat (as it could be in certain instances of early Irish or German legal codes). It can be diagnosed equally in our contemporary court rooms when such courts must deal with, say, Indigenous representatives who may invoke oral traditions in the form of songs or stories. Such oral traditions, however, in the words of philosopher Jill Stauffer in "Law and Oral History" (2020), "do not conform to legalist expectations about evidence," and thereby cannot be properly understood and lodged in that context. The court room evinces certain values about what may count *as* testimony, let alone what *kinds* of testimony are or are not valuable. The court room is thereby not value neutral; it also prioritizes certain forms of life and minimizes others. What Adorno is inviting us to do is to extend our analysis far beyond courts, suggesting that the objects and institutions around us are seldom neutral, frequently proscribing or inculcating certain values and/or sensibilities. And those values and sensibilities may contribute to the production of needless suffering.

The complexity of modern subjectivity, in turn, requires an expanded understanding of suffering. Needless suffering frequently affects physical wellbeing, but it can equally or additionally affect emotional or psychic wellbeing. And, in fact, it may even be the case that individuals are harmed by having their freedom or possibilities constrained without even knowing that this is happening. Horkheimer and Adorno stress in their "Theses on Need" (1942) that even our needs are a "social category" in the sense that they shift over time in response to historical developments. Contemporary institutions, from the family to the market to the state, not to mention dynamic notions like race, gender, nation, class, and ability, each affect how humans experience the world. Such phenomena are not static: the family can take many forms, the modern nation-state once didn't exist, and who counts as Black or what it means to be a woman, for example, shift across different places and times (and have done so throughout history). Around these phenomena arise certain kinds of suffering dependent on (themselves historically shifting) notions of guilt, shame, or conscience (think, for example, of the kinds of suffering that arise from internalizing racist norms or being labeled a "race traitor"). Systemic needless suffering can lead to psychic harms that cannot be reduced simply to physical suffering (which may of course also be present). The psychic harms, for example, of racism, antisemitism, or sexism can be separated from (and oftentimes must be alleviated differently from) the material harms these phenomena produce. The sorts of material prospects experienced around job, education, or even basic safety in a sexual or racial system of oppression is not the same as the sort of psychic anguish that may be experienced by living in such a world. For an example, see Jonathan Lear's remarkable *Radical Hope* (2006), which elaborates the distinct psychic harms that followed in the wake of the American annihilation of the Crow Nation.

In "Traditional and Critical Theory," Horkheimer offers a deeper context for these points when he writes that all facts are "socially performed." How we "see and hear," indeed how we sense and know things are, Horkheimer claims, are "inseparable from the social life process as it has evolved over the millennia." Such an evolution occurs at both ends of the knowing process: "through the historical character of the object perceived and through the historical character of the perceiving organ." To begin to get a grip on this point, just think of the cliché claim that the Eskimo have countless words for snow. While this claim is in fact false on its face (there are not such countless words for snow nor does any group even accept the colonially imposed name of Eskimo), it does suggest a deeper truth: what and how humans perceive is affected by historical conditions. Note that we are now further specifying the notion of "second nature" highlighted in the last chapter (and thereby also broadening the ways in which it can be affected by ideology). Whether human beings are understood as a "creature made in God's image" or a "featherless biped" makes a difference. More starkly, whether something is termed "demonic possession" or "gender dysphoria" affects what's seen, what might be done, and what can or cannot be imagined. As noted earlier, is the arrival of Columbus a discovery or an invasion? Our concepts matter, as do their origins and shifts. There are here potential connections to the critical theory of Michel Foucault (1926–1984) who drew philosophical conclusions from the genealogy of particular concepts. (Such a method is well presented in philosopher Colin Koopman's *Genealogy as Critique* [2013]; in this context, it is worth citing Foucault's own remarks in a 1978 interview when he notes that: "When I recognize all these merits of the Frankfurt School, I do so with the bad conscience of one who should have known them and studied them much earlier than was the case. Perhaps if I had read those works earlier on, I would have saved useful time, surely: I wouldn't have needed to write some things and I would have avoided certain errors.")

The ways in which modern society and modern subjectivity—our world and our experiences and perceptions of that world—are both shaped by historical forces suggests a thoroughgoing complexity, requiring an approach that spans many disciplines. The Frankfurt School pursues such an approach, frequently combining insights from disciplines like philosophy, political theory, economics, psychoanalysis, sociology, aesthetics, music theory, literature, among many others. The present moment has shifted, though, and to this list may be added new disciplines and insights, like, for example, critical theories of race and gender, approaches around artificial intelligence, developments in bioethics, and so forth. The Frankfurt School may be supplemented by or put into conversation with views that originate outside of the Western canon of thinking, including developments in anti-colonial theory, a project pursued in the philosopher Amy Allen's *The End of Progress: Critical Theory in Postcolonial Times* (2016). This is not to say that the Frankfurt School overlooked suffering outside of the Western world. Adorno frequently noted, for example in *Metaphysics* (1965), that his invocations of "Auschwitz" were meant to refer "not only Aus-chwitz but the world of torture which has continued to exist after Auschwitz" (in the lecture in which he made this statement, the specific reference was to Vietnam).

Relatedly, the historical and temporal scope of which events are salient is equally capable of being broadened. The Frankfurt School, after their arrival in the United States, once considered an ambitious research project into antisemitism that would examine the phe-nomenon in its deep context, moving from historical events like the first crusade to "Jew baiting" in 13th century England to the French revolution to the Nazi genocide (the details of this project can be found in "Research Project on Anti-Semitism" [1941]). Similar approaches must be taken to many contemporary phenom-ena, not least of which is the Nazi genocide itself, which, as noted in the previous chapter, had some of its roots in colonial rule. It is not by accident, for example, that the possibility of death camps emerges from the possibilities afforded by concentration camps, which were used extensively in German colonial rule over the Herero and Nama peoples in Africa (who already in 1904 and 1908 experienced genocidal violence in such camps). Of course, any analysis of the Nazi genocide cannot minimize or overlook the centuries of antisemitism in Europe. The point is that if we are to pursue critical theory now, we must combine the approaches of the Frankfurt School with subsequent developments in, for example, critical race theory and anti-colonial theory, and *vice versa*. Such a combination is warranted exactly by a shared conception of history, which Benjamin captures well with the idea that "there is no doc-ument of civilization which is not at the same time a document of barbarism."

4. THEORY AND PRACTICE

Given the breadth of critical theory, either as the Frankfurt School imagined and practiced it, or as it would need to be pursued now, the connection between theory and practice is not immediately obvious. In "Traditional and Critical Theory," Horkheimer nota-bly claims that the critical theorist "and his [sic] specific object are seen as forming a dynamic unity with the oppressed class." On one hand, given the focus on the amelioration of needless suffering, it makes sense that critical theory would be connected to those oppressed by society. On the other hand, the notion of an—that is, *one*—oppressed class is no longer feasible, if it ever was. Because he was interested in the suffering engendered by capitalism, Marx focused in large part on the immiseration of the working class. Over time, though, Marx himself realized that things were more complex (without ever losing sight of the suffering of the working class).

Contemporary critical theory proceeds with the understanding that there are multiple, mutually implicated sites of oppression. An early fierce expression of this is the Combahee River Collective, a group of Black, anti-capitalist lesbians, who named themselves after Harriet Tubman's (1822–1913) raid at the Combahee River in South Carolina in 1863 (a raid which freed 750 enslaved Blacks). Their name is meant exactly to suggest how they consciously see themselves as involved in the long history of Black struggle in the United States. In a statement issued in 1977, the Combahee River Collective note that they see as their "particular task the development of integrated analysis and practice based upon the fact that the major systems of oppression are interlocking." They go on to stress the extent to which they felt that as Black lesbian women their particular kinds of suffering did not register either within the Civil Rights movement (where they felt excluded as Black *women* in light of the patriarchal elements of the movement), or within the feminist movement (where they felt excluded as *Black* women given racist elements in the movement). Here once again we can see how notions of needless suffering and notions of freedom or liberation come to be practically intertwined. What the Combahee River Collective highlights is the way in which even movements towards liberation may recreate forms of oppression. From this statement, it is possible to draw a line to the now prominent idea of intersectionality introduced by legal scholar Kimberlé Crenshaw in "Demarginalizing the Intersection of Race and Sex" (1989). Crenshaw similarly stresses how the distinct kind of needless suffering experienced by a Black woman is "greater than the sum of racism and sexism," and that "any analysis that does not take intersectionality into account cannot sufficiently address the particular manner in which Black women are subordinated." Such insights remain relevant: just think, for example, of how American society currently responds to a disappeared White woman versus a disappeared Black woman or Indigenous woman. The former may elicit wide-ranging media coverage, while the latter may have difficulty even appearing on official records (in the case of Indigenous women, for example, things are so dire that they are murdered at a rate ten times that of other women—indeed, murder is the third highest cause of death for Indigenous women).

To be clear: none of the above is meant to suggest that only those with certain identities can engage in politics aimed at reducing needless suffering or that those with particular identities should care only about the needless suffering that affects them; rather the claim is that certain identities may reveal distinct kinds of needless suffering. As Demita Frazier, one of the founding members of the Combahee River Collective, stresses and recounts in "Rethinking Identity Politics" (1995):

> I never believed that Combahee, or other Black feminist groups I have participated in, should focus only on issues of concern for us as Black women, or that, as lesbian/bisexual women, we should only focus on lesbian issues. ... We worked in coalition with community activists, women and men, lesbians and straight folks. ... We understood that coalition building was crucial to our own survival.

Such an approach is not foreign to the Frankfurt School, and philosophers inspired by the Frankfurt School like Nancy Fraser and Amy Allen have explicitly merged the Frankfurt School with later developments in feminist, anti-colonial, and critical race theory, arguing that critical theory requires a responsiveness to a wide array of needless suffering. Given Marx's suggestion in a letter in 1843 that critique is "the self-clarification of the struggles and wishes of the age," such approaches may be part of critique itself (as, of course, also Marcuse's own involvement in the Black civil rights and student movements in the late 1960s also shows—more on this later in the book).

Critical theory is then meant to maintain a connection to worldly struggle; the needless suffering it considers is not mere abstraction. This is one way to understand how Adorno, a notoriously impenetrable writer, nonetheless gave countless (and quite clear) radio addresses upon returning to Germany after the end of Nazism. Axel Honneth, a member of the third-generation of the School and himself a director of the Institute for Social Research, put the idea as follows in "Is There an Emancipatory Interest?" (2017):

> Critical theory is nothing but the continuation, by means of a controlled scientific methodology, of the cognitive labor that oppressed groups have to perform in their everyday struggles when they work to de-naturalize hegemonic patterns of interpretation and to expose the interests by which these are motivated.

Critical theory thereby has a deep relation to oppressed and/or marginalized groups and their experience, using its scholarly approaches to aid their efforts at ending their oppression or marginalization. Critical theory is never neutral. Given this, critical theory then also frequently questions accepted ways of understanding the world, since it is exactly the status quo that maintains needless suffering.

To return to the question of practice, then, note that critical theory can operate along two related domains. On one hand, at the level of cognition and perception, critical theory can orient what we see in the world and how we see it. On the other hand, at the level of action and orientation, critical theory can direct what we might do, or point to how we ought to act. Developments in the former may lead to more possibilities in the latter, and vice versa. Critical theory may be as international in scope as the theory of crisis discussed at the conclusion of the previous chapter, or it may be as national as, say, showing that a particular government program must be called "torture" rather than "enhanced interrogation techniques." It may focus on mass trends or on the most minute details. With each case, possibilities for action emerge in a variety of realms, whether social, political, or aesthetic. Practical developments in each of these may, in turn, suggest new scholarly inquiry. For example, to stick with an example just cited above: making the case that certain intelligence gathering practices are torture rather than enhanced interrogation techniques embeds these practices in quite different histories (say, the archive of pain and sadism versus the archive of information gathering or medicine). Such developments may allow us to register features of the world we might otherwise miss: say, the extent to which some academics in the contemporary   discipline   of   psychology   became   sorts   of collaborators with the CIA's torture program, something chronicled by the contemporary philosopher Tamsin Shaw in "The Psychologists Take Power" (2016). And this may in turn suggest ways in which academic practices need to be reworked.

5. CRITICISM: IMMANENT AND OTHERWISE

In "Traditional and Critical Theory," Horkheimer presents critical theory as "part of the development of society." This is to see it as a kind of "constructive" criticism that aims to improve society: the reduction of needless suffering makes society better. When framed in this way, critical theory uses the current standards of society for its critique. So, for example, when Horkheimer criticizes the capitalist order, he notes that capitalism itself proposes "the course of history as the necessary product of an economic mechanism." Through its development, the capitalist order itself raises the possibility of a society that is intentionally constructed to benefit all rather than as a mere byproduct of competition. Horkheimer sees these two options as inherent to the present norms of capitalism. Since the market is always humanly constructed, it may be constructed in ways that are less and more responsive to needless suffering. The present capitalist order itself thereby contains "a protest against this order of things, a protest generated by the order itself," leading to "the idea of self-determination for the human race, that is the idea of a state of affairs in which man's [sic] actions no longer flow from a mechanism but from his own decision." An analogous approach towards a different feature of society is found in Martin Luther King, Jr.'s (1928–1968) "I Have a Dream" (1963) speech, where he references a "promissory note to which every American was to fall heir." When he claims that "we refuse to believe that the bank of justice is bankrupt," he means exactly to note that the United States has somehow not lived up to its own standards. Philosophers term this sort of criticism immanent criticism because it does not import an external standard by which to criticize society, instead the standards are immanent—inherent—to the society in question. Such an approach has much in common with approaches that animate the history of Black social criticism in the United Sates. As James Baldwin (1924–1987) claims in *Notes of a Native Son* (1955), it is exactly because he loves "America more than any other country in this world" that he will "insist on the right to criticize her perpetually." It is also an approach harnessed by Hegel and by Marx. The Frankfurt School certainly sometimes used such an approach, but at other times they shied away from it.

To see why this might be the case, note philosopher Michal Rosen's claim in *Hegel's Dialectic and Its Criticism* (1984) that "immanent critique, whatever it is, is not so much a method as a commitment to take one's method from the exigencies of the particular critical situation." To the extent that the Frankfurt School was at times suspicious of society as a whole, such a method may be untenable, since the present norms of society may themselves be questionable. For example, Adorno famously claims in *Minima Moralia* that "there is no correct life in the one that is false." If that's true—if the problem with society is of such scope and scale—then current norms may not be helpful. Other members or associates of the School presented views similar to Adorno's:

Whoever has emerged victorious participates to this day in the triumphal procession in which current rulers step over those who are lying prostrate. According to the traditional practice, the spoils are carried in the procession. They are called "cultural treasures" (Benjamin).

The life of the general public arises blindly, accidentally, and defectively out of the chaotic activity of individuals, industries, and states. The irrationality expresses itself in the suffering of the majority of human beings (Horkheimer).

The destructiveness of the present stage [of human civilization] reveals its full significance only if the present is measured, not in terms of past stages, but in terms of its own potentialities. There is more than a quantitative difference in whether wars are waged by professional armies in confined spaces, or against entire populations on a global scale; whether technical inventions that could make the world free from misery are used for the conquest or for the creation of suffering; whether thousands are slain in combat or millions scientifically exterminated with the help of doctors and engineers; whether exiles can find refuge across the frontiers or are chased around the earth; whether people are naturally ignorant or are being made ignorant by their daily intake of information and entertainment. It is with a new ease that terror is assimilated with normality, and destructiveness with construction (Marcuse).

Adorno thus calls the contemporary world an "open-air prison" in "Cultural Criticism and Society" (1949), suggesting in *Negative Dialectics* that even while "no universal history leads from savagery to humanitarianism," there perhaps is one "leading from the sling-shot to the megaton bomb." He claims this history "ends in the total menace which organized mankind poses to organized men." In such a wrong world, Adorno suggests, "there can be no right consciousness." Invoking the norms of such a problematic society may itself be problematic. For this reason, Adorno at times evinces a deep suspicion of immanent critique, noting in the aforemen-tioned "Cultural Criticism and Society" essay that "the alternatives—either calling culture as a whole into question from outside under the general concept of ideology, or confronting a culture with the norms that it has crystallized out of itself, cannot be recognized by critical theory." Other times, for example in *Minima Moralia*, he puts the idea as the thought that "there is not a crevice in the cliff of the established order" into which we might even "hook a finger-nail" to get immanent criticism going.

One way to register the force of Adorno's point is to think about the development of certain legal concepts. For example, prior to the development of legal concepts like genocide in the 1940s or sexual harassment in the 1970s, the experience of these phenomena could only be organized haphazardly (even though, of course, the phenomena themselves surely existed—just think of the Armenians exterminated by the Ottomans from 1915–1917 or the countless working women considered to be sexually available to their male supervisors, employers, or co-workers). Critique had to proceed in ways that pointed *beyond* current legal norms. This is no easy task, requiring the development of both conceptual and imaginative capacities. In a way, though, even this example is imperfect, since at least for both genocide and sexual harassment we had other norms that might serve as proxies: say, murder or harassment (even though neither one of these may capture the exact kind of suffering that genocide or sexual harassment produces). This may not be the case for other kinds of suffering, which may be impossible to regis-ter by means of current norms, but which nonetheless produce effects that require accounting for by society. Two formal illustra-tions here could be the experience of Nora in the Henrik Ibsen

(1828–1906) play *A Doll's House* (1879), where the protagonist Nora feels like she must flee even though she can point to no particular moral norm that would justify the action, or the ways in which legal structures simply cannot register the particular testimony of a victim due to a lack of understanding of the suffering involved, a possibility suggested and considered in some parts of Jean-François Lyotard's (1924–1998) *The Differend* (1983). More concrete cases would be structural forms of needless suffering that affect children and the very development of their subjectivity, experiences which have led to the development of notions like intergenerational trauma. Taking such a long epigenetic view, we likely have not yet grasped the full scope of the suffering involved around phenomena like child soldiers or Western residential schools aimed at "reeducating" Indigenous populations (used broadly and brutally, for example, in Canada and the United States).

6. THE NORMATIVE GROUNDS OF CRITICAL THEORY: THE INSTITUTIONAL CONTEXT

Questions around the norms that would animate the pursuits of critical theory then connect to broader questions around the relationship between critical theory and society. For example, contemporary social struggles are increasingly ambiguous, nowadays perhaps even bound up with the structures of oppression they aim to combat (think, for example, of practices like greenwashing or rainbow washing). Corporations, even as they operate gruesome sweatshops or brutally exploit, can nonetheless commit millions of dollars to "diversity, equity, and inclusion" (which itself has become an industry). Even revolt is increasingly sold or used to peddle wares, a phenomenon that the musician Frank Zappa (1940–1993) diagnosed decades ago, suggesting that this was why he believed more in "evolution rather than revolution." In response, though, we may say as Cavell does in *The World Viewed* (1971) that "the interesting question for us cannot any longer be whether a serious impulse or idea will be debased or imitated or skinned for show." Cavell notes that even "the Beethoven Ninth will be used to throw out the news." The urgent question then is "whether room continues to be made for the genuine article, and whether we will know it when we see it." The genuine thing may always be subject to fickleness, faddishness, or outright cooptation. Movements that should persist sometimes fail, while those that shouldn't persist sometimes do (and this apart from the ways in which those threatened by social struggles may explicitly work to undermine movements for change—think here, for example, of the FBI's COINTELPRO program, well detailed in David Cunningham's *There's Something Happening Here* [2004]). Worries about the social nature of struggles against oppression led Honneth, in works like *The Struggle for Recognition* (1996) and, with Nancy Fraser, in *Redistribution or Recognition?* (2003), to frame social struggles as ultimately struggles for recognition. Such struggles, Honneth argues in *Freedom's Right* (2014) and in *The Idea of Socialism* (2015), must be anchored to institutions exactly of the sort that exist in liberal democracies, so that "all members of society" have "the opportunity to participate in institutions of recognition." Only in being anchored to such institutions do they have the possibility of being efficacious over time, and only then can they weather the vagaries of chance or cooptation. For Honneth, then, the achievements of critical theory would no longer be tied to "the existence of a social movement with corresponding aims," but rather "the capacity to bring about institutional reforms within the given social reality."

On one hand, the present rise of authoritarian elements through and in such institutions across the West raises the question of whether Honneth may not just be pushing the problem back a step. On the other hand, the basic impulse pursued by Honneth (and as I'll shortly note by Habermas) may speak to the questions of what sort of institutions we might need to pursue any amelioration of needless suffering. The question that seems to be most crucial here though is a question about the normative basis of criticism altogether: how can the claims of critical theory be justified? To bring this into focus, note that even a member as seemingly bleak as Adorno does not entirely reject society entirely. On one hand, Adorno does claim in *Negative Dialectics* that "all post-Auschwitz culture, including its urgent critique, is garbage." On the other hand, he tempers the thought, explaining that "whoever pleads for the maintenance of this radically culpable and shabby culture becomes its accomplice, while the man who says no to culture is directly furthering the barbarism which our culture showed itself to be." Such paradoxical claims may suggest that there simply is no normative basis. Jürgen Habermas, the most prominent second-generation theorist of the Frankfurt School, suggested in *The Theory of Communicative Action* (1981) that from its very beginning, "critical theory labored over the difficulty of giving an account of its own normative foundations." More recently, Honneth has also claimed in *Pathologies of Reason* (2009) that there is "no doubt that the basic historical–philosophical and sociological assumptions of the Frankfurt School can no longer be defended."

Reviewing Habermas's response to this problem is worthwhile. In *Knowledge and Human Interests* (1968), Habermas claims that certain interests are fundamental to human life. The continuing reproduction of humankind requires that humans labor to create the world around them, and that they interact with each other to do so. These two requirements—labor and interaction—are underwritten by technical and practical interests that allow for the development of the kinds of knowledge humanity produces, broadly understood as falling either into the empirical-analytic sciences or the historical-hermeneutic humanities. In broad strokes, the former kind of knowledge allows for greater technical mastery with regard to nature, while the latter allows for a greater understanding of ourselves, each other, and the world in which our mastery of nature occurs. Human knowledge and interest have a fit moderated by the world. And just as in an individual human life, the two can come to fall apart. Practical need in an individual (needless suffering) necessitates psychoanalysis and then critical self-reflection and change; in society, practical need (needless suffering) necessitates critical theory and then critical social reflection and change. As Habermas puts it in *Knowledge and Human Interests*, in each case, "the pressure of suffering is also immediately an interest in enlightenment; and reflection is the only possible dynamic through which it [such an interest] realizes itself."

While Habermas abandons this project for reasons related to developments in his own thinking (more on this shortly), it is equally likely that he realizes that it rests on a questionable analogy between psychoanalysis and critical theory. As Joel Whitebrook notes in *Perversion and Utopia: A Study in Psychoanalysis and Critical Theory* (1996), there is "an ambiguity in the concept of self-reflection." On one hand, it may point to a sort of "reconstruction of the presuppositions of knowledge and action," with the implication that some kind of ignorance is the problem. Such ignorance can be corrected by making explicit what appears to be implicit: we bring something that is unknown to consciousness. On the other hand, notably in the case of psychoanalysis, what's unconscious may be so because there are particular unconscious forces *making it impossible* for this unknown element to come to consciousness (as in the case of, say, repression and desire). In such a case, these forces must be met with particular techniques. Unlike in the case of an individual undergoing psychoanalysis, though, the distinction raises questions about *who* the exact agent of critical theory is, bringing to the fore again all of the questions around normative justification.

In *The Theory of Communicative Action,* Habermas shifts the terrain of critical theory, focusing instead on the centrality of language and communication for human life. On such a view, the normative foundations of critical theory can be found through an exploration of the universal standards of rationality inherent to communication. Of course, communication can bring us together as much as it can tear us apart. Nonetheless, built into communication is the possibility to assess how agreement in language might be achieved in cases of disagreement. Habermas suggests that we have reached a point in history where such discourse (his technical term for this reflective capacity about communication) is the default means employed for settling conflict (as opposed to, say, violence or divination or whatever else). This historical claim is developed through the elaboration of two formal dimensions of the modern world: "lifeworld" and "system." "Lifeworld" refers to the world of our ordinary shared saliences: common assumptions, meanings, possibilities, standpoints, and so forth. Such a world is "living" to the extent that it both exhibits the constancy necessary for modern life and allows for the development and emergence of novelty. Without the former constancy, the world could not be shared in mutual understanding, while without the latter potential for novelty, the world could not shift in response to human lives. The lifeworld is perpetually open to revision, albeit not all at once. "System" refers to the closed world of pre-established purposes, where the parameters of human activity are determined in advance, now chiefly by the operations of money and power. In such a world, the possibilities for discourse—for reflection on how to settle disagreement—are circumvented or already foreclosed.

Each world serves a purpose, allowing for features of the modern world to continue their operation. Yet the lifeworld has priority, for the system is in fact parasitic on the lifeworld. Furthermore, as Habermas stresses, the system increasingly colonizes—monetizes—more and more elements of the lifeworld. In doing so, possibilities for communication (and discourse) are undermined, becoming proscribed solely by the operations of money or power ("appendages of the machine" is apt once again). To the extent that the system is parasitic on the lifeworld, such colonization destroys each. This situation leads Habermas to think of the ills involved here as a sort of social pathology (analogous to a pathology in medicine, where something misfunctions in otherwise well-established patterns of development). Thus, Habermas thus notes in a response to *A Theory of Communicative Action* that "social pathologies can be understood as forms of manifestation of systemically distorted communication."

7. THE NORMATIVE GROUNDS OF CRITICAL THEORY: BEYOND THE INSTITUTIONAL CONTEXT

But we may in fact question the very use of any notion of development in this context. The entire frame in fact presupposes the soundness of a particular story about the historical moment, a story that may debatable: indeed, even the extent to which current practices around discourse are settled may be questioned. Equally, underwriting such claims seems to be a notion of or a story about human progress, where modern social life is seen as an improvement on prior forms of social organization. Both Habermas and Honneth in fact undertake claims aiming to present such accounts (in Habermas as a story, in Honneth as an explicit claim). As Honneth puts it in *Pathologies of Reason*, critical theory explicitly "relies on the possibility of viewing history with reason as its guiding thread." There are many potential issues here, and readers who are steeped in the work of Habermas (or Honneth) may balk at my suggestion on this front, especially since I cannot defend it in the required depth here. (I would refer such readers to Amy Allen's *The End of Progress* for details about such a story about progress.)

The first-generation of the Frankfurt School, though, eschewed any such story. Adorno stresses in *Negative Dialectics* how there is no universal history that "leads from savagery to humanitarianism." He entertains, in fact, the possibility that the opposite may be true, that there is a universal history that leads from "the slingshot to the megaton bomb." Adorno pursues this option by suggesting that such a negative universal history must both "be construed and denied." Such a history must be construed because construing is the only way to soberly confront where we are as a species: on the brink of destruction and global catastrophe, thoroughly enveloped in a variety of needless suffering exactly because we have organized ourselves in a particular way. Such a history, however, must also be denied because it is not settled. To the extent that it is a human history, how it will turn out is still an open question. *Things could be different.* Progressive and regressive accounts of history are thereby two sides of the same coin, each always threatening to justify the status quo, which must be rejected due to the needless suffering it produces.

To return to the question of normative justification, perhaps it is enough to point out, as Adorno does in his *Problems of Moral Philosophy* (1963) lectures, that "we may not know what absolute good is or the absolute norm, we may not even know what man is or the human or humanity—but what is inhuman we know very well indeed." Critical theory may start—and be justified—where the critical theorist finds themselves. The only necessary expertise is the recognition of needless suffering. And everyone is potentially an expert. Perhaps this is all the justification that we need. On such a view, critical theory becomes in part the practical task of communicating such expertise about the world: that it produces *this* suffering in *this* way. The task demands, as Adorno puts in "Theses on the Language of the Philosopher" (1930), that we "must find the words that are alone legitimized by the state of truth in them," we must understand exactly where "truth dwells at the historical hour." This is a point as much about discerning features of the world as expressing what we have discerned. Each of these is made difficult as much by the complexity of the phenomena as the ways in which phenomena may be hidden by ideology.

An analogy strikes me here with what's sometimes termed "ordinary language philosophy," at least as how it was practiced by philosophers like J.L. Austin (1911–1960) and Stanley Cavell

(1925–2018). Such philosophers equally stressed the importance of language, but in a way distinct from Habermas. (It must be noted that Habermas also invokes Austin and "speech act theory" in *Theory of Communicative Action,* but for quite different purposes and that Marcuse launches a full blown criticism of Austin in *One Dimensional Man,* but he does so in a way that profoundly misreads him— for more on the nature of such a common misreading, although without reference to Marcuse, see Cavell's "Austin at Criticism" [1965].) For Austin and Cavell, we are each authoritative when we speak, and our speech may be understood as itself a sort of act, where at the very least we are inviting someone to see what we see. Austin and Cavell thereby both made a career of examining what we might say in particular contexts (and why and how). Austin stresses in "A Plea for Excuses" (1956) that:

> [W]hen we examine what we should say when, what words we should use in what situations, we are looking again not *merely* at words (or "meanings", whatever they may be) *but also at the realities we use the words to talk about*: we are using a sharpened awareness of words to sharpen our perception of, though not as the final arbiter of, *the phenomena* (emphasis in the original).

This is why Cavell will ultimately say in *The Claim of Reason* (1979), that our claims are "claims to community." To try to get a grip on this view, let's start with an unrelated example. Imagine you have a leak and call a plumber. In addition to diagnosing the problem, the plumber may also initiate you into viewing the malfunction of your pipes in the same way that they do. Of course, the perspective of the plumber may be rejected (and either for good reasons or poor ones—the plumber may be a poor communicator, or he may even be a swindler). In such a case, Cavell notes that "we have to conclude that on this point we are simply different; that is, we cannot here speak for one another." The plumber's perspective is not thereby invalidated; rather there just is no shared perspective, in fact "there is no us (yet, maybe never)." What's ultimately the case and wrong with any such claim is that it was made "to the wrong party." Unlike in plumbing, where it is generally settled who is an expert, and to the extent that many are capable of registering the many kinds of needless suffering around us, the suggestion is that we be willing to broaden the scope of who may count as a possible expert in the realm of critical theory, especially since we are each steeped in a shared second nature (albeit in perhaps differently reflective ways).

To understand critical theory as somehow related to ordinary language philosophy offers another context for Adorno's claim in *Negative Dialectics* that "cognition needs not less subjectivity, but more." To have a voice, to be a self, means risking rebuke or isolation, but it also means acknowledging that we always potentially speak for others, who may come to see as we do. Speech is not merely the transfer of information; it is rather itself an activity full of practical import. As Austin puts it in "Other Minds" (1946): "even if some language is now purely descriptive, language was not in origin so, and much of it is still not so." Everything hinges on finding the right words for the situation, and in this way, critique has a sort of anarchic dimension, where its parameters cannot be located solely in the realm of social movements nor in the realm of institutions, but rather perpetually haunts each, capable of transforming the boundaries between the two, often in unruly or unpredictable ways. On such a view, as Adorno puts it in *Negative Dialectics*, "the need to give voice to suffering" becomes "a condition for *all* truth."

8. CRITICAL THEORY AND SUBJECTIVITY

It is still plausible then to speak here of justification, objectivity, and truth. When a plumber sees something, anyone can come to see what they see if they are initiated into that way of seeing things. The same is true in, say, mathematics or music. Cognitive or sensible capacities can be refined in ways that allow features of the world to be perceived that previously could not be. On such a view, the world may reveal possibilities to those who are trained to see them. Note here that the world itself is inviting such possibilities for perception; they are not merely invented, even though they are accessible only to those with certain kinds of training. Such possibilities may then only appear to certain kinds of subjects. Explanation and education emerge as crucial, but their emergence only reinforces the idea that objectivity must not be seen as entirely divorced from human sensibility (a point alternatively pursued by contemporary philosophers like David Wiggins, Sabina Lovibond, and John McDowell). This background offers another way to inflect Adorno's claim in *Negative Dialectics* that "direct communicability to everyone is not a criterion of truth." Such truth, though, as David Wiggins puts it in "A Sensible Subjectivism?" (1987), is "indispensably sustained by the perceptions and feelings and thoughts that are open to criticism that is based on norms that are open to criticism."

There are, of course, dangers here—as noted earlier, there is the possibility of cooptation, destruction, fickleness, irony, and whatever else. These dangers, though, may be an unavoidable feature of being human. To truly approach everyone as a potential expert in critical theory is to approach such encounters with a sense of modesty or humility. It is striking, for example, that when asked about possibility making a list of cardinal virtues, Adorno, in *Problems of Moral Philosophy*, claims that he can "think of nothing except for modesty." With his typical pithiness, he says "we must have a conscience, but may not insist on our own conscience." Relatedly, rather than attempting to subvert the question of normative foundations merely to problems of identity—this historical account is wrong or right owing to what kind of person is making it, or, say, this or that is or isn't Eurocentric—the focus must always be on needless suffering. In such a case, it's obvious that such suffering can be produced by European practices as much as non-European ones, all without denying that the former indeed has a disproportionate and hegemonic priority in the production of suffering in the present historical moment. To approach things in this way is to make of ourselves students of needless suffering. Such studentship mitigates the kinds of dangers cited above, for rather than settling things once and for all, we are always open to the possibility of a changed perspective, a changed sensibility, a changed world. Allow everyone the possibility of being a critical theorist and you sharpen the possibilities of critical theory even if these possibilities may be misused; such misuse is easier snuffed out by the heighted awareness that comes from the expansion of critical theory being proposed. It may be the case, then, that sometimes what's required is an approach that's immanent, taking the norms or values of present society as the means for critique, while at other times, it may be that a transcendent approach is required, where new values must be invented or pursued for the purposes of critique (and the two may interact, each vivifying the other). What the two modes have in common is the deep connection between reality and our conceptual capacities. As Adorno puts it in *Negative Dialectics*, concepts are "moments of a reality that requires their formation."

In *The Idea of Critical Theory*, Raymond Geuss termed a similar approach a "contextualism" to the extent that any such an approach always depends on a specific historical context. This is the tenor in which Adorno's famous "new categorical imperative" must be understood. As he notes: "a new categorical imperative has been imposed by Hitler upon unfree humankind: to arrange their thoughts and actions so that Auschwitz will not repeat itself, so that nothing similar will happen." Adorno is here referencing the categorical imperative of Immanuel Kant (1724–1804), who wrote in the *Groundwork for the Metaphysics of Morals* (1785) that morality demands that humans pursue actions whose maxim (rule or reason or justification) can be willed in such a way that "it should become a universal law." For Kant, morality is in large part a matter of determining correct abstract universal principles. Adorno instead argues that a specific situation—Hitler and Auschwitz—requires a wholesale reorientation of how we think and act. Part of such a reorientation is a broadening of moral theory to include more than abstract principles. Adorno thereby explicitly speaks of a "practical abhorrence of the unbearable physical agony to which individuals are exposed." Our sensibility and subjectivity are each a significant feature of the new categorical imperative, which comes to be activated in virtue of being a human being at this historical moment.

Because anyone can be initiated into such a sensible subjectivity, any person may be capable of bringing distinct insights to bear on the tradition. Such insights may thereby be intimately related to a transformative practice. There are then potentially deep connections here to the sort of critical pedagogy advocated by the philosopher Paulo Freire (1921–1997), as when he stresses in *Pedagogy of the Oppressed* (1968) that the pursuit of freedom requires us to "see the world unveiled." Questions around practice are never divorced from questions about our vision and its potential refinement. Critical theory then operates along a sort of continuum, where sometimes it involves activity aimed at transforming our capacities (conceptual, imaginative, sensible, or otherwise), while at other times it involves activity aimed at transforming our world (social, political, economic, or otherwise). Each of these, though, is an activity, and thereby fundamentally practical. Critical theory may then be seen through and through as a practice, albeit one with differing dimensions. And that practice, as Horkheimer puts it in "Traditional and Critical Theory," is the pursuit of an "emancipation from slavery," it "never aims simply at an increase of knowledge as such."

If the modern world is fundamentally wrong, however, everywhere deforming individuals, then it may in fact *not* be possible to attain the sort of critical consciousness required for critical theory. Or at least it may not be possible to know when such a consciousness has been achieved. In this way, as the first-generation of the Frankfurt School seemed to think, and as Amy Allen highlights in her recent *Critique on the Couch* (2020), critical theory may in fact need psychoanalysis exactly because the picture endorsed by later generations of the Frankfurt School through their adoption of the work of developmental psychologists is already a sort of capitulation to the status quo, and thereby a sort of psychoanalytic counterpart to the kind of progressive history discussed and dismissed above. In the same lectures cited above in *Problems of Moral Philosophy,* it is notable that Adorno cautions his students to be wary of anyone who says that we "are making our stand and can do no other" (a reference to Martin Luther's refusal to recant his position). Adorno points out that "this gesture contains exactly the same positing of self, the same self-assertion as positivity." There is a tension here underwritten by the basic situation of subjects in the modern world. Critical consciousness may be foreclosed (by, say, privilege or complete deprivation), difficult (by, say, the entire everyday existence of modern life), or uncertain (by, say, gaslighting or even the very modesty Adorno recommends). In *Negative Dialectics*, Adorno claims that it may ultimately be a bit of "undeserved luck" about who arrives at a critical perspective. He notes that in such a case, "criticizing privilege becomes a privilege." This privilege becomes even more important since not everyone may immediately be able to "understand, or even perceive, all things" (note Adorno is not making the claim that not everyone can *ever* do so, only that not everyone can immediately do so). This task, of saying what people seem unable to "see or, to do justice to reality, will not allow themselves to see," thereby becomes an imperative. The thoroughgoing contingency and uncertainty that's emerged here, however, suggests that the very idea of a self must be more closely examined.

SUGGESTED READING

FRANKFURT SCHOOL WRITINGS AND SECONDARY SOURCES

Allen, Amy. *The End of Progress: Decolonizing the Normative Foundations of Critical Theory*. Columbia University Press, 2016.

Adorno, Theodor W. "Cultural Criticism and Society." Translated by Samuel Weber and Sherry Weber. In *Prisms*, 17–35. Cambridge: MIT Press, 1983.

———. *Minima Moralia*. Translated by Edmund Jephcott. London: Verso, 2005.

———. *Negative Dialectics*. Translated by E.B. Ashton. New York: The Continuum Publishing Company, 1973.

———. "Theses on Need." Translated by Martin Shuster and Iain Macdonald. *Adorno Studies* 1: 101–4.

———. "Research Project on Anti-semitism." *The Stars Down to Earth and Other Essays on the Irrational in Culture* (Routledge, 1994), 181–217.

Burke, Donald A., Colin J. Campbell, Kathy Kiloh, Michael K. Palamarek, and Jonathan Short, eds. *Adorno and the Need in Thinking: Critical Essays*. Toronto: University of Toronto, 2007.

The last collection includes a translation of Adorno's essay "Theses on the Language of the Philosopher."

Celikates, Robin. "Critical Theory and the Unfinished Project of Mediating Theory and Practice." In *The Routledge Companion to the Frankfurt School*, edited by Peter Gordon, Max Pensky, Espen Hammer, and Axel Honneth, 206–20. London: Routledge, 2018.

Finlayson, James Gordon. *Habermas: A Very Short Introduction*. Oxford University Press, 2005.

Finlayson, James Gordon. "The Persistence of Normative Questions in Habermas's Theory of Communicative Action." *Constellations* 20, no. 4 (2013): 518–32.

Fraser, Nancy, and Axel Honneth. *Redistribution or Recognition? A Political-philosophical Exchange*. London: Verso, 2003.

Habermas, Jürgen. *The Theory of Communicative Action: Volume 1: Reason and the Rationalization of Society*. Vol. 1. Boston: Beacon Press, 1985.

Habermas, Jürgen. *Knowledge and Human Interests*. New York: John Wiley & Sons, 2015.

Honneth, Axel. "Is There an Emancipatory Interest? An Attempt to Answer Critical Theory's Most Fundamental Question." *European Journal of Philosophy* 25, no. 4 (2017): 908–20.

Honneth, Axel. *The Idea of Socialism: Towards a Renewal*. New York: John Wiley & Sons, 2016.

Honneth, Axel. *Freedom's Right: The Social Foundations of Democratic Life*. New York: Columbia University Press, 2014.

Honneth, Axel. *Pathologies of Reason*. New York: Columbia University Press, 2009.

Honneth, Axel. *The Struggle for Recognition: The Moral Grammar of Social Conflicts*. Cambridge: MIT Press, 1996.

Marcuse, Herbert. "The Foundation of Historical Materialism." In *Studies in Critical Philosophy*. Translated by Joris de Bres. Boston: Beacon Press, 1973.

Whitebook, Joel. *Perversion and Utopia: A Study in Psychoanalysis and Critical Theory*. Cambridge: MIT Press, 1996.

These are the various other central works of critical theory cited and/or elaborations of some central questions discussed here.

ON CRITIQUE/CRITICISM

Finlayson, James Gordon. "Morality and Critical Theory: On the Normative Problem of Frankfurt School Social Criticism." *Telos* 146, no. 7 (2009): 7–41.

Finlayson, James Gordon. "Hegel, Adorno and the Origins of Immanent Criticism." *British Journal for the History of Philosophy* 22, no. 6 (2014): 1142–66.

Huddleston, Andrew. "Adorno's Aesthetic Model of Social Critique." *A Companion to Adorno* (2020): 237–49.

Ng, Karen. "Ideology Critique from Hegel and Marx to Critical Theory." *Constellations* 22, no. 3 (2015): 393–404.

ORDINARY LANGUAGE PHILOSOPHY

Austin, J.L. *Philosophical Papers*. Oxford: Oxford University Press, 1970.

Cavell, Stanley. *The Claim of Reason: Wittgenstein, Skepticism, Morality, and Tragedy*. Oxford: Oxford University Press, 1979.

Laugier, Sandra. *Why We Need Ordinary Language Philosophy*. Chicago: University of Chicago Press, 2013.

Norris, Andrew. *Becoming Who We Are: Politics and Practical Philosophy in the Work of Stanley Cavell*. Oxford: Oxford University Press, 2017.

BROADER PHILOSOPHICAL APPROACHES REFERENCED IN THE CHAPTER

Crenshaw, Kimberlé. "Demarginalizing the Intersection of Race and Sex: A Black Feminist Critique of Antidiscrimination Doctrine, Feminist Theory and Antiracist Politics." *u. Chi. Legal f.* (1989): 139.

Koopman, Colin. *Genealogy as Critique: Foucault and the Problems of Modernity*. Bloomington: Indiana University Press, 2013.

Nussbaum, Martha. "Capabilities as Fundamental Entitlements: Sen and Social Justice." *Feminist Economics* 9, no. 2–3 (2003): 33–59.

Rosen, Michael. *Hegel's Dialectic and Its Criticism*. Cambridge: Cambridge University Press, 1984.

MORAL PHILOSOPHY REFERENCED AT THE END OF THIS CHAPTER IN ORDER TO PROPOSE AN UNDERSTANDING OF CRITICAL THEORY

Lovibond, Sabina. *Ethical Formation*. Cambridge: Harvard University Press, 2002.

———. *Realism and Imagination in Ethics*. Minneapolis: University of Minnesota Press, 1983.

McDowell, John. *Mind, Value, and Reality*. Cambridge: Harvard University Press, 1998.

Wiggins, David. "A Sensible Subjectivism?" In *Foundations of Ethics: An Anthology*, edited by Russ Shafer-Landau and Terence Cuneo, 145–57. Oxford: Wiley-Blackwell, 2007.

ADORNO'S MORAL THEORY

Bernstein, J.M. *Adorno: Disenchantment and Ethics*. Cambridge: Cambridge University Press, 2001.

Freyenhagen, Fabian. *Adorno's Practical Philosophy: Living Less Wrongly*. Cambridge: Cambridge University Press, 2013.

Gandesha, Samir. "Adorno, Ferenczi, and a New 'Categorical Imperative after Auschwitz.'" *International Forum of Psychoanalysis* 28, no. 4 (2019): 222–30.

Shuster, Martin. *Autonomy after Auschwitz: Adorno, German Idealism, and Modernity*. Chicago: University of Chicago Press, 2014.

2

SELF

1. SUBJECTIVITY AND MATURITY

The Frankfurt School sometimes defends a somewhat traditional understanding of human subjectivity: the self is associated with reaching a certain level of maturity. Adorno ties it explicitly to the philosopher Immanuel Kant's (1724–1804) suggestion in "What is Enlightenment?" (1784) that such maturity occurs when humans move beyond a "*self-incurred* tutelage" (emphasis added). In an interview in 1969 with Hellmut Becker (1913–1993), co-founder of the Max Planck Institute for Human Development, Adorno highlights Kant's use of the German word "Unmündigkeit" for tutelage. He stresses that its opposite, "Mündigkeit" (which has no exact analogue in English but is often translated as meaning both "maturity" and "responsibility"), remains relevant and involves "the resolution and courage to rely on oneself without the guidance of another" and "the capacity and courage of each individual to make full use of his reasoning power." Autonomy could be another useful frame of reference for the term.

In mainstream Anglophone philosophy, questions of the self are oftentimes considered as derivative of broader metaphysical questions about the relationship between the mind and the body. The self appears to possess mental properties and physical ones: we are beings who move around in the world but also beings who can have thoughts about that world as we do so. Our movements are potentially observable by others, while our thoughts are not. These features of human life lead to various positions that can be located

DOI: 10.4324/9781003200963-3

on a continuum between dualist options (mental and physical things are different and irreducible to one anther) and monist options (either the mental or the physical is "really" real and the one can be reduced to the other)—a useful discussion and summary of the various options is John Heil's *Philosophy of Mind* (2019).

The Frankfurt School falls into a very different tradition of thinking about these issues, a tradition that in many ways begins with Rousseau. In "Discourse on Inequality" (1755), Rousseau argues that the self is fundamentally social, a sort of social achievement. Our selfhood is intimately related to questions of acknowledgment and recognition, and who we are is affected by how others see us. The kind of self that gets actualized is intimately related to the sort of society to which that self belongs. This tradition then receives some of its most powerful and detailed formulations in the work of Kant and the German Idealists. For this tradition, the fundamental questions surrounding the self are not metaphysical, not about what sort of substance the self is, but rather normative, about how the self justifies and understands itself irrespective of these metaphysical questions, in relation to others. For this tradition, such normative questions must be approached in different ways from metaphysical ones.

To make a start on bringing this approach into focus, think of attending a musical performance. When I have the experience of, say, watching Kristin Hayter perform, I have the experience of hearing her voice, the piano, various ambient sounds, crowd noise, and so forth. The music also perhaps elicits in me, and perhaps the audience around me, an emotional response. Equally, I see her moving on stage in front of me even as the audience and I potentially move in response to her. At any moment, I can focus my self-conscious attention on any of these features of my experience. Equally, I can also reflect on the fact that I am having this experience, in whole or in part. I can thereby make judgments about the nature of such experience. I can decide that Kristin Hayter is a "good" musician, perhaps even a "brilliant" one. Note that such a decision, such a judgment, is mine alone. The rest of the audience may disagree (so much so that they may all leave—I may literally be the only one left; it may even be that Kristin herself thinks she's terrible, but I may *still* disagree). Such an occurrence would allow me to make additional judgments: I may conclude that the reason these people are leaving is because they simply do not understand or cannot handle the subject matter of her music and its expression. The question of how I ought to judge this performance can only be settled for me and by me. Of course, it may be the case that I seek input from others, or am influenced by them, or biased by implicit or explicit indoctrination, or whatever else, but it is still the case that I ultimately *can* decide what criteria and what information are relevant to my judgment. The question then becomes whether my decision operates explicitly through reflection or implicitly through a process of social formation by means of the sort of habits, thoughts, beliefs, desires, and so forth that have been inculcated as a bit of second nature (ideology is again relevant here).

Notice, though, that were I myself to become a musician, then things would shift: it would no longer be up to me to settle whether I was a "good" musician. I may claim to be one, but unless I am recognized as such by others (likely other musicians), then it is impossible for me to be one without such recognition. This point is importantly entirely separate from whether I will make music or continue to do so, since I may do so irrespective of whether my music is recognized by anyone, ever. Note that operative here are thereby two sets of relations of recognition. There is a class of musicians that I recognize as "good," and they, in turn, are capable of recognizing me. In order for me to consider them a "good" musician, I must recognize them as such, but in order for me to be considered one, they must recognize me as such. Their recognition of me seemingly cannot occur without my recognition of them (e.g., if I do not recognize them as "good" musicians then their recognition of me would mean nothing to me and thereby have a one-sided character that leaves the matter in at least one way unsettled). The philosopher Jean-Paul Sartre (1905–1980) once noted it is impossible for me to know I am a great novelist unless others agree. Such knowledge extends across the range of human affairs, even to my claims for human standing or respect. Bringing this tradition into focus gives added depth to the point made earlier in this book: that needless suffering involves not just material or bodily suffering, but also the range of intersubjective sufferings that may follow these, pointing, say, to the sort of suffering produced by discrimination, exclusion, or expulsion (just for example). Early member of the Frankfurt School Leo Lowenthal (1900–1993), in his "Address Upon Accepting the Adorno Prize" (1989), highlights the importance of this tradition and such themes to the Frankfurt School, noting that such a tradition must remain central, for "the disavowal of any intersubjective critical interpretation, and thus of the possibility of a society that is potentially free of suffering is an explicit and implicit component in the discourse of the liquidation, death, dwindling, and disappearance of the subject" (and Lowenthal's remarks are equally useful for highlighting the theme of this chapter—the extent to which the subject, the self, is crucial to the project of critical theory).

To bring this broader philosophical tradition into focus, note that some of the questions emerging here revolve around responsibility: what is the nature of the responsibility that a subject has for their claims (me for mine and others for theirs)? How can such responsibility be justified and unpacked and understood? For example, when I make certain claims, like, say, "this candy is hard," then I also commit myself to the inclusion and exclusion of other claims (like, respectively, say, "this candy is solid" and "this candy is not soft"). We may multiply such claims beyond these relatively innocuous ones: for example, when someone claims that "Whites are the master race," then they also claim that "non-Whites are inferior" and/or "non-Whites are made to be ruled."

Kant's *Critique of Pure Reason* (1781) presents a robust first exploration of the normative basis of such aspects of human cognition and experience. While the details of Kant's argument are beyond the scope of this book, note again how Kant is uninterested in what kind of being or thing the thinking subject of such responsibility is. This is so much the case that he refers to the subject simply as "this I or he or it (the thing) which thinks." Instead, Kant is interested in how we so much as can even come to make judgments. The Frankfurt School may be seen to stand in this same tradition, with the caveat that much of their focus operates on ways in which relationships between self and self, and, self and other come to be warped or undermined or qualitatively affected by the kinds of needless suffering around us. Normative questions have an irreducibly social component, though, and any understanding of the self cannot be divorced from such social components. Furthermore, what places the Frankfurt School most forcefully in this tradition is the aforementioned notion of maturity, which stipulates that such questions cannot be ignored or bypassed, but must be addressed, again and again, as historical circumstances themselves shift in relevant ways.

2. SUBJECTIVITY, STOICISM, AND MARXISM

Contrasting the approach of the Frankfurt School around needless suffering to the approaches of a couple of other historical options can bring this point into much sharper focus. For example, there is a way in which such normative questions around suffering can be dissolved. Take, for example, Stoicism, a school of philosophy inaugurated thousands of years ago. For the Stoic, the mind is a sort of "inner citadel," where the ills of the outside world can be cordoned off so that they do not disturb the self. The Stoic Marcus Aurelius (121–180), himself no stranger to needless suffering having lost eight of his fourteen children, nonetheless wrote in his *Meditations* (161–180) that even when you kiss a son goodnight, you must resign yourself to his non-existence and "whisper to yourself, 'He may be dead in the morning.'" It is allegedly always possible to respond to any needless suffering by adjusting how that suffering is seen by the human mind. Of course, this may require training (thus his writing meditations), but as Aurelius puts it, "we have the power to hold no opinion about a thing and not to let it upset our state of mind." The Stoic may thereby agree that the world is full of needless suffering and the Stoic may even be personally involved in politics with the aim of opposing such suffering (many Stoics were in fact oftentimes ardent critics of imperial Rome). But the Stoic remains fundamentally indifferent to the political system around them since they can exercise their rational capacities in any system. Only this employment of rational capacities matters, and social questions have no ultimate bearing on personal virtue, which is either pursued or not.

Such an approach to the self is anathema to the Frankfurt School since it is at bottom a conformism to the status quo. As noted already in the first chapter, in his programmatic essay "Traditional and Critical Theory," Horkheimer, following Marx, stressed the extent to which humans profoundly shape their world, both for better and for worse. Needless suffering is not a cosmic tragedy, but rather a humanly created catastrophe. For this reason, the Frankfurt School sometimes locates Stoicism as a sort of precursor to modern bourgeois coldness, which Adorno sees as a cruel indifference to the suffering of others. In *Minima Moralia,* Adorno argues that the modern world seems to require such coldness, committed structurally to the cultivation in people of a "coarseness, insensibility, and violence." Think fundamentally of the sort of abstraction that's required to navigate a modern city, where we frequently literally step over the groans of the homeless to get to our destinations, or the sort of crudeness that accompanies most visits to the doctor in the United States, where patients are moved through areas like livestock, or where we simply imbibe the latest statistics around death and suffering with our weather forecasts and morning coffees (and this is not even to mention the explicit ways in which the success of one group oftentimes structurally requires the immiseration of another).

If Stoicism promotes a dissolution of any normative approaches to suffering, certain forms of Marxist thought equally solve such normative approaches by seeing them as a necessary feature of history. As Nikolai Bukharin (1888–1938) claims in *Historical Materialism* (1925): "society and its evolution are as much subject to natural law as is everything else in the universe." Later, he puts it simply as the idea that, "if society is to continue to develop, socialism will inevitably come." Such views see revolution as a necessary feature of the historical process, thereby suggesting that any normative assessment of needless suffering is already settled to the extent that such suffering exists to put us on the path to revolution. There are versions in which such suffering may even be embraced to the extent that it accelerates the eruption of revolution.

Such an approach suggests an understanding of the self that abdicates responsibility for and to the present historical moment. The maturity advocated by Adorno and others, however, requires the development of the human capacity for judgment and discernment and responsiveness to the present moment (even as this can be deformed in the ways discussed so far). With an eye towards the conclusion of the last chapter, such maturity also determines what sort of action the present moment suggests, including drawing the very distinction between pursuing theoretical versus practical engagement at any moment. In this vein, in his *Introduction to Sociology* (1968) lectures, Adorno stresses that once certain practical possibilities for action appeared closed off to Marx, he then "spent decades in the British Museum writing a theoretical work on national economy. That he did so without having engaged in much praxis in reality is not a matter of mere biographical accident"; it is rather the "imprint" of "an historical moment."

Such a focus on the development of human capacities for judgment and thought is also why Horkheimer, in "Traditional and Critical theory," can locate critical theory as the "heir" of "philosophy as such." To make sense of this claim, note that from philosophy's earliest history, it was always an enterprise that had a peculiar relationship to ordinary life. Socrates, for example, was called "out of place" or "unclassifiable." The philosopher Pierre Hadot (1922–2010) elaborates this as follows in *Philosophy as a Way of Life* (1995):

> One does not know how to classify him [the philosopher], for he is neither a sage nor a man like other men. He knows that the normal, natural state of men should be wisdom, for wisdom is nothing more than the vision of things as they are, the vision of the cosmos as it is in the light of reason, and wisdom is also nothing more than the mode of being and living that should correspond to this vision. ... For such a man, daily life, as it is organized and lived by other men, must necessarily appear abnormal, like a state of madness, unconsciousness, and ignorance of reality. And nonetheless he must live this life every day, in this world in which he feels himself a stranger and in which others perceive him to be one as well.

There are resonances here with the way in which critical theory has thus far been framed in this book: ordinary life cannot be accepted at face value. A crucial difference, however, is that for the ancient philosophers and their inheritors, development of the self required an investigation into the fundamentally rational nature of the world and/or its laws, a nature that may be hidden but that is nonetheless accessible to human rational thought. As noted in the Introduction, though, such a view of the world as rationally designed, began to unravel in Western culture especially after the terror of the Lisbon earthquake.

Kant and the German Idealists respond to this shift away from seeing the world as rationally designed by understanding more deeply the very possibilities and limits of human reason. In doing so, they also reformulate the contours of philosophy. This is why Horkheimer notes that in so being the heir of philosophy, in "relating to matter" and "to human production," critical theory ultimately "agrees with

German Idealism." Horkheimer qualifies this agreement by also pointing out that, with Kant and German Idealism, there is ultimately an "intervention of reason in the processes whereby knowledge and its object are constituted," but, against Kant and German Idealism, such an intervention does not occur "in a purely intellectual world, but coincides with the struggle for certain real ways of life." These claims require some explanation, cutting to the heart of the Kantian revolution in philosophy, and also to the core elements that animate the Frankfurt School conception(s) of the self. In ways still to be specified, the Frankfurt School combines three revolutionary moments in German philosophical thought: Kant and German Idealism, Marx, and Freud. From each, critical theory draws radical conclusions about the nature of the self, which together underwrite the possibilities for maturity in this context.

3. SUBJECTIVITY AND THE WORLD: KANT, HEGEL, AND MARX

As suggested earlier, philosophy prior to Kant often proceeded with an idea of the self as passive observer of a well-ordered world. The aim was to discover a natural order already there (oftentimes thought to have been placed there by divine fiat). Kant himself was struck by the fact that during his time, camps represented by two brilliant thinkers, Leibniz (mentioned already earlier) and Isaac Newton (1643–1727), fundamentally disagreed about the basic nature of reality (namely, the character of its spatial properties, even as each independently invented calculus). Struck by the fact that philosophy allegedly seemed to make no progress throughout its long history, such disagreement presented to Kant just another example of some fundamental failure in philosophical method. In response, Kant pursued a "Copernican" revolution in philosophy, so named so because he aimed to put the subject at the center of philosophy just as Copernicus put the sun at the center of astronomy. Kant thereby famously asked in the *Critique of Pure Reason* whether more progress might be made in philosophy if instead of viewing experience as a passive endeavor, we instead asked whether it might be the case that the subject is active in experience, so that "objects must conform to our cognition." This claim should not be understood in any way to suggest that humans somehow create their experience; rather Kant is interested exactly in how the human mind makes experience possible, what it contributes to its constitution.

This last claim can be unpacked by remembering that Kant sees experience as fundamentally normative. Note that our experience of the world, in all its rich sensuousness, is discrete: at every moment, and from moment to moment, there come in countless bits of sensory matter. (Think just of the experience of reading this page, where there is the visual stimuli of the various elements that make up a letter, a word, a sentence, a page, the surrounding visuals of where you're reading; the sounds, ambient and local, breathing, heartbeat, and whatever other noises; the physical qualities of what you're reading this on, the way the book or electronic reader feels to you; the sorts of tastes and smells that are occurring as you do so, etc.) Kant's revolutionary position in the *Critique of Pure Reason* is that the experience we have of the sensible world—where things are, what they are, how they are—occurs, in part, because our mind organizes the disparate discrete bits of sensibility into a unified whole. Exactly because the human mind has the power to reflect on—to take a reflexive stance towards—its own experience, philosophy can then explore those elements that the human mind contributes to the matter delivered to our senses (thus a *critique* of pure reason: a critical reflection on what human reason contributes for experience to be possible and thereby also on the limits of all possible knowledge in this realm). In his lectures *Kant's Critique of Pure Reason* (1959), Adorno stresses that this novel aspect of Kant's approach was exactly "the reflection of reason on itself" and that this "reflexivity is what lies at the heart of the Copernican revolution." Experience thereby is in part possible because the mind imposes concepts on the sensible matter supplied to it. The philosopher Robert Brandom suggests in *Tales of the Mighty Dead* (2002) that we may say that "for Kant, concepts are rules determining what one has committed oneself to by applying the concept in judging or acting—and so what would count as a reason entitling one to or justifying such a commitment."

The complex history of German philosophical development following Kant's revolution continues to be the topic of numerous books. It features well-known and less well-known figures of German Idealism like Friedrich Henrich Jacobi (1743–1819), Salomon

Maimon (1753–1800), Johann Gottlieb Fichte (1762–1814), Friedrich Schelling (1775–1854), and Georg Wilhelm Hegel (1770–1831). This tradition was no less important for the Frankfurt School, especially Kant and Hegel. (Hegel, for example, was the topic of Marcuse's *Hegel's Ontology and the Theory of Historicity* [1932], which prompted his entrance into the Institute for Social Research, while Adorno and Horkheimer's earliest philosophical experiences involved Kant's philosophy.) While the issues involved here are mammoth, one way to understand the problem that occupies these figures, and that receives a striking formulation in Hegel, is a certain suspicion about the alleged radicalness of Kant's project. (This is one way to understand Marcuse's opening line in *Reason and Revolution* [1941] that German Idealism might be called the "theory of the French revolution.") While Kant was correct to highlight the ways in which human experience was normative, he allegedly failed to recognize the ways in which our normative commitments are themselves a product of historical processes. On such a view, the conceptual capacities that organize sensible matter into experience themselves shift over time as our form of life shifts. Hegel thus famously claims in the *Philosophy of Right* (1820) that "philosophy is its own time comprehended in thought." Adorno echoes this sentiment when he notes, in the aforementioned lectures on Kant, that Hegel interprets history "as the determination of subject and object, but in a way that distances them fundamentally from their general definition as constant, unchanging entities." The Hegelian claim is that a true Copernican revolution in our understanding of the relation between self and world is satisfied only through an exploration of how the formal properties of reason emerge as the result of historical processes.

Marx similarly charges Hegel as being insufficiently radical. For Marx, the basic features of Hegel's account are to be commended, but it is now Hegel who must be radicalized because he fails to grasp how our normative commitments ultimately have a material basis linked to how society is economically organized. In the second afterword to the German edition of *Capital* (1873), Marx draws a sharp contrast between himself and Hegel, arguing that where for Hegel "thinking" is primary, for him (Marx), such thinking "is nothing else than the material world reflected by the human, and translated into forms of thought." Capitalism, with its concomitant class struggle, thereby has a profound effect on human experience to the extent that it fundamentally alters how we conceptually organize the sensible matter presented to us. Marx's philosophical shift is decisive for the emergence of critical theory. Marcuse notes in *Reason and Revolution* that, while keeping with the impulse of Kant's Copernican revolution, Marx reveals that there is more at stake here than philosophy, for now "the whole problem is … no longer a philosophical one, for the self-realization of man [sic] now requires the abolition of the prevailing mode of labor, and philosophy cannot deliver this result." What's emerging here is a normative standpoint that sees the relationship between our knowledge of the world and our knowledge of ourselves as mediated by historical processes which are themselves mediated by material conditions. And these material conditions, in turn, appear to depend certain kinds of social change.

These quotes from Marx may make it seem as if the relationship between economic realities and human cognitive developments is somehow causal or direct. This is certainly not the case for the Frankfurt School, who adamantly reject any such mechanical conception of the relationship between the two. Horkheimer explicitly aims to chart a middle path between Hegel and Marx in his programmatic "The Present Situation of Social Philosophy and the Tasks of an Institute for Social Research" (1931), where he rejects "such dogmatic convictions." Horkheimer argues that any reading that claims that "ideas are primary, while material life, in contrast, is secondary or derivative" is "an abstractly and thus badly understood Hegel." Similarly, any reading that claims that "the psyche of human beings, personality as well as law, art, and philosophy, are to be completely derived from the economy, or mere reflections of the economy" is equally "an abstractly and thus badly understood Marx." There just is no such "complete correspondence between ideal and material processes" in either direction. Contemporary scholarship on Hegel and Marx echoes Horkheimer's sentiments as when, for example, the philosopher Susan Buck-Morss stresses the influence of the Haitian revolution on Hegel's thought in *Hegel, Haiti, and Universal History* (2009), or when the sociologist Kevin B. Anderson highlights how Marx thought about racism and colonialism in the context of economic development in *Marx at the Margins* (2020).

4. SUBJECTIVITY AND THE WORLD: FREUD, PSYCHOANALYSIS, AND MATERIAL PROCESSES

Following in the wake of these German philosophical developments, critical theory pursues an interdisciplinary, multi-pronged investigation of the mediation between "ideal and material processes" and how they contribute to the formation of the self. Horkheimer stresses in "The Present Situation of Social Philosophy and the Tasks of an Institute for Social Research" that "the question today is to organize investigations stimulated by contemporary philosophical problems in which philosophers, sociologists, economists, historians, and psychologists are brought together in permanent collaboration." Horkheimer frames a possible line of inquiry as follows:

> [W]hich connections can be demonstrated between the economic role of a specific social group in a specific era in specific countries, the transformation of the psychic structure of its individual members, and the ideas and institutions as a whole that influence them and that they created?

Critical theory may pursue "large philosophical questions on the basis of the most precise scientific methods." The incredible scope of critical theory—a theory concerned with the entirety of society—comes into sharp relief. To this picture, though, Horkheimer adds another feature, noting that the "correspondence between ideal and material processes" is ultimately a question around "the complicating role of the psychical links connecting them." Horkheimer himself pursues the details of such an account in various essays, most explicitly in "Egoism and Freedom Movements: On the Anthropology of the Bourgeois Epoch" (1936). In this tour de force, Horkheimer outlines on one hand a theory of how particular historical circumstances produce specific general psychological characteristics, and on the other hand a detailed account of how modern history produces a bourgeois character, defined in large part by individualism and cruelty. Here's how Horkheimer describes it:

> Each one is the center of the world, and everyone else is "outside." All communication is an exchange, a transaction between solipsistically

> constructed realms. The conscious being of these individuals can be
> reduced to a small number of relations between fixed quantities. The lan-
> guage of logistics is its appropriate expression. Coldness and alienness are
> the direct result of this basic structure of the epoch: nothing in the
> essence of the bourgeois individual opposes the repression and annihila-
> tion of one's fellow human beings. On the contrary, the circumstance
> that in this world each becomes the other's competitor, and that even
> with increasing social wealth there are increasingly too many people,
> gives the typical individual of the epoch a character of coldness and indif-
> ference, one that is satisfied with the most pitiful rationalizations of the
> most monstrous deeds as long as they correspond to his interest.

While I have omitted the lengthy and extensive historical research
that Horkheimer pursues to establish these claims, it is striking how
he is able to situate disparate historical movements against various
kinds of authority—from Cola di Rienzo (1313–1354) in Italy to
the Reformation to the French revolution—as all contributing to
the emergence of a particular kind of subjectivity. Such subjectivity
is in fact progressive at a certain historical moment (when its individualism and resolve is in the service of opposing authority) but
can become regressive at a subsequent historical moment (as when
a "more rational system becomes technically possible over the
course of centuries" but is nonetheless incapable of being actualized
because present conditions do not allow it to emerge).

While there is more to say about all of this, and this is an essay to
which I will return in subsequent chapters, Horkheimer's invocation of a historically produced character and psychic links brings to
the fore the final German influence on how the Frankfurt School
understands the self—Sigmund Freud (1856–1939). Although the
progenitor of psychoanalysis, Freud very much saw himself as part
of the same German philosophical tradition that Kant inaugurated.
In "The Unconscious" (1915), Freud explicitly frames "the psychoanalytic assumption of unconscious mental activity" as "an
extension of the corrections begun by Kant in regard to our views
on external perception." Freud continues, stressing that "just as
Kant warned us not to overlook the fact that our perception is subjectively conditioned," so we also must acknowledge that "psychoanalysis bids us not to set conscious perception in the place of the
unconscious mental process." Into the Copernican revolution,

Freud aims to inject depth: he agrees that the subject stands at the center of experience, but he argues that the subject available to ordinary reflection—even of the most philosophically sophisticated kind—is the tip of the iceberg. The conscious subject is a mere portion of a greater reservoir of id (Freud's technical term for the conglomeration of libidinous drives that exist, generally unconsciously, in every individual). As Freud puts it in *The Ego and the Id* (1923), "in each individual there is a coherent organization of mental processes; and we call this his [sic] ego. It is to this ego that consciousness is attached." While Freud's own views about how the ego is formed undergo change through his work, what's important for the present story is the picture he presents in his late work, especially in *Inhibitions, Symptoms, and Anxiety* (1926), where he stresses that the ego is "the organized portion of the id." Freud there points out that "we should be quite wrong if we pictured the ego and the id as two opposing camps," rather the entire aim of the method of psychoanalysis as Freud conceived it was to allow for a "free intercourse" between the unconscious and conscious elements that constitute every subject. For Freud, it is the analysis and interpretation of our dreams, slips, jokes, pathologies, disorders, and so forth that offer us access to the depths of our (unconscious) subjectivity. And psychoanalysis, according to Freud, again with a nod to the German philosophical tradition, is itself the pursuit of a sort of mediation between the conscious and unconscious (so much so that Freud claims in "The Unconscious" that "a complete divergence" or "a total severance of the two systems" of conscious and unconscious is exactly the "condition of illness").

Critical theory combined the approaches of Marx and Freud (even as these themselves built on Kant and German Idealism). With Marx, the Frankfurt School explores how economic conditions alter the world and human subjectivity, especially the extent to which they contribute to the rise of needless suffering. With Freud, they explore how their conditions create additional needless psychic suffering and why subjects often appear incapable of recognizing the full range of their suffering. In many ways, the necessity of such a program was suggested, although not pursued in the same way, by the Marxist philosopher Karl Korsch (1886–1961), who claimed, in *Marxism and Philosophy* (1923), that the sort of revolutionary radical change that Marx envisioned "was never seized because the *socio-psychological* preconditions for its seizure were lacking" (emphasis added). Freud's work could offer insight into why conditions of increasing immiseration did not seem to lead to revolution or change. (We may diagnose here then a deepening of Marx's theory of crisis, discussed already in the Introduction, which it should now be clear cannot be understood exclusively or solely in mechanical or economic terms.) Freud was thereby central to the establishment of critical theory, so much so that the Frankfurt Psychoanalytic Institute came to be housed in the same building as the Institute for Social Research. This centrality should not be taken to mean that the Frankfurt School saw the mediation between mental and material life occurring *only* in the unconscious realm. As their interdisciplinary program maintained, such an approach occurs in a variety of realms and registers. (With an eye to the present moment, just think of the ways in which commodified culture inculcates in its participants a range of biases about, say, gender or race, both consciously and unconsciously.) In the words of historian Martin Jay in *The Dialectical Imagination* (1973), such a program, especially with its integration of Freud, was incredibly "bold and unconventional." Erich Fromm (1900–1980) was central to the Frankfurt School's integration of Freud and Marx. In early essays like "Psychoanalysis and Sociology" (1929), "Politics and Psychoanalysis" (1930), Fromm explicitly synthesized the two figures. With an eye to this discussion, Fromm notes in "The Method and Function of an Analytic Social Psychology" (1932) that he pursued this synthesis exactly because "Marx and Engels could not explain how the material basis [of society] was reflected in man's [sic] head and heart."

Freud's early work on human drives was central to the Frankfurt School. In this work, Freud argued that humans possess two basic sets of drives: those aiming at self-preservation and those aiming at libidinous satisfaction. Drives towards self-preservation were relatively invariable and generally available to consciousness. For example, hunger can only be repressed for so long. Drives towards libidinal satisfaction, however, admit of great variability. As Fromm summarizes things in "The Method and Function of an Analytic Social Psychology," such sexual drives can be "postponed, repressed, sublimated, and interchanged." When unsatisfied in various ways, such drives may shift from the conscious realm to the unconscious realm. They are, in Fromm's words, "much more elastic and flexible than the instincts for self-preservation." Freud thus notes in *Three Essays on the Theory of Sexuality* (1905) that in thinking about drives we must "loosen the bond that exists in our thoughts between drive and object." In short, sexual drives can be satisfied by a range of objects and a range of activities.

Such malleability was of great interest to Fromm and to the Frankfurt School. From the fact that from their infancy every human being has another human being as a model (for better or for worse), Freud claimed in *Group Psychology and the Analysis of the Ego* (1921) that "individual psychology is simultaneously social psychology." In "The Method and Function of an Analytic Social Psychology," Fromm glosses Freud's thought as the idea that "every society has its own distinctive libidinal structure, even as it has its own economic, social, political, and cultural structure." Different kinds of human organization affect how sexual drives develop. In Fromm's words, "the environment, social reality" is a crucial "modifying factor." With an eye especially to the capitalist form of organization, Fromm points out that "the role of primary formative factors goes to the economic conditions," but "the family is the essential medium through which the economic situation exerts its formative influence on the individual's psyche." Such a point now regularly appears in various contemporary analyses of capitalism and might be unpacked as the idea that capitalism orients itself through a certain familial structure, one that requires, say, a "breadwinner" and a "caretaker." Such a structure, may, in turn, be maintained through the performance of distinct gender roles (men vs. women), the glorification of particular virtues ("grit" or "resiliency"), and the preponderance of certain disorders or feelings (say, anxiety or loneliness). (And there are here, for example, many potential avenues of connection to theories about the performativity of gender as in the contemporary critical theorist Judith Butler; to the ways in which capitalism requires the free reproductive capacities and labor of women for maintenance of its work force, as in the work of critical theorists Selma James and Mariarosa Dalla Costa, and to the ways in which economic configurations affect conceptions of sexuality, as in, for example, Christopher Chitty's [1983–2015] sketch of sexuality under hundreds of years of capitalism in *Sexual Hegemony* [2020].)

Fromm thought a theory of social character was the most compelling way to explain "the shared, socially relevant, psychic attitudes and ideologies—and their unconscious roots in particular—in terms of the influence of economic conditions on libido strivings." Fromm first pursues such a theoretical approach with "The Dogma of Christ" (1930). He argues that the development of early Christian belief could be traced to the social and economic situation of Roman imperial rule. Such rule, in combination with a social caste system among Jews, led to certain radical impulses, so that "the first Christians were a brotherhood of socially and economically oppressed enthusiasts held together by hope and hatred." These early Christians differed from other oppressed groups under imperial rule only in the fact that their prospects for change, because subject to Jewish and Roman rule, were entirely hopeless, and it is this "complete hopelessness of realization [that] led the early Christians to formulate the same wishes in fantasy." While a fascinating work, for present purposes, its most interesting feature is the clue it gives to the method that Fromm pioneers. He explains that whereas ordinary "psychoanalytic research is concerned primary with neurotic individuals," the sort of "social-psychological research" that he is pursuing "is concerned with groups of normal people." Every society allegedly affects the development of basic sexual drives in ways that allow us to tease out a social character created by the ordinary ways in which these drives develop within particular social groups.

Essentially this understanding of the relationship between psychoanalysis and social-psychological research underwrites the Institute's first empirical study of German workers in 1929. While likely formulated collaboratively, the study was directed by Fromm. It might be said to attempt to respond exactly to Karl Korsch's question about why the working class did not incline towards revolution. Fromm and other members designed a questionnaire that was sent to a little over three thousand workers. It inquired into objective details about a respondent's political membership in addition to their social and economic status. At the same time, it also asked a range of informal questions about their attitudes towards politics, authority, and other elements of society. Alleged correlations between various answers were used to categorize study participants into authoritarian, radical, or reformist social characters. By current sociological standards and protocols, the design is rudimentary. Nonetheless, the study offered some powerful predictive conclusions, not the least of which was the claim that, even though the left "had the political loyalty and votes of the great majority of workers," these workers generally harbored authoritarian attitudes. The left "had by and large [thereby] not succeeded in changing the personality structure of its adherents in such a way that they could be relied upon in critical situations." The Frankfurt School was here prescient, as the rise of Hitler only too well illustrated. For a variety of reasons, this study was never published until years after Fromm's death (and then by someone not associated with the Institute), but the study is explicitly mentioned in the first published collective research project by the Institute, *Studies on Authority and the Family* (1936). Like the earlier study of German workers, this was a collaborative project that also had an empirical component: a questionnaire answered by thousands of youngsters in several European countries. They responded to questions about familial life and conceptions of family. The published study, however, was quite uneven, consisting of this empirical work and of theoretical reflections that did not particularly reference the empirical work in meaningful ways (although it was still quite compelling, making useful interventions into how we might think about the sort of traits that familial life produced under capitalism).

5. FROMM, PSYCHOANALYSIS, AND THE FRANKFURT SCHOOL

Around the time of this study is when a fissure between Fromm and the School emerged, exactly around psychoanalytic theory, including explicitly differing conceptions of selfhood and subjectivity. Before turning to these differences, and especially keeping with the spirit of a critical theoretical interest in material conditions, it is worth noting that there was potentially also an economic dimension to the fissure. The Institute increasingly had greater expenses given its move and its inclination, when interested, to help those fleeing the Nazi regime. In 1939, Fromm was asked to continue at the Institute without his salary (perhaps because he had a working income through a successful therapeutic practice, although only a year earlier Fromm had asked in a letter to borrow money to help his mother flee Germany, a request which Horkheimer did not grant). Fromm declined this proposed arrangement, negotiating instead a buyout by the Institute of his tenured appointment for the sum of $20,000 (the equivalent of almost $500,000 in today's terms). I mention this not to suggest that the intellectual disagreements that emerged here were not serious or authentic, but rather to say that the split may have been overdetermined. One way to register this point is to note that the Frankfurt School integration of psychoanalytic theory continues to the present day and involves a variety of oftentimes incompatible approaches. There is in fact still debate about which kind of psychoanalytic theory best serves the interests and needs of critical theory (a topic well explored in Amy Allen's recent book *Critique on the Couch* [2020]).

To bring the disagreement between Fromm and the School in the late 1930s into focus, let me fast-forward for a moment to the likely most well-known study associated with the Institute, *The Authoritarian Personality* (1950). Involving Adorno and published as part of the "Studies in Prejudice" sequence of books sponsored by the American Jewish Committee (a Jewish non-profit that funded elements of the Institute's work in the United States), the study is in many ways a sort of extension of the earlier study on German workers (other notable books in this series include Leo Lowenthal and Norbert Gutermann's study of the methods of American ideologues in *Prophets of Deceit* [1949] and Norbert Gutermann's *Rehearsal for Destruction* [1949], a study of antisemitism in imperial Germany). *The Authoritarian Personality* involved a much more sophisticated series of quantitative and qualitative questions aimed at discerning personality traits which could then be ranked by means of their alleged intensity along four scales: AS scale (antisemitism), the E scale (ethnocentrism), PEC scale (political-economic conservatism), and the F scale (fascism). The F scale was the great innovation of this study, allowing for the identification of a "potentially fascistic individual." In one of the study's chapters, "Types and Syndromes," Adorno reflects on the study's use of types. Adorno stresses that contemporary society has such a mass character that the use of types is justifiable, and in fact "holds good for our own standardized mass culture to even higher a degree than for previous periods." In such a mass society, it should not be neglected "that large numbers of people are no longer, or rather never were, 'individuals' in the sense of traditional nineteenth-century philosophy." In his Remarks on the study, however, Adorno pushes the thought further, musing that perhaps the mass character of society is becoming so extreme that we are entering a phase of human history where "the individual, in the sense of an equilibrium between ego, superego, and id, can no longer be regarded as the characteristic form of today's human beings." In such a case, "psychology may begin to become obsolescent inasmuch as individual actions can no longer be explained adequately in terms of the individual's own psychological household."

Emerging here is a crossroads for critical theory as the Frankfurt School pursued it. Because several lines of salience meet here, it is worthwhile to demarcate each of them. The locus of concern here is the issue of the relationship between psychoanalytic theory and the historical moment. Freud's position is that there are basic sexual drives whose development is affected by one's familial life. Fromm's early work, and the subsequent work of the Frankfurt School, stressed how historical circumstances may affect how these drives develop to the extent that their development is affected by shifts in the structure of the family. So, for example, the German workers study may reveal how familial life was affected by World War I, where fathers suffered great trauma or were absent due to having perished in the war (not to mention the more "common" psychoanalytic processes Freud diagnosed with something like the Oedipus complex). Several possible responses emerged from this picture, each representing options and sub-options that have been sometimes pursued by critical theory.

For Fromm, this led to a questioning of Freud's drive theory as ethically objectionable to the extent that Freud's theory required us to see, say, patriarchal relations as somehow natural (the aforementioned Oedipus complex is taken to be an alleged feature of being human as opposed to a possible historical configuration). This led him, as he reports in a letter to an Institute colleague in 1936, to conceptualize drives as themselves already historical artifacts, so that the "drives which motivate social behavior are not, as Freud assumed, sublimations of sexual instincts," but rather "the products of social processes." This is the fulcrum that separates him from the rest of the Frankfurt School. Adorno pursues criticism of Fromm on this point even in his late lectures *Philosophical Elements of Society* (1964), where he points out that "one can show in detail that the attempt to directly sociologize psychology failed because individuals in their individual formation are largely archaic and are not connected to the sociopsychological stimuli around them so directly." What's at stake in this criticism, though, is a conception of self and society. While both Adorno and Fromm agree that history affects the development of sexual drives, they differ around the exact mechanisms by which this happens. (In this way, then, they both reject a traditional reading of Freud and the Oedipus complex as an ahistorical process.) Adorno stresses that if one takes Fromm's view, then the self comes to be too much assimilated to society. In such a case, the procedures of psychology are entirely irrelevant, for the only thing that matters is changing society. Adorno compares psychology in such a case to a massage, where one works on symptoms but is not able to affect the underlying disorder that gives rise to the muscular pain in the first place. Equally, Adorno stresses that Fromm's picture also gives rise to a too tidy view of both these drives and society, for while Adorno agrees that "this deep layer of the individual is, of course, also of a social nature," it is not immediately accessible, for "the images and fundamental constellations one encounters in the unconscious themselves also refer back to social conflicts." While drives may be historically affected, their origins in prior social conflicts may now be forgotten or unknown, since contemporary social development has prevented accessing them or has covered them over with other things. Once again, there is an interpenetration between history and nature, where each is defined in terms of the other, but this situation is such that each is a conglomeration of sedimented pasts, oftentimes inaccessible in historically contingent ways, all while appearing as wholly natural (and thereby seemingly ahistorical).

As Adorno noted in his remarks on *The Authoritarian Personality* and in the preface to *Minima Moralia*, perhaps we are entering a phase of history where even the very notion of an individual, let alone an individual capable of critical theory, is untenable. If psychology is merely to be like a superficial massage, something incapable of getting to the root issues, then it becomes difficult to see how, on Fromm's picture, change could ever happen, for society appears to be producing individuals who are no longer capable of critical reflection. Fromm appears to recognize something like this problem since his later work increasingly glosses human beings as having a sort of invariable existential dimension, so that there exist "basic existential dichotomies," "fundamental psychological phenomena," and "existential needs" (just to name a few formulations throughout the years). There is here, then, seemingly a commitment to both the fundamentally historical nature of human mindedness (diagnosed via social character) and to something like an invariant human nature. In *Escape from Freedom* (1941), Fromm presents "the striving for justice and truth" as "an inherent trend of human nature." He explains this invocation of a "trend of human nature" by noting that "the only way to account for this striving for justice and truth is by the analysis of the whole history" of humankind. Wherever someone is powerless, "justice and truth are the most important weapons" in fighting for "freedom and growth." Fromm extends the thought, noting that in every human childhood there is an experience of powerlessness, and so thereby "in this state of powerlessness traits like the sense of justice and truth develop and become potentialities common to man as such." Fromm then concludes the thought with the idea that "*although character development is shaped by the basic conditions of life and although there is no biologically fixed human nature, human nature has a dynamism of its own that constitutes an active factor in the evolution of the social process*" (emphasis in the original). It is hard to know exactly how to take Fromm here. Even as he denies a human nature, he at the same time invokes it. Such a suspicion seems to be confirmed when he later writes about the subject in *Man for Himself* (1965) that only if a human being recognizes "the human situation, the dichotomies inherent in his [sic] existence and his capacity to unfold his powers, will he be able to succeed … to be himself and for himself and to achieve happiness by the full realization of those faculties which are peculiarly his—of reason, love, and productive work." Fromm's last work, *To Have or To Be* (1970), evinces a similar ambiguity, speaking of "two basic character orientations," but doing so while pursuing a historical story starting from "the beginning of the industrial age." There is potentially more to be said here about Fromm's work but suffice it to say that any invocation of an invariant human nature was a non-starter for other members of the first-generation of the Frankfurt School. As Horkheimer had noted in the aforementioned "Egoism" essay and explicitly in "Remarks on Philosophical Anthropology" (1935): human nature is "continuously influenced and changed by a manifold of circumstances."

Adorno equally argues that Freud's conception of drives cannot be abandoned, for it is central to the pursuit of critical theory in the present. On one hand, such drives prohibit an all too easy conformism to present society. As Adorno puts it in "Social Science and

Sociological Tendencies in Psychoanalysis" (1946), "the stress on totality as against the unique, fragmentary impulses, always implies the harmonistic belief in what might be called the unity of the personality, [a unity that] is never realized in our society. It is one of the greatest merits of Freud that he has debunked the myth of this unity." The "neurotic" individuals with whom psychoanalytic theory is concerned are of interest exactly because they are the byproduct of a fundamentally wrong world, while the groups of normal people that Fromm would make the interest of theory are exactly a dead end because they have adjusted themselves to a world that is fundamentally wrong. A denial of drive theory then ultimately lends "the glamor of the humane to an inhuman world." In opposition to any conformism, or to the contemporary psychiatric focus on "cognitive behavior therapy," Adorno rejects any attempt to reconcile oneself to an inhuman world. In reconciling ourselves in this way, we ultimately "treat a dehumanized society as if it were already a human one." Fromm's abandonment of drive theory leads either to conformism or to a problematic notion of a timeless human nature. On the other hand, these same drives may equally hold out some hope, for if properly harnessed, they might point beyond the current status quo, towards utopian possibilities that otherwise would not appear. Archaic drives sedimented in our psychological inheritance, while dormant now, may, if activated or unearthed, point beyond the present moment. We may think here of Benjamin's question in another context in "On the Concept of History": "doesn't a breath of the air that pervaded earlier days caress us as well?" Such archaic drives may also, in Adorno's words, allow us to "take utopia seriously and want it to materialize," viewing "reality with no illusions." Viewing society in this way is to acknowledge "the petrified conditions under which we live, and become as hardened as they are, in order to break them." Freud's early drive theory then serves as a sort of bulwark against conformity and defeat to present conditions.

6. PSYCHOANALYSIS AND HISTORY: HORKHEIMER, ADORNO, AND MARCUSE

This commitment to drives allows Adorno to formulate an even more serious objection to Fromm, but it is an objection that cuts in all directions, making any path towards the kind of maturity invoked at the beginning of this chapter ever more difficult. Note that the sort of critique of patriarchy that Fromm pursued against Freud continues to animate present-day critiques of Freud. Yet it is also possible to read Freud as himself a sort of diagnostician of patriarchal society, someone who maps its psychoanalytic currents. This was, for example, the reading popularized by Juliet Mitchel's landmark *Psychoanalysis and Feminism* (1974). It was also the approach to Freud that Adorno suggests in the aforementioned "Social Science and Sociological Tendencies in Psychoanalysis" (and in later works like "Sociology and Psychology" [1967]). Adorno begins the earlier paper by noting that when we "speak incessantly about the influence of society upon the individual," we "fail to see that the individual himself, nay, the very category of individualization is a social product." Adorno stresses that when Freud understood the individual as "a coherent organization of mental processes," he was already embarking on a historical understanding of the self, one that betrayed the social achievement of the possibility of such an organization. Such an achievement, though, must itself be understood as having its possibilities defined by the historical moment. Although the self is an organization of mental processes, it may be the organization of quite conflicting drives. Freud's theory thereby offers a sophisticated understanding of the modern world, where atomism rules and where conflicting social processes oftentimes exist simultaneously. As Adorno puts it, "the so-called atomistic psychology of Freud's is the adequate expression of a reality in which men are atomized and are separated one from the other by an almost unbridgeable gulf." The suggestion is that experience in modernity may itself already always be fragmentary, incomplete, full of gaps and contradictions, perhaps incapable of unproblematic integration into a properly functioning individual. For Adorno, this is "the deepest justification" for "delving into the archaic depth of the individual and treating it as if it were absolute." Freud's drive theory thereby cannot be abandoned, for the presence of these conflicting—and perhaps from the perspective of the present moment sometimes even alien drives—allows us properly to understand and respond to contemporary society, where "the relationships of men [sic] today are neither determined by their will nor even by their drives but by socio-economic materializing over the heads of the individual members of society."

Into this last line are compressed several possibilities that the Frankfurt School worked out. They can be brought to the fore by returning to Horkheimer's contribution to the aforementioned *Studies on Authority and the Family*. In his contribution, "Authority and the Family" (1936), Horkheimer argued that there was an important relationship between the formation of the ego, the structure of the bourgeois family and its concomitant demand for authority, and the sort of psychoanalytic relationships and economy it necessitated. Thus, he writes that:

> At the beginning of the bourgeois age the father's control of his household was doubtless an indispensable condition of progress. The self-control of the individual, the disposition for work and discipline, the ability to hold firmly to certain ideas, consistency in practical life, application of reason, perseverance and pleasure in constructive activity could all be developed, in the circumstances, only under the dictation and guidance of the father.

In other words, it is exactly through the sort of mechanisms that Freud described that an ego capable of critical theory could be formed. It is only when the authority of the father is internalized in the development of a superego that a subsequent possibility arises for conflict. In such cases, the superego can be questioned by the ego creating a model for all subsequent critical theory. Such an ego, in its possibilities for critique and critical theory, might be seen as a fingerhold by which maturity becomes possible.

As already hinted above, though, Adorno stresses how we may be entering a moment where the sort of ego formation that Freud describes has become impossible. Adorno presents a picture of such a state of affairs in a remarkable fragment titled "The Problem of A New Type of Human Being" that he composed likely in 1941 for a planned book he'd worked on for several years called *Current of Music* (unpublished during his lifetime, but published posthumously through Bob Hullot-Kentor's work). Adorno describes such a new type of person as a "person whose being lies in the fact that he no longer experiences anything himself, but rather lets the all-powerful, opaque social apparatus dictate all experiences to him, which is precisely what prevents the formation of an ego, even of a 'person' at all." Elsewhere in the essay, he glosses such a loss of individuality in the following terms:

> The individual seems to be on the way to a situation in which it can only survive by relinquishing its individuality, blurring the boundary between itself and its surroundings, and sacrificing most of its independence and autonomy. In large sectors of society there is no longer an 'ego' in the traditional sense. As all the traditional culture with which educators wish to bring people into contact presupposes the ego, however, and appeals to the ego, the very possibility of cultural education is now highly problematic from the outset.

While the full strength of this diagnosis will depend on grasping the way in which the Frankfurt School understands modern society (the topic of the next chapter), the basic picture should be relatively clear: the various structures and institutions of contemporary society are such that even the possibility of ego formation is in jeopardy. It is possible to cite here the breakdown of the traditional family structure so that children are increasingly raised only with the exceedingly weak authority of television, video games, or other products of the culture industry; or with only the administration of failing school systems; or without any significant authority altogether. In "Social Science and Sociological Tendencies in Psychoanalysis," Adorno describes the situation as a moment of narcissism, where because of the atomism of contemporary society, any sort of genuine connection to others becomes impossible, and thereby narcissism becomes the norm, having "its ultimate root in the almost prohibitive difficulties of any spontaneous and direct relationships between men today, which forces the individual, as it were, to throw his [sic] unused libidinous energy upon himself."

The category of narcissism invoked here is Freud's technical term, which he first introduces in "On Narcissism" (1914) to cover a state where the subject's sexual energy is directed inwards. Adorno's invocation requires some explanation, however, since Adorno is invoking the way in which the term develops in Freud's later work. In "On Narcissism" Freud conceives the ego as first focusing all its sexual energies on itself. The noted psychoanalyst Hans

Loewald (1903–1963) suggests in "Ego and Reality" (1949) that what's being referenced here is a primordial state that first exists in the womb, where "there are no boundaries and therefore there is no distinction between the two [ego and external reality]." In his "Introductory Lectures on Psycho-Analysis" (1917), Freud gives sleep as an example of a regression to such a state, where "in a sleeper the primal state of distribution of the libido is restored— total narcissism, in which libido and ego-interest, still united and indistinguishable, dwell in the self-sufficing ego." Take such infantile narcissism as a limit case, helpful for understanding the more developed notion of narcissism that Adorno invokes. Adorno's suggestion is that the modern world produces a situation where the ego is so underdeveloped that things look more and more like infantile narcissism, where there is little differentiation between anything: the ego hardly exists and thereby operates at the whim of the various drives that society administers in various degrees of totalization (this aspect still has to be described, forming the topic of the next chapter). Such a reduction of the ego through administration also implies the repression of a range of unsatisfied drives. Because modern society allows for the satisfaction of only a very limited range of drives, it is possible to speak here, as Marcuse does in *Eros and Civilization* (1955), of "surplus repression." For Marcuse, society represses significantly more than is necessary for the development of the ego. Surplus repression might thereby be seen as a sort of psychoanalytic counterpart to the structural conditions giving rise to the needless suffering at the heart of critical theory. In "Social Science and Sociological Tendencies in Psychoanalysis," Adorno describes the ego formed under such conditions as "a system of predominantly disconnected scars, painfully and never quite successfully integrated into a 'pattern.'" In *Civilization and its Discontents* (1929), Freud ominously argues in an analogous way that, "it is not easy to understand how it can become possible to deprive an instinct of satisfaction. Nor is doing so without danger. If the loss is not compensated for economically, one can be certain that serious disorders will ensue." Freud, in other words, is stressing that if libidinal energies do not find some sort of alternatives for satisfaction, then they will not disappear, but will instead produce other effects, finding other means of expression. (So, when Freud says "compensated for economically," he means in the "economy" of drives, which, as noted, have a plasticity, being capable of exchangeability.) Adorno will thereby suggest in "Social Science and Sociological Tendencies in Psychoanalysis," that "the narcissism characteristic of our time is a desperate attempt of the individual to undo some of the social wrongs he [sic] has to suffer from." And, as noted earlier, this is exactly why Adorno rejects the sort of modern forms of psychology in vogue now: they ultimately acquiesce to and justify such a society—as he puts it, "the cured personality of our time would be reduced to a mere focal point of conditioned reflexes."

In *Eclipse of Reason* (1947), Horkheimer adopts the same position about the totalizing structure of a societal world that increasingly manipulates the development of only certain kinds of drives and desires without the mediation necessary for ego formation. But he glorifies a possibility of a "resistant individual" who has avoided such a deformation. Such an individual "is overcome by a passion to realize what his father represented in his childish imagination, namely, truth." He continues that such an individual, presumably because he had the authority of a father in a traditional bourgeois family, "at least is successful in the process of internalization to the extent of turning against outside authority and the blind cult of so-called reality." In a nostalgic vein, Horkheimer stresses that the critical theory pursued by such an individual, "his criticism itself, theoretical and practical, is a negative reassertion of the positive faith he had as a child." This seems to raise all the problems noted above: why think such individuals currently exist? And even if they do, they seem to do so only by chance and thereby do not help us meaningfully think about questions of critical theory. Even more problematically, as first suggested by Jessica Benjamin in "The End of Internalization" (1977) and subsequent articles, on such a view, it seems that elements of consciousness where "resistance might be located—critical reason, individuation, integrity, and ultimately resistance itself—are tied to the process of internalizing authority." Benjamin points out that in such a case it appears that "rejection of authority can only take place through its prior acceptance." Benjamin is correct, but the objection is fatal only to the extent that the sorts of authority Horkheimer exalts appear to be linked to patriarchy as a structural form of domination. But not all authority is patriarchal. Authority may be necessary for ego development, but not domination. For example, making sure that a child internalizes my authority so that they, say, do not cross into a busy street or burn themselves on a hot stove is different from forcing them to then take on my authority in every other aspect of their lives. Patriarchy is oftentimes linked to the psychological internalization of authority, but it need not be—the two are surely separable.

If Horkheimer hearkens to a kind of nostalgia grounded in historical circumstances that no longer exist, Marcuse pursues a kind of fantasy akin to the infantile narcissism that Freud describes. Just as Adorno harnesses the image of infantile narcissism to describe a social situation where the ego is so small as to be almost non-existent leading towards a oneness with existing reality, Marcuse in *Eros and Civilization* pursues an analogous picture, except now cast in a positive light, as describing a possible utopian possibility. He writes that: "the striking paradox that narcissism, usually understood as egotistic withdrawal from reality, here is connected with oneness with the universe." Earlier in the book, he refers exactly to the image above of a primordial unity in the womb, where there was an "integral peace which is the absence of all need and desire— the Nirvana before birth." Marcuse stresses that such oneness is "beyond all immature autoeroticism"; instead "narcissism denotes a fundamental relatedness to reality which may generate a comprehensive existential order. In other words, narcissism may contain the germ of a different reality principle." It is important to note here, though, that the use of notion of a self in such a case may be entirely inaccurate, and so rather than proposing a particular conception of the self, Marcuse is really proposing a different conception of society, one wherein selves in fact do not—cannot—exist, or at least do not do so in a way comparable to how they do now. In any case, Marcuse is not suggesting that present-day society already somehow allows for such a psychological developments, but he does believe in *Eros and Civilization* that present-day society harbors this possibility. As noted above, the strength of this claim can also only be assessed once a more complete picture of how the Frankfurt School understands society is presented. Once that's accomplished, then we must also turn back again to the question of maturity. It should be noted also that Adorno keeps his distance from both options.

SUGGESTED READING

BACKGROUND IN KANT AND GERMAN IDEALISM

Bowie, Andrew. *From Romanticism to Critical Theory: The Philosophy of German Literary Theory*. London: Routledge, 1996.

Franks, Paul W. *All or Nothing: Systematicity, Transcendental Arguments, and Skepticism in German Idealism*. Cambridge: Harvard University Press, 2005.

Henrich, Dieter. *The Unity of Reason: Essays on Kant's Philosophy*. Cambridge: Harvard University Press, 1994.

Kant, Immanuel. *Foundations of the Metaphysics of Morals and What Is Enlightenment?* Translated by Lewis White Beck. 2nd ed. Upper Saddle River: Prentice-Hall, 1997.

Neuhouser, Frederick. *Diagnosing Social Pathology: Rousseau, Hegel, Marx, and Durkheim*. Cambridge: Cambridge University Press, 2022.

Pinkard, Terry. *German Philosophy 1760–1860: The Legacy of Idealism*. Cambridge: Cambridge University Press, 2002.

Pippin, Robert B. *Hegel's Idealism: The Satisfactions of Self-Consciousness*. Cambridge: Cambridge University Press, 1989.

———. *Modernism as a Philosophical Problem: On the Dissatisfaction of European High Culture*. 2nd ed. Oxford: Blackwell, 1999.

Rousseau, Jean-Jacques. "Discourse on the Origin of Inequality." Translated by Donald A. Cress. In *Basic Political Writings*, edited by Donald A. Cress, 25–81. Indianapolis: Hackett, 1987.

Shuster, Martin. *Autonomy after Auschwitz: Adorno, German Idealism, and Modernity*. Chicago: University of Chicago Press, 2014.

INTRODUCTIONS TO FREUD

Lear, Jonathan. *Freud*. 2nd ed. London: Routledge, 2015.

Whitebook, Joel. *Freud: An Intellectual Biography*. Cambridge: Cambridge University Press, 2017.

CRITICAL THEORY AND PSYCHOANALYSIS

Adorno, Theodor. "Sociology and Psychology I." *New Left Review* 46, no. 1 (1968): 79–97.

———. "Sociology and Psychology II." *New Left Review* 47, no. 1 (1968): 79–97.

Allen, Amy. *Critique on the Couch: Why Critical Theory Needs Psychoanalysis*. New York: Columbia University Press, 2020.

Allen, Amy, and Brian O'Connor. "Transitional Subjects: Critical Theory and Object Relations." New York: Columbia University Press, 2019.

Fong, Benjamin Y. *Death and Mastery: Psychoanalytic Drive Theory and the Subject of Late Capitalism.* New York: Columbia University Press, 2016.

Fromm, Erich. *The Crisis of Psychoanalysis: Essays on Freud, Marx and Social Psychology.* New York: Holt, Rinehart, and Winston, 2014.

———. *The Dogma of Christ and Other Essays on Religion, Psychology and Culture.* New York: Holt, Rinehart, and Winston, 1964.

Kiloh, Kathy. "Marcuse, Adorno, and the Drives." In *The Marcusean Mind*, edited by Eduardo Altheman, Jina Fast, Nicole K. Mayberry, and Sid Simpson, 571–98. London: Routledge, 2024.

Marcuse, Herbert. *Eros and Civilization: A Philosophical Inquiry into Freud.* Boston: Beacon Press, 1974.

Mitchell, Juliet. *Psychoanalysis and Feminism: A Radical Reassessment of Freudian Psychoanalysis.* New York: Pantheon Books, 1974.

Whitebook, Joel. *Perversion and Utopia: A Study in Psychoanalysis and Critical Theory.* Cambridge: MIT Press, 1996.

AUTHORITY AND MATURITY

Adorno, Theodor W. *The Authoritarian Personality.* London: Verso Books, 2019.

Adorno, Theodor W., and Hellmut Becker. "Education for Maturity and Responsibility." *History of the Human Sciences* 12, no. 3 (1999): 21–34.

Bowie, Andrew. *Adorno and the Ends of Philosophy.* Cambridge: Polity, 2013.

Horkheimer, Max. *Critical Theory: Selected Essays.* Translated by Mathew J. O'Connell. New York: Continuum, 1972.

———. *Eclipse of Reason.* New York: Oxford University Press, 1947.

Hullot-Kentor, Robert. "A New Type of Human Being and Who We Really Are." *Brooklyn Rail* 10, no. 11 (2008).

Kiloh, Kathy J. "Adorno's Materialist Ethic of Love." In *A Companion to Adorno*, edited by Peter E. Gordon, Espen Hammer, and Axel Honneth, 601–13, 2020.

Macdonald, Iain. "Cold, Cold, Warm: Autonomy, Intimacy and Maturity in Adorno." *Philosophy & Social Criticism* 37, no. 6 (2011): 669–89.

THE SPLIT WITH FROMM

Kamau, Caroline. "On Erich Fromm: Why He Left the Frankfurt School." In *Revisiting the Frankfurt School*, edited by David Berry, 185–206. London: Routledge, 2016.

McLaughlin, Neil. "Origin Myths in the Social Sciences: Fromm, the Frank-furt School and the Emergence of Critical Theory." *Canadian Journal of Sociology/Cahiers canadiens de sociologie* (1999): 109–39.

Additionally, the books by Jay, Wiggerhaus, and Wheatland cited in the Introduction address the split.

3

SOCIETY

1. MODERN SOCIETY

Given the simple fact that individuals are raised and educated—it is not too much to say formed—in a broader social whole, it is crucial to examine society in addition to the self. What's striking is how insightful the Frankfurt School's understanding of society remains. For example, here is Marcuse's description of society in *One Dimensional Man* (1964):

> The main trends are familiar: concentration of the national economy on the needs of the big corporations, with the government as a stimulating, supporting, and sometimes even controlling force; hitching of this economy to a world-wide system of military alliances, monetary arrangements, technical assistance and development schemes; gradual assimilation of blue collar and white collar population, of leadership types in business and labor, of leisure activities and aspiration in different social classes; fostering of a pre-established harmony between scholarship and the national purpose; invasion of the private household by the togetherness of public opinion; opening of the bedroom to the media of mass communication.

Marcuse specifies the account more, noting that in modern (capitalist) society, even the various functions of particular individual subjects are normalized. As he puts it, "assimilation in needs and aspirations, in the standard of living, in leisure activities, in politics derives from an integration." Such an integration occurs due to the "the material process of production." In an essay from the same year, "Industrialization and Capitalism in the Work of Max Weber"

DOI: 10.4324/9781003200963-4

(1964), Marcuse seems presciently to hearken even to the moment of big data, when he notes that

> [T]he formal rationality of capitalism celebrates its triumph in electronic computers, which calculate everything, no matter what the purpose, and which are put to use as mighty instruments of political manipulation, reliably calculating the chances of profit and loss, including the chance of the annihilation of the whole, with the consent of the likewise calculated and obedient population.

He depressingly notes that, "the masses themselves elect their leaders into the shell of bondage." Such one-dimensionality is analyzed in a variety of contexts by the Frankfurt School, whether industrially or culturally (and the difference itself becomes muted).

This last thought highlights how, in addition to the social state of affairs described above (which, of course, can and will be specified even more), there is a subjective component: a great many people appear quite satisfied with the status quo. Marcuse muses in *One Dimensional Man* that if "individuals are satisfied to the point of happiness with the goods and services handed down to them by the administration, why should they insist on different institutions for a different production of different goods and services? And if the individuals are preconditioned so that the satisfying good also include thoughts, feelings, aspirations, why should they wish to think, feel, and imagine for themselves?" Horkheimer and Adorno have a related, analogous assessment in *Dialectic of Enlightenment* (1944/1947), especially when they claim that the sort of abstraction associated with capitalism "stands in the same relationship to its objects as fate." Poignantly and tongue in cheek, they point out that in such a modern world, "each human being has been endowed with a self of his or her own, different from all the others, so that it could all the more surely be made the same."

For the Frankfurt School, there appears to be no predetermined definition of society beyond such extreme fungibility. As Adorno puts it in "Society" (1969): society "is essentially process." Such a process, in turn, appears to have taken a life of its own. Even as it is acknowledged that it is a human creation, the humans embedded in it now increasingly appear as cogs, mere "appendages of the machine" in Marx's words. Marx stresses how everyone—capitalists as much as workers—are functions of this process, structured by their class membership. Such "character masks" (in Marx's words) do not refer to the psychological character mentioned in the last chapter, but rather to the objective conditions of individuals in society. ("Character mask" has largely been absent from English discussions of Marx due to translation choices—the Frankfurt School, working with the original German, however, refers to the notion.) This point leads Adorno to question whether human beings even truly live in such a society. As he writes in his "Introduction" to *The Positivism Dispute in German Sociology* (1969): "the state of universal mediation and reification of all the relations between human beings sabotages ... objective possibility ... can this world be experienced at all as something living?" Adorno may here be invoking a sense of biological life that prioritizes the possibility of novelty, as claimed by the scientist Ilya Prigogine (1917–2003) and the philosopher Isabelle Stengers, when they write in *The End of Certainty* (1996) that such biological life is "related to the creation of unpredictable novelty, where the possible is richer than real." What life in contemporary capitalism seems to foreclose is such unpredictable novelty (of course, our lives are still filled with a variety of novel gimmicks, down to the latest iPhone and the most recent *Fast and Furious* film). Self and society are thereby intimately related to the extent that modern society deforms the possibilities for life to unfold in ways that exist outside of the sphere of exchangeability (and thereby determinability).

Note that even the contemporary French far-right agitator and conspiracy theorist Renaud Camus invokes a similar picture of modern society. In 2017, he told the *New Yorker* that "the very essence of modernity is the fact that everything—and really everything—can be replaced by something else, which is absolutely monstrous." That critical theory and the far right can invoke a similar sketch of modern life, even as they draw exceedingly different conclusions from it, points to the ubiquity of the situation they describe. It also suggests that such a high-altitude view requires additional specification so that we may better assess the kinds of conclusions that we ought to draw here. The broader picture can be traced to the way in which capitalism has affected the production of human value more generally and to how the economic sphere has expanded far beyond economics into seemingly all domains of human life.

2. COMMODITY EXCHANGE AND HISTORY

To bring this into sharper focus, note that commodity exchange is central to the modern world. Commodity exchange is not itself a novel development, however, since it predates modernity. Its scope, though, is a novel development. The first line of Marx's *Capital* thereby notes that "the wealth of societies in which the capitalist mode of production prevails appears as an *immense* collection of commodities" (emphasis added). Marx begins his analysis with trying first to understand what exactly a commodity is, since it "appears at first sight" an "extremely obvious, trivial thing," but on further examination, an analysis of it "brings out that it is a very strange thing, abounding in metaphysical subtleties and theological niceties." In the opening pages of *Capital*, Marx proposes an interesting analogy, suggesting that the "value-form of the commodity" should be seen as the "economic cell-form" of society. Just as we may study living cells so as to understand the biological features of human life, so may we study the "economic cells" that compose human social life.

The analogy is especially apt when it's understood that, just like biological life, economic life also shifts over time (society, as suggested, is a process). While humans have produced and exchanged commodities for thousands of years, it is only recently that (1) they have begun to do so on the scale that they do so now, importantly necessitating also that (2) they now produce commodities solely for the purpose of exchanging them. It is only now that human needs must for the most part be satisfied by means of a capitalist market. It is also important to note here that while Marx's account remains incredibly insightful, the scope of capitalism has advanced far beyond Marx's milieu.

Like Marx, the economist Karl Polyani (1866–1964) also stresses the historical nature of capitalism: it is only recently that commodity exchange by means of the market became the dominant feature of human life. In *The Great Transformation: The Political and Economic Origins of Our Time* (1944), Polyani points out that prior "to our time no economy has ever existed that, even in principle, was controlled by markets." Polyani reveals how previously, markets were a subsidiary feature of human life, mere "accessories of economic life." Broader economic life—human exchange—was governed by a great variety of social systems (what we might call an entire form of life).

To get a grip on this point, think, for example, the way in which work, finance, religion, and so forth were tied together during feudalism. (This is not to suggest that feudalism was better, but only to note that it also provided for human needs in certain ways.)

What's striking about Polyani's *The Great Transformation* is that exactly in order better to understand commodity exchange, he pursues a typology of the various ways in which humans have embedded economic life in broader social currents. For example, one way is explored in Marcel Mauss's (1872–1950) *The Gift* (1925), which shows how ancient societies used gifting as a means of exchange. In such societies, exchange was governed by social standing. In giving or receiving a gift, a particular social relation was actualized. Such activities, in turn, had their own logics, where one gift may lead to a drive to "give more" so as to achieve a particular relation between parties. We can find such economies even in the present day, whether in practices like Ayni among the Andean communities in Ecuador, or even in the kinds of gifting that occurs among hipster scenes in the United States. As Polyani noted in *The Great Transformation*, in such cases, "the broad principle of reciprocity helps to safeguard both production and family sustenance." Redistribution is another means by which humans have managed economic exchange. Under this rubric is captured everything from the earliest centralized states in, say, Babylonia to contemporary so-called "welfare states." Exchange is here governed by passing first through a central entity (usually a state, although not exclusively so). For such exchange, taxes or tribute may be collected and then redistributed amongst the population according to whatever value system is prominent. Such exchange can occur internally or externally, such as when foreign states or peoples are plundered, their wealth redistributed among the conquerors. Redistribution may thereby be equal or unequal, fair or unfair.

Polyani highlights how it is only in the modern period that the notion of a *self-regulating* market comes to prominence in human life. Its provenance is made possible by the rise of commodity exchange, especially by the development of what Polyani calls three "fictitious commodities": labor, land, and money. The "fictitious" nature of each of these can be brought to the fore through a consideration of the feudal system that precedes the rise of capitalism. In the feudal system, land was not a commodity to be bought and sold.

Who owned land and how ownership of land could shift was governed by social norms themselves anchored in a religious worldview. Land came by divine right; it was not generally acquired by purchase. Furthermore, the possession of land brought with it duties to feed those who worked the land (workers, who, conveniently, also worked the land because of divine fiat). Labor operated analogously: a guild structure made possible how and when workers operated and who could become a worker. Guilds also fit into a broader social structure and did not operate by market exchange. Money also operated similarly: money was a byproduct of the social system, there so that social life could proceed as it needed; it was not the reason for the whole. Polyani in fact points out that neither land, nor money, nor labor is in this earlier system "produced for sale." It is by no means obvious, then, that labor, land, and money should have come to be seen as commodities. Yet, in reading these lines, it is likely puzzling to most readers why we *wouldn't* see them as commodities; the capitalist perspective is now so dominant as to make Polyani's puzzlement itself puzzling. Indeed, the situation is now even more dire than when Polyani wrote, for now 'time is money' or, in some circles, in fact, 'everything (or even everyone) has a price.' In *Negative Dialectics*, Adorno glosses the present state of affairs with the thought that "the exchange principle" dominates and that through it, "non-identical individuals and activities become commensurable and identical." This is so much the case that the spread of the exchange principle in fact "comports the whole world towards identity, towards totality." A concrete example may help these abstract points along.

It's 2023. You walk into an American supermarket. You are immediately confronted with a panoply of goods. They all have prices. Just to name a few possibilities: apples may be $3.50, chickens $4.00, chocolate bars $3.75, water $2.00, lettuce $5.00, steaks $8.00 (it's on sale), and eggs $7.50 (sadly, there's been another bird flu). There are massive corporate industries behind each of these. They account for how the commodity is produced, how it's marketed, how it's transported, and increasingly how it's regulated. To purchase this lettuce or this chicken or this carton of eggs, (1) it must have been produced by someone working at a water plant or a chicken farm, (2) it must have been packaged by someone else, (3) it perhaps (hopefully?) must have been vetted by quality control, (4) it must have legal representation who can respond to issues that arise in any of the above, and (5) it must have lobbyists who look out for how the law may be shifted to produce more profit; it also (6) must have been transported to your store, (7) which means it must have been marketed to purchasers for the store, which means that (8) its sales must be analyzed in order determine whether more or less need to be bought, which in turn (9) requires that accountants at the production firm determine if more or less must be produced, which may suggest that (10) it be tracked by data scientists in conjunction with other products to see if certain variants or partnerships are more or less profitable, and so forth. In each of these domains there are: (a) additional industry standards and perhaps regulations, (b) various ways in which workers are paid for their labor or not, (c) struggles about how much or how little workers must work, (d) debates about hazards to health or environment, (e) complaints about lazy employees or terrible bosses, (f) regions of the world perhaps made uninhabitable by this work, (g) groups of people displaced, harmed, or destroyed by this industry, (h) species or groups of animals made extinct or injured, (h) perhaps even wars or skirmishes fought around the work, and so forth. This is why Marx will speak in *Capital* of "commodity fetishism," highlighting the fact that the entire system functions by conceiving value in a distinct way so as to cover over all of the complex—and often brutal and perverse—mechanisms and structures that are required for things to continue as they do.

These products reach your store, but none of this is apparent to you. If you're lucky, at best, you might see a list of ingredients. But mostly you just see the product. This product, in at least one important way, is also like every other: it can be bought with money. Money is an equalizer, it makes everything comparable, it allows for exchange between things. Such exchangeability is so ubiquitous and so closely linked to money that it likely doesn't even strike you as mysterious. Just imagine, though, how incredible it would have appeared to someone in an earlier age to be able to exchange, say, a pair of sandals for a Bible by means of money. Part of Marx's point in *Capital* is that everything becomes commodified exactly because capitalism's drive for profit is limitless. Relatedly, the ubiquity of exchange and its ordinariness for us is the result of the functioning, in Marx and Engels's words in *The German Ideology* (1846), of an entire "mode of life." Later in *Capital* Marx will note that, "precisely this finished form of the world of commodities—the money form" in fact "conceals the social character of private labour and the social relations between the individual and workers, by making those relations appear as relations between material objects."

The nature of this concealment forms a large part of Marx's investigation; it is also not unrelated to the concerns of the Frankfurt School. Consider that in earlier phases of human history—and in some places now—a particular commodity was produced for a particular use or function. This spear, say, was made so that it could be used for spearing game. Marx theorizes in *Capital* that when communities began to encounter one another, it is then that commodity exchange came on the scene, exactly "where communities have their boundaries," right "at their points of contact with other communities." This leads eventually to the production of commodities "especially for the purpose of exchange." This other spear, say, is now made so that it can be exchanged for the net that someone else makes. Commodities may now be seen as having a "use-value" (what need will this be used for) versus a value or "exchange value" (what commodity will this be exchanged for). With either perspective, it is human labor that creates value, as Marx puts it, although here he is echoing thinkers like Adam Smith (1723–1790) and John Locke (1632–1704).

3. COMMODITIES, LABOR, AND THE PRODUCTION OF VALUE

Sticking with the story of this book thus far (especially as pursued in the Introduction), it may seem as if Marx's critique—and that of the Frankfurt School—is fundamentally about "class struggle": that the problem of capitalism is a problem of crisis engendered by the status of who's wealthy and who's in power, ultimately about who owns the means of production. This is indeed a problem, but it is not the only—or perhaps even most pressing—problem in capitalist society. What's been described thus far may be a spur to critique, but it is not the entirety of the critique, nor perhaps even the thorniest issue. The philosopher Moishe Postone (1942–2018) thereby distinguishes two perspectives when he differentiates in *Time, Labor, and Social Domination* (1993) between a critique that prioritizes "class domination, rooted in private ownership of the means of production" and a critique that prioritizes "an abstract, impersonal, structural form of domination underlying the historical dynamic of capitalism." The latter perspective is of chief interest here, and it is the pursual of that interest that forms Marx's foremost contribution to modern thought. As he notes in *Capital*, prior to him no one ever "once asked the question" of "why labour is expressed in [exchange] value, and why the measurement of labour by its duration is expressed in the magnitude of the value of the product." He explains in a footnote to this claim that, "the value-form of the product of labour is the most abstract, but also the most universal form of the bourgeois mode of production; by that fact it stamps the bourgeois mode of production as a particular kind of social production of a historical transitory character." We must thereby understand the historically specific way in which value is produced in capitalism, and not make "the mistake of treating it as the eternal natural form of social production." In short, Marx, is asking why monetary value seems increasingly to underwrite all values in modern society. Adorno pursues a similar interest when he notes in *Introduction to Sociology* that such an abstraction is "really the specific form of the exchange process itself, the underlying social fact through which socialization first comes about." Marx's core claims require some explanation, but their basic orientation should be coming into focus. Naively we tend to think of the commodity simply as a product that admits of a variety of use-values (i.e., it can be bought and sold and then used for whatever purposes the purchaser wants). But on closer analysis, the commodity is in fact an abstract form that encloses how human beings relate to anything at all: the world, each other, and even themselves.

Central to this story is money. Classical economists all assume, as Adam Smith puts it in the *Wealth of Nations* (1776) that labor is "the real measure of the exchangeable value of all commodities." What Marx stresses in response, however, is that any proper analysis of the form of value in commodity exchange always presupposes money. Neither use-value nor exchange-value are basic terms, rather each one appears only through the presence of money. As Marx puts it in *Capital*, "what appears to happen is not that a particular commodity becomes money because all other commodities express their values in it, but, on the contrary, that all other commodities universally express their values in a particular commodity *because* it is money" (emphasis added). Adorno summarizes the idea in *Introduction to Sociology* as the thought that "exchange takes place" exactly "through money as the equivalent form." One way to grasp this point is just to note that if you can't sell something you produced for the purpose of gaining money; it doesn't matter how much labor went into it: it has no value (not even a use-value since if it is made to be sold, it wasn't made to be used—i.e., the distinction between use-value itself only makes sense in contrast to exchange-value). Value emerges only when commodities can somehow be made equivalent. This is why Marx is deeply interested in the *form* of value, in how commodities may come to be taken as equivalent.

Marx presents the following history. Exchange emerges first, likely in trade between communities. Different communities become good at producing different things. One community may, let's say, have a knack for producing spears, another corn, a third nets, and a fourth wood. Initial exchange may have been haphazard. In one case a net may, say, be equivalent to two spears or to a dozen corn. What Marx highlights is that in such cases a commodity either occupies the relative form (its value is relative to another commodity) or the equivalent form (the value of the other commodity is equivalent it). The value of a commodity can only emerge with one or the other form, for it is exactly only the form that brings value into focus. Value emerges when something is equivalent relative to something else. There is also, then, an important asymmetry here: it is when a commodity cannot be traded for some other commodity that this commodity has no value. Human communities are of course much more complex than the above example. Even if such an early commodity had only a small number of exchangeable products, exchanging them would have meant needing to keep a very large ledger with all the various possibilities for each commodity in exchange to all the others. The decision may be made, then, to use just one commodity as a universal equivalent. This is the birth of money. This commodity—whether it is a spear, a corn, or a coin—can come to be equivalent to any other commodity. Every commodity now stands relative to money and is equivalent to money. Once money is on the scene, this feature "remains the same no matter how many metamorphoses and forms of existence the commodity goes through."

Pause for a moment to consider the picture emerging. Imagine that the universal equivalent is a spear. In such a case, the spear will no longer be defined by how well it spears things. In Marx's words in *Capital*, the spear is now a "thing in which value is manifested." Such a manifestation involves the fact that *this* is now its use-value: it is used for valuing, or it has, in Marx's words, the "form of value," so it is as if "its value form were given by nature." To stick with this example, note that making a spear requires a particular set of skills: perhaps wood-working, metal-working, chopping, tying, and so forth. Because the spear occupies the equivalent form, though, such particular labor now becomes an expression of abstract labor: it can be equivalent to the labor that goes into picking corn, making a net, chopping wood, or whatever else can be exchanged for the spear. When the spear becomes money, it becomes potentially anything. This is the power of money. And so labor that occurs in private can now become public when it stands equivalent to the labor required to make the spear; the particular becomes the general, the abstract. As Marx puts it in *Capital*, "the magic of money" is that it can be "the direct incarnation of all human labor."

There are myriad reasons for why a spear is not an efficient form of money. But the example is worthwhile since it allows us to register the *power* of money to the extent that we can follow the form of money without usual preconceptions. We come to see how the form of money is defined by occupying a particular position in exchange. Value emerges when relative and equivalent form is on the scene; value is a byproduct of exchange by means of these formal properties. Marx thereby claims that value "does not have its description branded on its forehead; it rather transforms every product of labour into a social hieroglyphic." Deciphering a hieroglyphic, just like understanding any language, requires understanding the social context that animates or makes meaning possible. Meaning cannot simply be found in a dictionary, for as a range of slang attests, we can always use words by projecting them into novel contexts without loss of understanding. Meaning, as philosophers may say, is use (of course, not only use). The social context here is notably the entire totality that makes up the form of life of capitalism. In the *Grundrisse* (1858), Marx reflects on the abstraction that animates the system, noting how the capitalist has an amazing ability to "come into relation with every *specific* labor." Money allows the capitalist to confront "the *totality* of all labors as potential," so that any "particular one it confronts at a given time is an accidental manner." Equally money covers over the unequal and contingent social relations that animate various labors and the values they produce and perpetuate (that the labor of one kind of worker is valued more than the labor of another). As Marx puts it in *Capital*,

> it is however precisely this finished form of the world of commodities—the money form—which conceals the social character of private labour and the social relations between the individual workers, by making those relations appear as relations between material objects, instead of revealing them plainly.

And such fungibility applies to all spheres of capitalist life. Marx notes in the *Grundrisse*, for example, that the conclusion he reaches "is not that production, distribution, exchange and consumption are identical, but that they all form the members of a totality, distinctions within a unity." In his lectures *Philosophy and Sociology* (1960), Adorno extends this analysis when he notes that there is a "significant structural relationship between money as the universal medium of equivalence and the coining of concepts that can be employed to stand in anywhere for anything."

4. COMMODITY, WORLD, REIFICATION: LUKÁCS, HUSSERL, AND LASK

Moving from Marx's picture to claims like Adorno's requires understanding the influence of the Marxist philosopher György Lukács (1885–1971) on the Frankfurt School. It is his technical notion of "reification" that best situates the transition from Marx to the Frankfurt School. In *History and Class Consciousness* (1923), Lukács pursues the idea that the "structure of commodity-relations" (the picture introduced above) must be understood as the "archetype" or "prototype" (we may equally say "model") of "all forms of objectivity and all corresponding forms of subjectivity in bourgeois society." This is a complex claim that is hardly obvious. One way to gloss the idea, at a very high altitude, as the philosopher Andrew Feenberg suggests in *The Philosophy of Praxis* (2014), is to take Lukács to be claiming that the economic form of capitalism also somehow "functions as the basis of the capitalist cultural system." The way in which society is organized economically affects our subjectivity and our institutional possibilities, whether political, social, artistic, or otherwise. The form of value in one sphere affects the form of value in others. Adorno in *Negative Dialectics* will claim something like this when he writes that: "the exchange principle, the reduction of human labor to the abstract universal concept of average labor-time, is fundamentally akin to the principle of identification. Exchange is the social model of the principle, and without this principle, there would be no exchange. It is through exchange that non-identical individuals and activities become commensurable and identical. The spread of the principle comports the whole world towards identity, towards totality."

As seen earlier, especially in his "Economic and Philosophic Manuscripts," Marx had a keen understanding of the effects of capitalist life on human subjectivity. Lukács importantly did not have access to these manuscripts. Despite being written by Marx in 1844, they hadn't yet been published when Lukács wrote *History and Class Consciousness*. (Marx's manuscripts were only published in 1932 when Lukács helped edit the mouse-gnawed manuscripts with David Ryazanov in Moscow; Ryazanov was sadly later murdered by the Soviets in 1938.) *History and Class Consciousness* thereby covers some of the same ground as these early manuscripts, but oftentimes using the philosophical apparatus that Lukács encountered in his own time. Marx was inspired to pursue his exploration of the commodity and value form by their effects on human subjectivity. Lukács, on the other hand, started with Marx's arguments about form but sought to expand them beyond this horizon, thinking explicitly about human subjectivity. In this way, as has been argued most recently and forcefully by Richard Westerman in *Lukács's Phenomenology of Capitalism* (2019), in addition to being influenced by Kant and the German Idealist tradition discussed in the last chapter, especially around the Hegelian notion of "second nature," Lukács's approach was also deeply influenced by his contemporaries, especially philosophers Emil Lask (1875–1915) and Edmund Husserl (1859–1938).

To the extent that Husserl influenced Lask, it is important to understand certain features of Husserl's project. Terming it "phenomenology," Husserl defines his project in *Ideas I* (1913) as the "science of the essence of consciousness." While an exceedingly complex approach, its basic feature was a consideration of what Husserl termed "the stream of mental processes." Such a stream, Husserl thought, could at any moment be descriptively analyzed, especially with regard to its formal characteristics given the sorts of content that showed up there. Across a great array of works and inquiries, Husserl showed how a careful analysis of the features of consciousness could reveal, for example, that imaginary objects are philosophically descriptively distinct from real ones, scientific or natural objects from aesthetic ones, features of objectivity descriptively different from subjectivity, and so forth. Husserl's approach, in short, was also deeply dependent on the radical shift in philosophical perspective described in the last chapter. In "Static and Genetic Phenomenological Method" (1921), Husserl later summarizes his approach as an interest in "modes of givenness" so that different objects within the stream of consciousness are given in different ways. In different kinds of experience, there is given to us an entire world, which we can then philosophically—phenomenologically—analyze in order to determine how certain things could have appeared there in the first place. Here's how Husserl summarizes the method in *The Crisis of European Sciences* (1936), noting that "first comes the straightforwardly given life-world, taken initially as it is given perceptually: as 'normal,' simply there, unbroken, existing." Once the phenomenological method is applied, however, "the life-world becomes a first intentional heading, an *index* or *guideline* for inquiring back into the multiplicities of manners of appearing." Such an inquiry leads to the presence of subjectivity, for certain things could only appear if a subject was somehow involved (again, the analogy to the radical shift in perspective elaborated in the last chapter should be coming into focus).

Lask did not operate exclusively in the phenomenological tradition, but his approach was surely influenced by Husserl (likely were it not for his early death during World War I, it's possible that he would have become part of the tradition of phenomenology—letters between him and Husserl show a mutual respect). In *The Logic of Philosophy and the Theory of Categories* (1911), Lask also notes a primal relation that predates any claims of knowledge, that first there is a "living in" the world and only then derivatively knowledge of it. As he puts it, "recognizing sensuous material is not a sensuous experience, but a non-sensuous attitude towards truth, not a 'living in' the sensuous, but rather a mere 'knowledge' of it.

There is immediate life only when unaffected, not when besieged by an enclosed form." This is not a distinction between two kinds of "things" or "realms." It is instead a pre-reflective unity that allows for the very distinction between subject and object. As Lask puts it, a "separation into two realms of the object and the "truth about it" must not be allowed," rather "the thing itself and the truth about it are one and the same." According to Lask, "the category and the material of the category" are merely two features of the same primal unity. Both Husserl and Lask stress, in a manner that would prove to be incredibly influential for phenomenology, the way in which humans first practically operate within a world, an entire horizon of salience, before they inquire into notions of subjectivity or objectivity, or any relationship between them.

In *History and Class Consciousness*, Lukács evinces a similar approach in rejecting any conception of a subject as fundamentally "a pure and purely formal subject." In *Record of a Life* (1971), Lukács in fact stresses that "historicity is the fundamental concept of social being, *and as such of all beings*" (emphasis added). He continues, in a way quite reminiscent of Lask, noting that "the categories, therefore, are components of objective reality." In fact, they "are forms of beings," where "it is not the case that history unfolds within the system of categories, but rather that history is the system of categories in the process of change." Just as in Husserl and in Lask, there is a primal reality that is first on scene, which is "lived in," but which shifts over time, and where—and this is the difference between Lukács and these thinkers—these shifts are understood through Marx's analysis of effects of capitalism. Put alternatively, the primal relation that makes possible both consciousness and its objects is understood through Marx's analysis of capitalism. Just as Hegel (and Marx) criticized Kant for neglecting the way in which history affects the formal possibilities for human experience, so does Lukács take himself to be expanding (by means of Marx's account) the role that history has on the formal accounts of Husserl and Lask. When in *History and Class Consciousness*, Lukács stresses that the "particular forms" beings take must be understood as belonging together because they have a "place and function in the totality," he is using Marx's analysis to historicize Husserl and Lask's approaches. On such a view, this totality or primal relation is "by no means an unmediated datum for thought," it is rather itself socially created.

Lukács claims that this becomes most readily apparent in capitalism, for in feudal society humans could not yet see themselves as social beings because "society was far too unorganized and had far too little control over the totality of relations between humans for it to appear to consciousness as *the* reality of humans."

"Reification" is the technical term that Lukács introduces to capture the pre-reflective unity that structures relations of subject and object under capitalism. In *History and Class Consciousness*, reminiscent of Marx, Lukács notes that while commodity exchange surely existed prior to modern life, it is with the rise of capitalism that this structure seems to "penetrate the very depths of human physical and psychic nature," ultimately "to penetrate society in all its aspects," having remolded everything "in its own image." This horizon or primal relation generates both a new subjectivity and a new "form of objectivity." Lukács diagnoses its two chief features as follows. First, there is an increasing rationalization in how reality is grasped and understood. Because everything is underwritten by abstract labor and commodity exchange and its concomitant value form, reality itself appears to have only these characteristics, so that we must be "able to predict with ever greater precision all the results to be achieved." When everything actually or potentially becomes commodified, then everything just is of a kind and so subject to manipulation and calculation. Second, and surely not unrelated, whatever might be subject and object within such a horizon becomes increasingly atomized. Humans are understood largely as inputs within an apparatus that operates independently according to abstract laws over which they can have no influence. The world thereby unfolds by means of "a process mechanically conforming to fixed laws and enacted independently of man's consciousness and impervious to human intervention." Lukacs calls it a "perfectly closed system" defined above all by a reduction of "space and time to a common denominator," where even time itself is degraded to "the dimension of space." Time is money, and the qualitative character of human temporality becomes instead a mechanical, quantitative succession of work (or repose in preparation for work). Spaces too share a common denominator: centers for rest are equally centers for profit, spectacle is repose, and vice versa. Clock time organizes all human experience. (While the mechanical clock is thousands of years old, it is not by accident that clocks become ubiquitous in households exactly when capitalism comes to prominence.) Lukács stresses in *History and Class Consciousness* how such a "ghostly objectivity" orients the entire horizon that makes up the modern world. The shift being described is not a mere psychological feature of modern humans, but rather already affects the very terms in which subject and object unfold and are understood. (Just think again of Polyani's triumvirate—labor, money, land: when these are understood as having an abstract value, then we are in a deep sense already speaking about the very parameters by which subject and object are structured.) Other intellectual precursors could of course be cited here: (1) the aforementioned notion of "commodity fetishism" in Marx and the concomitant story of value discussed above, and (2) Max Weber's account of "intellectualist rationalization," where, as he notes in "Science as a Vocation" (1919), the world comes to be entirely "disenchanted" in modernity, so "that principally there are no mysterious incalculable forces that come into play" and instead all things can now be mastered "by calculation."

This general picture is influential for how the Frankfurt School approaches its own understanding of society. So while Adorno is wary of Lukács's support for the Soviet Union (he remarks in *Introduction to Dialectics* [1958] that some of Lukács's works during this period should "never have seen the light of day"), Horkheimer, Marcuse, and Adorno are nonetheless deeply influenced by Lukács's account. Due to this wariness, Adorno appears instead frequently to invoke the economist and philosopher Alfred Sohn-Rethel (1899–1990), but as Andrew Feenberg has pointed out in "Lukács's Theory of Reification and Contemporary Social Movements" (2015), Sohn-Rethel's account of how human experience is already always determined by capitalist form is "similar if not identical" to Lukács's account. Relatedly, with an eye to the centrality of Marx's notions sketched above, Adorno argues in the *Introduction to Sociology* lectures that "the concept of exchange is, as it were, the hinge connecting the conception of a critical theory of society to the concept of society as a totality." Echoing Marx, Adorno points out in the same lectures that "the true unit which stands behind money as the equivalent form is the average necessary amount of social labour time." The emergence of abstract labor time equally requires that "the specific forms of the objects to be exchanged are necessarily disregarded; instead, they are reduced to a universal unit." And in his lectures on the *Philosophical Elements of Society* (1964), Adorno also highlights how such a system of exchange "in fact presupposes the class system." This is the case because the alleged prospect of wage labor is a "leonine contract" (a fabled contract between a lion and a mouse where of course the lion will always dictate the terms): if they do not engage in wage labor, then "the workers will face hunger and have nothing to live on." In *Negative Dialectics*, Adorno summarizes things with the claim that, "society stays alive, not despite its antagonism, but by means of it; the profit motive, and thereby the class relationship, make up the objective motor of the process of production on which everyone's life hangs, and whose primacy has its vanishing point in the death of all." While later members of the Frankfurt School like Habermas and Honneth tend to temper these explicitly Marxist elements, they also pursue and develop accounts of reification. For example, Habermas's *Theory of Communicative Action* (1981) presents reification as the process by which elements of the "lifeworld" are colonized by the instrumental logics of the "system," while Honneth's *Reification* (2008) argues that reification is best understood as a "forgetfulness of recognition," where what's forgotten or overlooked is the primordial relationship that any subject must first have to another subject in order first to become a subject themselves.

5. ABSTRACTION AND ADMINISTRATION

This thick account of capitalism from Marx to Lukács is the means by which some of the boldest claims of the Frankfurt School should be contextualized, especially in works like Horkheimer and Adorno's *Dialectic of Enlightenment* and Marcuse's *One Dimensional Man*. Horkheimer and Adorno claim that in *Dialectic of Enlightenment* that,

> abstraction, the instrument of enlightenment, stands in the same relationship to its objects as fate, whose concept it eradicates: as liquidation. Under the leveling rule of abstraction, which makes everything in nature repeatable, and of industry, for which abstraction prepares the way, the liberated finally themselves become the "herd."

Marcuse presents a similar image in *One Dimensional Man* when he writes that, "the quantification of nature separated reality from all inherent ends," so that "man and nature become fungible objects of organization." Such a view also offers a way to situate Marcuse's concept of "technological rationality," first introduced in "Some Social Implications of Technology" (1941) but also pursued in *One Dimensional Man*. Marcuse argues that the rise and eventual ubiquity of technology is not neutral; rather it alters the entire horizon by which subject and object come to be constructed. He deploys a memorable and fruitful example in "Some Social Implications of Technology":

> A man who travels by automobile to a distant place chooses his route from the highway maps. Towns, lakes and mountains appear as obstacles to be bypassed. The countryside is shaped and organized by the highway. Numerous signs and posters tell the traveler what to do and think; they even request his attention to the beauties of nature or the hallmarks of history. Others have done the thinking for him, and perhaps for the better. Convenient parking spaces have been constructed where the broadest and most surprising view is open. Giant advertisements tell him when to stop and find the pause that refreshes. And all this is indeed for his benefit, safety and comfort; he receives what he wants. Business, technics, human needs and nature are welded together into one rational and expedient mechanism. He will fare best who follows its directions, subordinating his spontaneity to the anonymous wisdom which ordered everything for him. The decisive point is that this attitude—which dissolves all actions into a sequence of semi-spontaneous reactions to prescribed mechanical norms—is not only perfectly rational but also perfectly reasonable.

The picture Marcuse presents can of course be multiplied in countless new contemporary contexts, many far less benign than the one that he describes.

Such technological rationality has, if anything, become far more predominant with technological development since Marcuse's time. Technology now reaches even more directly and forcefully into the world. Just think, for example, of augmented reality devices. Here, the entire technological apparatus explicitly prescribes values and proscribes certain imaginative possibilities, thereby already setting the horizon for human experience. The underlying motive is the profit motive, but this aspect comes to be increasingly covered over and mediated by quite complex technological developments so that activities that contribute to rising profits are not immediately understood as such by the subjects involved with them. Think, for example, of the ways in which *Pokémon Go,* putatively a kid's video game, in fact, in the words of Shoshana Zuboff in *The Age of Surveillance Capitalism* (2019), "provided a living laboratory for telestimulation at scale as the game's owners learned how to automatically condition and herd collective behavior, directing it toward real-time constellations of behavioral futures markets, with all of this accomplished just beyond the rim of individual awareness." In the game, players download an app that allows them to collect various Pokémon creatures by looking at the world through their phone in order to "find" these creatures—of course, the locations at which these Pokémon are found were in fact locations that provided profit to the game's creators in the form of explicit payment from firms or in the form of data that they could later sell about how people behaved in response to being directed to certain locations. As Zuboff described it in an interview, "the incentives of the game to reward, punish us, shape our behavior, to actually get us to the places that were going to pay Niantic Labs for our presence, our bodies, our feet, falling on their floors." This is an explicit example that can easily make the broader point clear, but Marcuse stresses also that there are countless implicit ones, where the technological horizon already always sets possibilities for what we see and what we do, and, indeed, even what and how we think. In *One Dimensional Man,* Marcuse summarizes the point as the idea that "in the medium of technology, man and nature become fungible objects of organization," so that "the world tends to become the stuff of total administration, which absorbs even the administrators."

Referring to the horizon that structures experience in even broader terms, Horkheimer and Adorno write in *Dialectic of Enlightenment* that "the abstract self, which alone confers the legal right to record and systematize, is confronted by nothing but abstract material, which has no other property than to be the substrate of that right." This leads to the ominous situation where "the equation of mind and world is finally resolved, but only in the sense that the two sides cancel out." With exactly the picture of capitalism implied thus far, "the identity of everything with everything is bought at the cost that nothing can be identical to itself." In other words, exactly because the subject itself becomes little more than the expression of a market that is continually in flux, both the world and the subject as a qualitatively unique entities are equally undermined. Marcuse concludes in *One Dimensional Man* with a similar picture, arguing that this is in fact "the pure form of servitude: to exist as an instrument, as a thing." So Marcuse can claim that "reification tends to become totalitarian."

Such claims may sound hyperbolic, but they are intended to be taken seriously. (One way to register this point is to understand that such totalitarian aspects are in fact entirely compatible with 'positive' developments—as it is often joked, albeit inaccurately, how in Mussolini's Italy, the trains ran on time.) Thus, for example, in his radio address, "Education after Auschwitz" (1966), Adorno refers to a "type of reified consciousness," where "people of such a nature have, as it were, made themselves akin to things." From here it is not a huge step to violence, since such people, "when possible … make others akin to things." Adorno stresses how such a view of self and others has its extension in the Nazi idea of "finishing off" or "polishing off" a person, as if victims are mere things in broader production processes. What's emerging here is a sort of continuum: on one end are explicit genocidal activities like administered extermination and ethnic cleansing while on the other end are common administrative features of the modern world that make everyone and everything alike. This is why putatively democratic regimes like the United States or Canada easily pursue genocidal actions towards its Indigenous populations ranging from outright extermination to death through migration to ethnic cleansing to annihilation through reeducation programs that destroy the cultural features of a people. On such a view, as Adorno puts it in *Negative Dialectics*, "genocide is the absolute integration, which is prepared anywhere human beings are made the same, 'polished off'" (and the entire trajectory and features of the prevalence of such a continuum, animating equally democratic and totalitarian regimes in the West, is captured poignantly in Raoul Peck's documentary *Exterminate All the Brutes* [2021]). And because such claims are tied to the formal features of human subjectivity as understood in the philosophical tradition, to the very distinction between subject and object as noted above with the discussion of Lukács, Horkheimer and Adorno are led to suggest in *Dialectic of Enlightenment* that, "one might say that the collective madness that ranges today, from the concentration camps to the seemingly most harmless mass-culture reactions, was already present in germ in primitive objectivization." Part and parcel of this entire account is also the idea that our very sensible uptake of the world is affected, so that our very sensibility becomes coarsened, less capable of qualitatively variegated experience, that our sensibility becomes, in Marcuse's words, "one dimensional."

6. HISTORY AND REASON

The exact nature of the historical story animating this entire account requires some discussion. To see this, note, for example, that there is here a historical account about the development of human subjectivity. The account is dialectical in the sense that a form of subjectivity that allegedly initially procured positive benefits for humanity and human development eventually turns into a form of subjectivity that threatens the possible destruction of humanity. The basic contours of such a position were proposed by Horkheimer in "Egoism and Freedom Movements: On the Anthropology of the Bourgeois Epoch" (mentioned also in Chapter 2). Horkheimer sketches a historical story about the various movements that led to the rise of bourgeois individualism from 14th century Italy to the French revolution, framing this rise as both a progressive response to feudal conditions (where joint cause was made with the masses), and as a repressive pursuit equally aimed at the consolidation of the power of the bourgeoisie themselves. This tension expresses a dialectical logic that then recurs in contexts following this period. Horkheimer thereby locates the fascist movements emerging during the moment he is writing his essay as a sort of recurrence of this earlier logic where "the forms they take seem to be a bad imitation of the movements previously discussed." Such recurrence is made possible by the fact that each of these otherwise unique historical situations are underwritten by a similar psychoanalytic logic of masses (see the conclusion of Chapter 2), where a subject with an underdeveloped ego can gain compensation through identification with a leader who can then channel the individuals in this mass towards the hatred or destruction of an 'out' group. Marcuse similarly uses the basic contours of this dialectic movement to think about the rise of technological rationality, noting in "Some Social

Implications of Modern Technology" that such rationality and the notion of truth it instantiates in the world "comes into striking contradiction with the form in which individualistic society had established its supreme values. The pursuit of self-interest now appears to be conditioned upon heteronomy, and autonomy as an obstacle rather than stimulus for rational action." (It was quite apt that Martin Jay in "Introduction to Horkheimer" [1982] once called Horkheimer's dialectical story a sort of "seed-bed" for the Frankfurt School.) Concepts that at one time aided in the pursuit of maturity now come to work against its possibility.

While the basic dialectical logic of the account is plausible enough, the exact historical scope of application may be disputed. For example, as the reference to Raoul Peck's documentary above about Europe's relation to colonialism suggests, perhaps Horkheimer's location of progressive tendencies within the bourgeoisie requires a sort of historical myopia. While at a certain moment these progressive tendencies can indeed be felt within Europe in how the bourgeoisie aligns with workers against feudal interests, *at the same exact moment*, these same bourgeoisie pursue brutal colonial and racial policies abroad. Acknowledging this requires us significantly to modify the historical details of Horkheimer's account and perhaps also to alter its psychoanalytic features. It also may require us to revise the ways in which we understand the very relationship between feudalism and capitalism. For example, in *Black Marxism* (1983), Cedric Robinson argues that capitalism was from its beginnings already inflected by racial categories, since these categories were in fact central to the feudal order where earlier subjects like the Jews, Irish, Roma, and others were already racialized and subjected to processes that we later recognized and termed as colonial (processes that the historian Robert Bartlett has pushed back even further than Robinson, to the 10th century in *The Making of Europe* [1993]). If this is to push the historical account by means of its specificity, there is also a way to push it by means of its lack of specificity. For example, while I have presented *Dialectic of Enlightenment* as a historical story about modern subjectivity, there are elements in the text that suggest a much less historical story, meant to apply to the development of human subjectivity altogether. (Related models may be the way in which the state of nature is invoked in political philosophy or the way in which Nietzsche suggests modern morality emerged from an alleged slave revolt in *On the Genealogy of Morality* [1886].) For example, Horkheimer and Adorno write that in their function, no difference may be "said to exist between the totemic animal, the dreams of the spirit-seer, and the absolute Idea." Habermas thus criticizes Horkheimer and Adorno, pointing out in *Philosophical Political Profiles* (1974) that Horkheimer and Adorno must claim that "*from the very start* the process of enlightenment is the result of a drive to self-preservation that mutilates reason." On such a view, if the problem is with human subjectivity as such, then the prospects for any sort of future historical solution to this predicament seems hopeless. I cannot here settle this question and it remains the subject of scholarly dispute to the present day (although I have responded to Habermas's criticisms in my earlier book, *Autonomy after Auschwitz* [2014]).

7. STATE CAPITALISM

But even if we reject Habermas's reading and do not expand the thesis of the *Dialectic of Enlightenment* in this strong and potentially self-undermining way, there is here still the unavoidable problem of how exactly to assess the current historical moment. Habermas himself captured this well when he noted in *The Philosophical Discourse of Modernity* (1985), that "the relation of history to reason remains constitutive for the discourse of modernity—for better or worse." Features of this problem can in fact be brought into focus by situating Friedrich Pollock's (1894–1970) thesis of state capitalism in "State Capitalism" (1941). Prompted foremost by an analysis of Nazi Germany, but equally also by developments in non-totalitarian regimes like the United States and Roosevelt's "New Deal," Pollock suggests that "19th century free trade and free enterprise are on the way out." The common feature of such states is that "the market is deposed from its controlling function to coordinate production and distribution." Instead, all such functions are "taken over by a system of direct controls." In the totalitarian version of state capitalism, such direct controls are administered by a totalitarian regime, while in the democratic version it is administered by a democratically elected regime. Their common feature is that each "signifies the transition from a predominantly economic to an essentially political era." Pollock thereby even optimistically muses that "government control of production and distribution furnishes the means for eliminating the economic causes of depressions, cumulative destructive processes and unemployment of capital and labor." The idea is that politics becomes primary to the extent that it emerges as the realm that can make Marx's theory of crisis largely irrelevant.

Different members of the Frankfurt School have differing responses to Pollock's claims. In this context, Habermas's own response in "Technology and Science as 'Ideology'" (1968) is instructive. Presented on Marcuse's seventieth birthday, the essay is in many ways a critique of Marcuse's notion of technological rationality, with Habermas arguing that the emergence of state intervention in the economy opens up possibilities for human political intervention in such a way that government action can be explicitly "designed to compensate for the dysfunctions of free exchange." Such intervention makes it possible to prevent technological rationality from entirely overwhelming the whole horizon (as long as we can distinguish, as Habermas does, between lifeworld and system—see Chapter 1). Even if this latter claim is found plausible, though, it is not obvious, or at least, it is open to dispute whether the present moment admits of this sort of state intervention. And exactly this element of Pollock's argument was subjected to skepticism almost immediately by other members of the Frankfurt School. For example, Franz Neumann (1900–1954) who joins the Institute in 1936 presses against Pollock's claim by suggesting in his mammoth analysis of the Nazi regime, *Behemoth* (1942), that what's going on in Nazi Germany is in fact irreducible to a one-sided expression of politics over economics. Rather, there is a much more symbiotic relationship between them, involving equally also other elements of society. As Neumann puts it:

> With regard to imperialist expansion, National Socialism and big business have identical interests. National Socialism pursues glory and the stabilization of its rule, and industry, the full utilization of its capacity and the conquest of foreign markets. German industry was willing to co-operate to the fullest. It had never liked democracy, civil rights, trade unions, and public discussion. National Socialism utilized the daring, the knowledge, the aggressiveness of the industrial leadership, while the industrial

leadership utilized the anti-democracy, anti-liberalism and anti-unionism of the National Socialist party, which had fully developed the techniques by which masses can be controlled and dominated. The bureaucracy marched as always with the victorious forces, and for the first time in the history of Germany the army got everything it wanted. Four distinct groups are thus represented in the German ruling class: big industry, the party, the bureaucracy, and the armed forces.

While Neumann does not offer analogous arguments against qualifying the democratic version of the state capitalism thesis, such arguments are not difficult to find. For example, very recently the historian Michael Joseph Roberto argued for a much more complex picture of the New Deal in *The Coming of the American Behemoth* (2018), suggesting that even many of its features were in fact underwritten by fascist tendencies operating in the United States.

There is continuing debate amongst scholars about exactly how compelling the rest of the School found the state capitalism thesis, since there are moments where some like Horkheimer praise it, while other moments where others, especially Adorno, appear to qualify or reject it. In some of its optimistic claims, it is obvious that Adorno and others simply find the thesis entirely false and unworkable. In a letter to Horkheimer from 1941, Adorno explicitly rejects any optimistic picture suggesting that if anything the thesis points to a "constant series of catastrophes." Adorno thinks that it is simply impossible that an antagonistic society could produce a non-antagonistic outcome. This insight first leads Horkheimer and Adorno to formulate a theory of "rackets," which although never developed properly is described in unpublished materials and letters as essentially a rule of gangs and rackets, where politics is little more than different groups of powerful individuals fighting over access to profits. Adorno's thought develops far beyond this view, though, especially in later years, when in "Late Capitalism or Industrial Society?" he argues that there exists a dialectical relationship between (1) a fundamentally antagonistic economy of commodity relations as underwritten by class struggle, and (2) state intervention as a mechanism of "self-defense" on the part of such an economy. State intervention on this view is not something that somehow completes or serves as a culmination to economic functioning but is rather simply "essential to the working of the system as a whole";

it is the way in which "capitalism discovered resources within itself that have postponed its collapse." State intervention thereby "confirms the survival ability of the system, but *indirectly also the theory of the breakdown of capitalism*" (emphasis added). In short, both Marx's theory of crisis and the discovery of political intervention as the mitigation of crisis remain true (this would be very much to pursue an account that runs formally parallel to Habermas's but that reaches a quite different historical assessment). On such a view, modern society oscillates between economic crisis and political intervention, each an appendage of the other, us cogs in its movement. Adorno's insights describe just as easily the present moment as his own, as the movement from the 2008 banking crisis (and bailout) to our current crisis demonstrates. War, pandemic, inequality, and a falling rate of profit continue (among many other ills). War rages between Russia and Ukraine right now, leading to global instability, and increasing geopolitical tension. In *Philosophical Elements of a Theory of Society*, Adorno wrote remarks intended to paint a picture of the Cold War, but they are just as apt to the present geopolitical moment: "the world reproduces itself economically only through the establishment of the armament apparatus, in the East and West, an apparatus that guarantees prosperity while devouring the national product and threatening humanity with annihilation."

To this already grim picture may be added the equally bleak picture of possible planetary environmental collapse. The Frankfurt School already stressed how the entire picture of capitalism that's been presented necessitates a very particular conception of nature: once capitalism becomes the dominant global form, everything is potentially profit, so that, as Horkheimer and Adorno put it in *Dialectic of Enlightenment*, nature exists to be "mastered through labor." Even drives to "conserve" nature have a basis in the same impulse, for they too prepare and delineate what nature is, can, and will be. Adorno thereby writes in *Minima Moralia* that "the more purely nature is preserved and transplanted by civilization, the more implacably it is dominated." Earlier, he had explained that "what passes for nature in civilization is by its very substance furthest from all nature, its own self-chosen object." Similar thoughts lead Marcuse to write in "Nature and Revolution" (1972) that the capitalist notion of nature is of "value-free matter, material for the sake of domination." Marcuse holds out hope that perhaps in a future society there will emerge "an experience of nature as a totality of life to be protected and 'cultivated.'" Many Indigenous groups and movements stress that exactly such an experience organized Indigenous approaches to nature (and here Marcuse's imperative can profitably be put into productive conversation with a recent manifesto like the Red Nation's *The Red Deal* [2021]).

8. THE CULTURE INDUSTRY, FREE TIME, AND POLITICS

Because modern society is a fundamentally antagonistic, destructive, and unstable system, it invites the possibility of administration. Adorno thereby notes in *Philosophical Elements of a Theory of Society* that "power relations cloak themselves in bureaucratic procedures." Such bureaucracy, the administered world, then becomes "independent, ultimately determined by economic motives or economic objectives." On such a view, as Adorno had already claimed in the Introduction to the *Positivist Dispute*, "society is a system in the sense of a synthesis of an atomized plurality, in the sense of a real yet abstract assemblage of what is in no way immediately or 'organically' united." If administration necessitates maintenance of the structure at the level of objective conditions, what Horkheimer and Adorno term the culture industry also necessitates the maintenance of the whole at the level of subjective conditions. "Culture industry" is their term for the great range of cultural products that now just form another branch of commodity production. Such products equally also keep the whole running smoothly, ideologically justifying or making palatable administration. In *Dialectic of Enlightenment*, Horkheimer and Adorno stress that "culture today is infecting everything with sameness." Various entertainment industries are intertwined with each other and with the whole, making for a seamless integration: "the dependence of the most powerful broadcasting company on the electrical industry, or of film on the banks, characterizes the whole sphere, the individual sectors of which are themselves economically intertwined." Even resistance (and it might be noted even critical theory) itself becomes just another product to be marketed and sold. The latest Rage Against the Machine album can be sold as easily as the latest Taylor Swift, Tyler Perry as easily as David Lynch, Jordan Peterson as easily as Noam

Chomsky. Classifications—no matter how radical or fine-grained—are exclusively "preempted by the schematism of production." The whole thing works so well exactly because the fundamental nature of society is already fragmented and antagonistic: "the culture industry can only manipulate individuality so successfully because the fractured nature of society has always been reproduced within it." In addition to the antagonism of society, the culture industry itself thereby directly contributes to the erosion of the self (as noted in the last chapter), since with the culture industry, "the most intimate reactions of human beings have become so entirely reified, even to themselves, that the idea of anything peculiar to them survives only in extreme abstraction: personality means hardly more than dazzling white teeth and freedom from body odor and emotions." Connections can easily be drawn here to the ways in which subsequent critical theory diagnoses how the culture industry inculcates habits of thinking around race, gender, sexuality, and ability. Horkheimer and Adorno aptly claim in *Dialectic of Enlightenment* that "the whole world is passed through the filter of the culture industry."

Even the experience of time comes to be organized by the culture industry and the economic system that underwrites it. Adorno highlights in "Free Time" (1969) how even alleged "free time is the unmediated continuation of labor as its shadow." The working day is such that it requires escape, and thus what Horkheimer and Adorno in *Dialectic of Enlightenment* call "the incurable sickness of all entertainment." This leads to at least two effects. On one hand, leisure time cannot truly be leisurely, instead congealing "into boredom," since genuine leisure could only exist if not somehow indexed to labor (and thereby understood somehow through labor). Adorno claims in "Free Time" that in such a social situation, leisure "must not demand any effort," but the close link between leisure and labor as two sides of the same coin makes that impossible. Subjects move from labor to boredom to consumption and then back to labor, moving between these "well-worn grooves of association." Leisure comes to have "something superfluous about it," where free time is such that "the maximum must be extracted from leisure," so that the entirety of life appears "like a job." To register this point, just think of the common adage: work hard, play hard. On the other hand, this stress on leisure as a site where no effort is exerted perverts another possibility for leisure time: that it be a time set apart from the instrumental labor of the market, but nonetheless be a time of great exertion, as when, for example, someone may spend their leisure time mastering a complex piece of literature, or creating a significant work of art or theory, or developing a skill important to them, or whatever else. Leisure time need not be a time of frivolous lack of exertion but may in fact be the last possible site of radical self-creation or communal activity.

The political landscape is equally affected—as Adorno notes in *The Authoritarian Personality*, "politics is viewed in much the same way as sport or the movies." To the extent that politics is consumed and pursued during leisure time, politics also comes to be understood "within the framework of 'entertainment'" (a feature of the modern world that the band Gang of Four stressed with their album *Entertainment!* [1979]). Politics even under the best of conditions is oftentimes disappointing. Under the sway of the culture industry, especially in comparison to its productions, politics appears as "drab, cold, dry," ultimately "boring." Or politics becomes thoroughly like entertainment (it is surely not too much to understand celebrity politicians like Obama or Trump through this lens). In either case, politics begins to resemble nothing different than cheering for a favorite team or athlete. Pick a team and stick with them until the bitter end (so poignantly and humorously exemplified in the "America Decides" episode of HBO's *Succession*). Or not. There are standard tropes and soundbites (and now algorithms) for either option. Thinking is not part of the process. Adorno introduces the term "ticket thinking" for this situation, highlighting how politics itself is standardized as a feature of the culture industry (To register this latter point, just think about the fact that running for the president of the United States now requires a billion dollars.) While not a member of the Frankfurt School, the suggestion of critical theorist Johannes Agnoli in *The Transformation of Democracy* (1964) that voters appear as mere consumers of political goods is relevant here.

9. POLITICS AND PSYCHOANALYSIS

In "Freudian Theory and the Pattern of Fascist Propaganda" (1951), Adorno argues that because of the way in which the ego is weakened through such conditions, subjects easily fall for the techniques of demagogues. Explored in Frankfurt School works like Leo Lowenthal and Norbert Guterman's *Prophets of Deceit* and in Adorno's own studies of Christian right-wing radio in *The Psychological Technique of Martin Luther Thomas's Radio Addresses* (1941/1975), Adorno diagnoses the psychoanalytic features of the work of these pundits as ultimately satisfying the desire of subjects for a larger ego (this account depends exactly on the Freudian story about ego formation recounted in the last chapter). Through an emotional identification with the leader, a subject introjects the leader into themselves, making the leader an ego ideal or superego in Freudian terms (a model for the social standards that an ego applies to itself). As Adorno summarizes it in the aforementioned essay, "by making the leader his ideal he loves himself, as it were, but gets rid of the stains of frustration and discontent which mar his picture of his own empirical self." Such a leader, Adorno notes, must be a "great little man" to the extent that he must both appear to be one of the people and also omnipotent. (Adorno uses the image of Hitler as a "composite of King Kong and the suburban barber," or, in the American context, with an eye towards Trump, Charles Coughlin [1891–1979], and many others in its history, someone who "suggests both omnipotence and the idea that he is just one of the folks, a plain, red-blooded American, untainted by material or spiritual wealth.") Adorno notes how this leads to a sort of hypnosis, since there is in fact no real ego ideal or superego (for the introjected leader in fact stands for nothing, has no values); there is thereby never any real criticism of the self. Because any positive content is lacking, negative qualities come to be substituted and dominant: out groups are constructed, and destructive tendencies are prioritized. Adorno highlights in "Freudian Theory and the Pattern of Fascist Propaganda" how this is all capable of playing out in any context, since its "effectiveness is itself a function of the psychology of the consumers," which is standardized. And such "standardization, in turn, falls in line with the stereotypical thinking, that is to say, with the 'stereopathy' of those susceptible to this propaganda and their infantile wish for endless, unaltered repetition." With an eye to the last chapter, in "Opinion Delusion Society" (1960/1961), Adorno argues that "the weakness of the ego nowadays, which beyond its psychological dimension also register the effects of each individual's real powerlessness in the face of the societalized apparatus," is exactly what leads to an "identification with the power and the glory of the collective."

Relatedly, in "Anxiety and Politics" (1957), an essay strikingly written only a little after he began to integrate psychoanalysis into his work, Franz Neumann stresses that there are basic structural issues experienced by any ego of whatever sort. To the extent that every society, every social configuration, whether progressive or regressive, requires some renunciation of instinctual drives, then such "psychological alienation" produces anxiety "as a permanent condition." This permanence emerges exactly because the drives will continue to clash with the internalized norms of society, thereby producing anxiety around this condition (Neumann here cites "On the Theory of Anxiety and Guilt" [1952] by the psychoanalyst Melanie Klein [1882–1960]). To such alienation, we may equally add the more "ordinary" kinds of alienation associated with existence in the modern world (Marx's alienation as discussed in Chapter 1). The anxiety that arises around such alienation is difficult to overcome or deal with, since we cannot immediately or easily make clear either the structural forms of oppression around us nor make easily available our repressed drives (here we may again propose a very mild and tempered analogy between critical theory and psychoanalysis). An unconscious solution that becomes plausible for an agent under the grip of such a situation is to convert this permanent, unavoidable anxiety into a pathological, neurotic anxiety. Such a pathology then becomes a means of avoiding this deeper, more existential, more permanent anxiety. Equally, as in Adorno's thought, such neurotic anxiety can in turn be "overcome by means of identification" with a charismatic leader or a cult of personality. A similar mechanism animates the retreat into conspiracy theories. With either, the identification with authority (or the acquiescence to conspiracy), complex structural conditions and their concomitant unavoidable psychological byproducts are converted to mere problems of individual neurosis that can then be addressed through the substitution in the ego of a leader or a conspiracy theory.

10. MATURITY

To return to the question of maturity raised in the last chapter, it is not too much to say that things look grim: society is totalizing; democracy is frail and perpetually on the verge disappearing; inequalities animate local and global contexts; subjects are formed with weak egos and limited powers of imagination; cultural products maintain docility, cynicism, or oftentimes even happiness in such conditions; and antagonism, contradiction, and crisis continue to threaten the whole, now possibly to the point of planetary collapse. Social domination, even in democratic polities, appears to be ubiquitous and vast. Think here again, for example, of Adorno's claim in "Working through the Past" that the "survival of National Socialism *within* democracy" was a greater threat than the survival of fascism against democracy (of course, given recent developments, we have good reason now to fear both). Equally, though, to return to the theme of this book: what drives things here is needless suffering, which oftentimes appears natural and thereby unavoidable. The need for social transformation, then, arises from the demand to bring such needless suffering to an end, with critical theory playing a crucial role in registering the full scope of this suffering and how it tends to be overlooked. Furthermore, social transformation demands that we potentially explore and rethink a wide range of our social institutions and processes. This is one way to situate, for example, the very first publication of the Institute for Social Research after its move to the USA, Georg Rusche and Otto Kirchheimer's *Punishment and Social Structure* (1939). In the conclusion, Kirchheimer stresses that, for example, even "the penal system of any given society is not an isolated phenomenon," but is rather an "integral part of the whole social system," thereby sharing "its aspiration and its defects." Rather than a fixed necessity, the entire penal system "provides the illusion of security by covering the symptoms of social disease with a system of legal and moral value judgments." While the book pursues evidence for such a claim through a variety of historical contexts, it is also not too difficult to highlight the American context (as already noted in the Introduction with works like Michelle Alexander's *The New Jim Crow*): social trends profoundly affect penal outcomes as in the three strikes laws for only certain kinds of crimes, sentencing differences between different versions of the same drug, the racialized makeup of prison and the labor practices therein, and so forth. It is also quite easy to draw here, as, for example, the philosopher Eduarto Mendieta has done, a direct line from such claims to the sort of prison abolition work that Angela Davis and others undertake. (Davis was a student of Marcuse and Adorno; more on this in the Conclusion.) I flag *Punishment and*

Social Structure not to pursue the topic in the required depth, but rather to make explicit that such a view of society highlights the great range of phenomena that become potentially of interest, bringing into focus also the immense scope of the problem(s) involved.

With that said, things are not entirely hopeless. In the "Free Time" essay mentioned above, Adorno notes that "it is obvious that the integration of consciousness and free time has not yet completely succeeded." Resistance is still possible. Adorno stresses that this possibility persists exactly because of the antagonistic, and thereby contradictory, nature of society, for "a society, whose inherent contradictions persist undiminished, cannot be totally integrated even in consciousness." The contradictions of society themselves guarantee that change remains a possibility, since they may alternatively suggest or demand change, and since they prevent complete integration. As noted in the beginning of this chapter, society is process. Adorno concludes "Free Time" by claiming that "we can here glimpse a chance of maturity, which might just eventually help to turn free time into freedom proper." Marcuse equally raises the possibility of a "great refusal" throughout his work. Such a refusal rejects current possibilities so as to hold out for something better. At the very least, this practically means civil disobedience, where, as Marcuse puts it in *An Essay on Liberation* (1969), "the mark of social repression" is nonetheless recognized "even in the most sublime manifestations of traditional culture, even in the most spectacular manifestations of technical progress." It may also suggest outright revolution. In either case, there are no guarantees, nor is the question of which option is best somehow settled. Marcuse stresses at the end of *One Dimensional Man* that "the critical theory of society possesses no concepts which could bridge the gap between the present and its future; holding no promise and showing no success, it remains negative." His claims and those of Adorno, though, are entirely compatible with the *possibility* of maturity and thereby a different world. Here the topic of the next chapter comes into focus, since it is art that seems to hold out the sparks that might help bring such maturity and such a different world into focus and then perhaps into existence. How this might be is far from obvious, and as we increasingly know all too well, the contradictions and obstacles appear to be greater and more numerous now. It is perhaps for such reasons that Marcuse's *One Dimensional Man* concludes with a quote from Walter Benjamin, that "it is only for the sake of those without hope that hope is given to us."

SUGGESTED READING

ONE DIMENSIONALITY, DIALECTIC OF ENLIGHTENMENT, AND/OR THE FRANK-
FURT SCHOOL IN RELATION TO HISTORY

Abromeit, John. "Genealogy and Critical Historicism: Two Models of Enlightenment in Horkheimer and Adorno's Writings." *Critical Historical Studies* 3,
no. 2 (2016): 283–308.

———. *Max Horkheimer and the Foundations of the Frankfurt School.* Cambridge:
Cambridge University Press, 2011.

Allen, Amy. "Reason, Power and History: Re-Reading the Dialectic of
Enlightenment." *Thesis Eleven* 120, no. 1 (2014): 10–25.

Horkheimer, Max, and Theodor W. Adorno. *Dialectic of Enlightenment, Philosophical Fragments.* Translated by Edmund Jephcott. Cultural Memory in the
Present. Edited by Mieke Bal and Hent de Vries. Palo Alto: Stanford University Press, 2002.

Hulatt, Owen. "The Place of Mimesis in the Dialectic of Enlightenment." In
The Routledge Companion to the Frankfurt School, 351–64. New York: Routledge, 2018.

———. "Reason, Mimesis, and Self-Preservation in Adorno." *Journal of the
History of Philosophy* 54, no. 1 (2016): 135–51.

Kellner, Douglas. "Marcuse." In *A Companion to Continental Philosophy*, edited
by Simon Critchley and William R. Schroeder, 389–96. London: Blackwell, 2017.

Kleinberg, Ethan. "One-Dimensional Man, One-Dimensional History:
Re-Reading Herbert Marcuse." *Journal of the Philosophy of History* 15, no. 3
(2021): 340–60.

Marcuse, Herbert. *One-Dimensional Man: Studies in the Ideology of Advanced
Industrial Society.* Boston: Beacon Press, 1964.

Noppen, Pierre-François. "The Anthropology in Dialectic of Enlightenment."
In *A Companion to Adorno*, edited by Peter Gordon, Espen Hammer and
Max Pensky, 207–20. London: Blackwell, 2020.

Schlipphacke, Heidi. "A Hidden Agenda: Gender in Selected Writings by
Theodor Adorno and Max Horkheimer." *Orbis Litterarum* 56, no. 4 (2001):
294–313.

Schmidt, James. "Language, Mythology, and Enlightenment: Historical Notes
on Horkheimer and Adorno's 'Dialectic of Enlightenment.'" *Social Research*
(1998): 807–38.

Shuster, Martin. "The Critique of the Enlightenment." *A Companion to Adorno*
(2020): 251–69.

The *Dialectic of Enlightenment* is such a complex and disputed text.
These are good entrypoints, but really just scratch the surface.

THE MARXIST BACKGROUND

Bonefeld, Werner. *Critical Theory and the Critique of Political Economy: On Subversion and Negative Reason*. London: Bloomsbury, 2014.

Bonefeld, Werner, and Chris O'Kane. *Adorno and Marx: Negative Dialectics and the Critique of Political Economy*. London: Bloomsbury, 2022.

Braunstein, Dirk. *Adorno's Critique of Political Economy*. Leiden: Brill, 2022.

Feenberg, Andrew. *The Philosophy of Praxis: Marx, Lukács and the Frankfurt School*. London: Verso, 2014.

————. "Realizing Philosophy: Marx, Lukács and the Frankfurt School." In *Critical Theory and the Challenge of Praxis*, edited by Stefano Giacchetti Ludovisi, 117–30. London: Routledge, 2016.

LUKÁCS, REIFICATION, AND READING LUKÁCS

Goldmann, Lucien. *Lukács & Heidegger: Towards a New Philosophy*. Translated by William Boelhower. London: Routledge, 1977.

Kavoulakos, Konstantinos. "What Is Reification in Georg Lukács's Early Marxist Work?" *Thesis Eleven* 157, no. 1 (2020): 41–59.

Lotz, Christian. "Categorial Forms as Intelligibility of Social Objects: Reification and Objectivity in Lukács." In *Confronting Reification: Revitalizing Georg Lukács's Thought in Late Capitalism*, edited by Gregory R. Smulewicz-Zucker, 25–47. Chicago: Haymarket, 2020.

Smulewicz-Zucker, Gregory R., ed. *Confronting Reification: Revitalizing Georg Lukács's Thought in Late Capitalism*. Chicago: Haymarket, 2020.

Westerman, Richard. "Lukács in the 1920s and the 2020s: The Practice and Praxis of Intellectual History." *Thesis Eleven* 157, no. 1 (2020): 24–40.

————. *Lukács's Phenomenology of Capitalism: Reification Revalued*. London: Palgrave-Macmillan, 2018.

————. "The Reification of Consciousness: Husserl's Phenomenology in Lukács's Identical Subject-Object." *New German Critique* 37, no. 3 (2010): 97–130.

These are novel readings of Lukács. Feenberg and Westerman were the scholars who first turned me onto understanding the ways in which Lask and Husserl and phenomenology was central to Lukács.

LASK AND PHENOMENOLOGY (IN THIS CONTEXT) AND FRANKFURT SCHOOL AND PHENOMENOLOGY

Abromeit, John. "Herbert Marcuse's Critical Encounter with Martin Heidegger 1927–33." In *Herbert Marcuse*, 131–51: Routledge, 2014.

———. "The Vicissitudes of the Politics of" Life": Max Horkheimer and Herbert Marcuse's Reception of Phenomenology and Vitalism in Weimar Germany." *Enrahonar: quaderns de filosofia* 62 (2019): 0039–58.

Crowell, Steven Galt. "Emil Lask: Aletheiology as Ontology." *Kant Studien* 87, no. 1 (1996): 69–88.

———. *Truth and Reflection: The Development of Transcendental Logic in Lask, Husserl, and Heidegger.* New Haven: Yale University, 1981.

Dallmayr, Fred R. "Phenomenology and Critical Theory: Adorno." *Cultural Hermeneutics* 3, no. 4 (1976): 367–405.

de Vries, Hent. *Minimal Theologies: Critiques of Secular Reason in Adorno and Levinas.* Baltimore: The Johns Hopkins University Press, 2019.

Gordon, Peter E. *Adorno and Existence.* Cambridge: Harvard University Press, 2016.

Hodge, Joanna. "Adorno and Phenomenology: Between Hegel and Husserl." *Philosophy Today* 63, no. 2 (2019): 403–25.

Wolff, Ernst. "From Phenomenology to Critical Theory: The Genesis of Adorno's Critical Theory from His Reading of Husserl." *Philosophy & Social Criticism* 32, no. 5 (2006): 555–72.

Zahavi, Dan. *Husserl's Phenomenology.* Palo Alto: Stanford University Press, 2003.

STATE CAPITALISM

Cook, Deborah. "Adorno on Late Capitalism." *Radical Philosophy* 89 (1998): 16–26.

Gangl, Manfred. "The Controversy over Friedrich Pollock's State Capitalism." *History of the Human Sciences* 29, no. 2 (2016): 23–41.

THE CULTURE INDUSTRY

Cook, Deborah. *The Culture Industry Revisited: Theodor W. Adorno on Mass Culture.* Lanham: Rowman & Littlefield, 1996.

Rebentisch, Juliane, and Felix Trautman. "The Idea of the Culture Industry." In *A Companion to Adorno,* edited by Peter Gordon, Espen Hammer, and Max Pensky, 19–32. London: Blackwell, 2020.

These are two excellent overviews, but the amount of scholarly ink spilled around the culture industry is too mammoth now to capture in any sort of compact list.

POLITICS, AUTHORITARIANISM, ETC.

Abromeit, John. "Frankfurt School Critical Theory and the Persistence of Authoritarian Populism in the United States." In *Critical Theory and*

Authoritarian Populism, edited by Jeremiah Morelock, 3–27. London: University of Westminster Press, 2018.

Gordon, Peter. "The Authoritarian Personality Revisited: Reading Adorno in the Age of Trump." *boundary 2* 44, no. 2 (2017): 31–56.

Marasco, Robyn, Christina Gerhardt, and Kirk Wetters. "The Authoritarian Personality." *Polity* 54, no. 1 (2022): 1–7.

McAfee, Noëlle. *Fear of Breakdown: Politics and Psychoanalysis.* New York: Columbia University Press, 2019.

Mendieta, Eduardo. "The Prison Contract and Surplus Punishment: On Angela Y. Davis's Abolitionism." *Human Studies* 30, no. 4 (2007): 291–309.

The *Polity* issue cited above (Introduction) is entirely dedicated to the *Authoritarian Personality* and features several essays.

4

ART

1. ART AND SOCIETY

The Frankfurt School attached great importance to art. Given the picture of society that emerged in the last chapter, and given the way that art is nowadays largely seen as commodified or disposable entertainment, readers may be puzzled by how this may be the case. Yet, art was an unchanging locus of concern for the Frankfurt School and some members in fact saw it as a crucial site for critical theory (for example, nine out of the nineteen volumes in Adorno's collected writings are about music). And between the Frankfurt School or its close associates or influences (for example, György Lukács, Sigfried Kracauer, Walter Benjamin), critical theory addressed itself to almost every major artistic and media form, and did so oftentimes in varied and complex ways. Because the output of the members of the Frankfurt School is so vast, this chapter is oriented around Marcuse's last published book, *The Aesthetic Dimension* (1977), and Adorno's *Aesthetic Theory* (1970), which appeared posthumously a year after his death (it was culled from drafts Adorno had been working on for decades). These two books situate art as a crucial pursuit in response to the state of affairs outlined in the prior chapters, and they may be understood as emblematic of the Frankfurt School in many regards. Much of the Frankfurt School's examination of art revolves around assessing or understanding its critical potential, especially its possibilities for being a source of some kind of perspective or value independent of the totalizing aspects of modern society.

DOI: 10.4324/9781003200963-5

To bring this approach into focus, note, for example, that if art is understood solely as a product of the culture industry, then it is just another branch—the cultural branch—of industrial commodity production. On such a view, as Adorno suggests in "The Culture Industry Reconsidered" (1975), art just is a product of a culture industry that "fuses the old and familiar into a new quality." The culture industry thereby creates "in all its branches, products which are tailored for consumption by masses, and which to a great extent determine the nature of that consumption." Such products, including cultural products, can be said to be "manufactured more or less according to plan." Art becomes nothing more than the cultural wing of capitalist commodity production and consumption (and like these other elements, it serves to pacify and administer human beings as much as anything else).

Equally, to the extent that art is exclusively understood as an expression of the culture industry and of society more generally, there may be strong ethical reasons for rejecting art if it is understood to be an element of a society that is, in Adorno's words, "wrong." Something like this thought led Adorno to write in "Cultural Criticism and Society" that "to write poetry after Auschwitz is barbaric." Later, in *Negative Dialectics*, Adorno quotes the playwright Bertolt Brecht (1898–1956), making the same point, that culture is ultimately a "mansion built of dogshit." The very existence of Auschwitz, and the events related to it, undermines art as a cultural product: "Auschwitz demonstrated irrefutably that culture has failed." That such brutalities "could happen in the midst of traditions of philosophy, art, and the enlightening sciences says more than merely that these traditions and their spirit weren't able to grab people and transform them." Culture is at bottom "garbage." This is one way in which any justification of art as a human product may be questioned in the face of the brutal suffering human culture continuously unleashes.

In response it may be claimed that the point of art is to bring about a better society. Such an instrumental view of art, however, raises questions about the specificity of art. It does not seem obvious why art would be preferable here as opposed to some social or political program, especially given everything that's just been said about art, the culture industry, and society. As Marcuse puts it in *The Aesthetic Dimension*: "in a situation where the miserable reality can be changed only through radical political praxis, the concern with aesthetics demands justification." Measures that aim to harness art towards such a political program do not bypass this question, but rather further complicate and specify it, since radical political change appears no less mysterious than art. Think here, for example, of "Socialist Realism," a Russian artistic movement officially coined after the Russian revolution as a means to vivify its then nascent possibilities for democratic socialism. Within a decade it had been coopted by Stalin's totalitarian politics. (Less dramatically, think of the fate of punk rock, the artistic counterculture of the 1960s, or hip-hop, each of which were quite easily coopted by the establishment so that whatever critical potential they had was dissolved.)

Adorno's opening line in *Aesthetic Theory* thereby registers something like the puzzlement that should accompany any consideration of art in the modern world: "it is self-evident that nothing concerning art is self-evident anymore ... not even its right to exist." In the cases above, if art is merely an extension of society, current or future, then perhaps our investigation should be into society rather than art. Works of art, in such a case, as Adorno puts it in "On Commitment" (1974), "merely assimilate themselves sedulously to ... brute existence." Marcuse and Adorno, and indeed the Frankfurt School more generally, however, never gave up the idea of conceiving art as a distinct domain of human life, at least potentially unassimilable or irreducible to other aspects of human life, and one that, thereby, required its own investigation.

2. ART, JUDGMENT, AND AUTONOMY

Emerging here is a historical account of mammoth proportions. While the full details and scope of such an account are impossible to present in any compact way, it suffices to highlight that, even with the most cursory understanding of Western art history, it's notable that for the large part of that history, the function of art was generally religious. Think, for example, just as easily of ancient Greek sculpture as of the religious art leading up to and through the Renaissance. Just as we saw views shift around the goodness of creation in the modern period (think of the shift effected by the Lisbon earthquake, cited in the Introduction), the way in which humans thought about art also began to shift. On one hand, something like the more traditional position was still popular, with art seen as participating in the broader apprehension of beauty, available to human perception most prominently (but not exclusively) through the experience of a divinely ordered natural beauty. Such apprehension was sensible and pleasurable, offering access to the perfection of creation. On such a view, human sensibility, like human rationality, offered a kind of knowledge of the world, wherein beauty and goodness, art and morality, were intimately related. Prominent figures in this tradition include Anthony Ashley Cooper, the Earl of Shaftesbury (1671–1713) and Alexander Baumgarten (1714–1762), who coined the modern usage of "aesthetics" as referring to the sensation of beauty (prior to this coinage, as taken from Greek philosophy, aesthetics just meant sensible perception). On the other hand, there were also theories that understood art and beauty as phenomena that have nothing to do with goodness or perfection, but are rather merely phenomena from which humans derive pleasure, in the same way that they derive pleasure from a delicious meal or a pleasing drink. David Hume (1711–1776) thus writes in his *Enquiry* (1748) that when Euclid gave the various "qualities of the circle," he did not anywhere say "a word of its beauty." The reason is that "beauty is not a quality of the circle," but rather "is such" that "either by the primary constitution of our nature, by custom, or by caprice, is fitted to give a pleasure and satisfaction" to us.

Kant inherited these two frames of reference with respect to art, but as in other areas of philosophy, he modified them significantly in order to produce a radical and novel position in the history of philosophy. In the *Critique of Judgment* (1790), Kant argues that art and beauty offer humans a distinct way of understanding their humanity. To see how this is the case, recall (as noted in earlier chapters) that for Kant perception is normative. According to Kant, perception occurs when the subject brings a concept to bear upon the matter of sensibility (in Kantian parlance: a perceiver *subsumes* the deliverances of sensibility under a general concept). I judge that something is so-and-so. When the concept is available to me prior to perception, then my judgment is determining: it determines that this bit of sensible matter is, say, a penguin. When I perceive something for which I have no prior concept like, say, a beautiful object, then my imagination and my conceptual capacities enter into what Kant calls a free play of these faculties, where one vivifies the other, multiplying the possible concepts that may be applicable to the beautiful object. With a beautiful object, I am aiming *to find* the concept that applies to it. A judgment that the object is beautiful testifies to the way in which this object resists the possibility of ending in a determinative judgment about the object. Instead, the beautiful object suggests more and more concepts that may be applicable to it. Such perception is thereby "merely reflective," for there is no determination by a concept but rather only reflection on possible concepts.

Such reflection allows ultimately for an even more robust exploration of the work of art and human beings. Because human beings all share the same capacities, Kant speaks of a "common sense." While the notion of a common sense has a long parlance in philosophy dating back to antiquity, in Kant, the possibility of such a common sense hinges on the fact that all human beings allegedly (1) experience the world by means of sensibility, (2) use concepts to organize that experience, and (3) possess an imagination to mediate between these two. In such a case, when someone perceives an object of beauty, they experience a free play between their conceptual capacities and imagination. They may then be justified in claiming that *anyone else* who also perceives such an object will have a comparable experience since they share the same basic cognitive makeup. The very experience of beauty allegedly depends on a shared humanity. This is why, in *Aesthetic Theory*, Adorno summarizes the historical situation as the idea that art, "after having freed itself from cultic function and its images, was nourished by the idea of humanity." In the *Critique of Judgment,* Kant also explicitly inflects the experience of beauty with a moral valence around being human, suggesting that beauty is a "symbol" of morality to the extent that beauty, like morality, hearkens to something that cannot be reduced solely or exclusively to the empirical realm (even as beauty and morality are each grounded in that realm). Reflective judgment and the lack of a determinate empirical concept underwrites this symbolism. Kant thus proposes beauty as a sort of initiation into the workings of morality, training us to value morality, for "the beautiful prepares us to love something" even "without interest," in fact "to esteem it, even contrary to our (sensible) interest."

What Kant introduces is a sort of logic of aesthetics or art, whereby beauty compels or demands agreement amongst humans.

And all of this with the possibility—indeed the understanding—that no such agreement necessarily will or does exist. It is a normative claim: when I find something beautiful, I am claiming that you also *ought* to find it beautiful. If you do not, then the very question of who we are as humans is somehow at stake, for the demand occurs exactly because of our shared human capacities. Exploring the contours of this demand forms the basis for a certain kind of deep understanding of what it means to be human, for oneself as much as for others. Cavell captures this sentiment well when he notes in "Aesthetic Problems of Modern Philosophy" (1965) that in such cases, a human being is saying to another: "look and find out whether you can see what I see, wish to say what I wish to say." Marcuse relatedly notes in *The Aesthetic Dimension* that "the inner logic of the work of art terminates in the emergence of another reason, another sensibility." Beauty or art that produces such a free play between our conceptual and imaginative capacities invites us to reflect on what we can and cannot see together and why, and how we can and cannot go on with each other in light of such shared capacities; it invites us to delineate what we do and do not share.

Because such aesthetic experience is not reducible to any other phenomena, depending as it does only on our common humanity in the face of an aesthetic object, it is plausible here to speak of an autonomy of art. From Kant to the present moment (through figures like the German Idealists, the Romantics, Arthur Schopenhauer, Friedrich Nietzsche, Martin Heidegger, and many others), the significance of art as such an autonomous human enterprise undergoes immense scrutiny. The Frankfurt School stands in this tradition, but with the caveat that any account of aesthetics must be contextualized historically, especially around the sort of needless suffering that this book has prioritized. Adorno thus claims in the opening lines of *Aesthetic Theory* that "as society became ever less a human one, this autonomy [of art] was shattered." He qualifies the statement, though, noting that "even prior to Auschwitz it was an affirmative lie, given historical experience, to ascribe any positive meaning to existence." (Think here of the notion of theodicy introduced in the Introduction, and also Susan Neiman's and Adorno's stress on the Lisbon earthquake as shattering the possibility of a successful theodicy.) To the extent that this Kantian tradition links the autonomy of art to an understanding of what it means to be human (and sometimes explicitly to morality), the brutal inhumanity of which humans are capable requires theoretical acknowledgment and contextualization, especially in the modern period, with its histories of colonialism, slavery, imperialism, and genocide. These are all reasons for why we may now equally say just as Adorno did that paradoxically "art is autonomous and it is not." Art may equally be taken to buttress humanity as much as inhumanity.

3. ART, HISTORY, AND SUFFERING

In this way, the approach of Adorno and the Frankfurt School also pushes against the Kantian account, for while the Frankfurt School also prioritizes the uniqueness or autonomy of art, it is not wed to, and indeed oftentimes vigorously rejects, beauty as an organizing principle of aesthetics. As Adorno puts it in *Minima Moralia:* "there is no longer beauty or consolation except in the gaze falling on horror, withstanding it, and in unalleviated consciousness of negativity holding fast to the possibility of what is better." Marcuse similarly writes in *The Aesthetic Dimension* that autonomy in art now "contains the categorical imperative: 'things must change.'" The relationship to Kant, as seen in the earlier chapters on subjectivity and critique, is one of harnessing the formal features of his account while updating its content by means of a deep reflection on the human historical developments since Kant, especially around needless suffering. With an eye to the history of philosophy, the Frankfurt School may then be said to be playing off Kant and Hegel against each other, since it was Hegel who first lodged a critique of Kant's aesthetics exactly by injecting into aesthetics a historical dimension in his *Lectures on Aesthetics* (1823), where he pursues a story about its alleged evolution through time (a position sketched quite compactly in Robert Pippin's recent *After the Beautiful* [2013).

What Adorno calls art's autonomy and its lack of autonomy exactly comes into focus when its historical, social basis is prioritized. Marcuse, for example, notes in *The Aesthetic Dimension* that "in its very elements (word, color, tone) art depends on the transmitted cultural material; art shares it with existing society." This is true no matter how radical or avant-garde the art may be—as Marcuse puts it, no matter how much art overturns the ordinary meanings of words and images, the transfiguration is still that of a given material." There is no art that somehow stands entirely apart from human society; even an art where "words are broken" or "new ones are invented" contains elements of sense, for "otherwise all communication would be severed" as Marcuse puts it. As earlier (see Chapter 2), there is here an analogy to ordinary language philosophy. Art is a sort of invitation to see things the way that the artist and/or the critic of that art sees them. This is why Cavell can, in *The World Viewed* (1979), compare forms of art to "forms of speech," for they are ultimately "ways of making sense." As Marcuse notes in *The Aesthetic Dimension*, though, there is a potential tension here around the autonomy of art, for "art is inevitably part of that which is and only as part of that which is does it speak against that which is."

This tension requires a balancing act. One way to understand how to balance here is to highlight that the Frankfurt School does not aim to give a theory of art or aesthetics applicable to all times and places. The whole point is exactly that our account of these must shift as the historical situation shifts. Adorno stresses in *Aesthetic Theory* that art is "understood only by its laws of movement, not according to any set of invariants." What animates the Frankfurt School approach to theorizing art, then, is exactly the historical situation as sketched thus far in this book: above all, the conditions of early and late capitalism, and all the needless suffering and pain that involves. In *Aesthetic Theory,* Adorno thereby makes the bold claim that "it would be preferable that some fine day art vanish altogether than that it forget the suffering that is its expression and in which form has its substance." Standing behind this remark is a sophisticated account about the relationship between art and the needless suffering that society engenders. That relationship requires more elaboration.

In *Aesthetic Theory*, Adorno notes that "art is expressive when what is objective, subjectively mediated, speaks, whether this be sadness, energy, or longing." When Adorno refers to "what is objective," he is referring to (needless) suffering, whose "expression is the suffering countenance of artworks." There is a potential ethical question here, however, about the relationship between the work of art and the suffering that it expresses. For example, if a work of art merely shows or exhibits suffering, whether forcefully or subtly, then it seems just to recreate society, double it. In such a case art is a mere extension or epiphenomenon of a fundamentally wrong society. Art may thereby (even if unintentionally) operate in the service of effecting a kind of acceptance of or acquiescence or reconciliation with the suffering of society through the pleasure gained from aesthetic experience. There is then a tension emerging here that is captured well by both Marcuse and Adorno in *The Aesthetic Dimension* and *Aesthetic Theory*, respectively:

> Auschwitz and My Lai, the torture, starvation, and dying—is this entire world supposed to be "mere illusion" and "bitterer deception"? ... Art draws away from this reality, because it cannot represent this suffering without subjecting it to aesthetic form, and thereby to the mitigating catharsis, to enjoyment (Marcuse).

> Even the sound of despair pays its tribute to a hideous affirmation (Adorno).

In his lectures on *Aesthetics* (1959), Adorno expands on this point, stressing that with works of art, "as soon as one violates the distance that lies in them, as soon as one relates the works directly to what one wants from them, one already 'de-artifies' them and destroys the very thing one hopes to get from them."

4. ON THE IMPORTANCE OF FORM

Animating this point is a complicated understanding of the relationship between form and content. From a high-altitude view, because society is fundamentally wrong, the general picture for Marcuse and Adorno is one where serious art responds to and resists society. How this might happen, though, is by no means straightforward. As seen in the last chapter, society has a massive culture industry dedicated to producing a range of aesthetic products aimed exactly at obfuscating and hiding the suffering it causes. If this wasn't problematic enough, there is also a basic formal point that any serious art that could be created is always a byproduct of that very same society, using its topics and forms (in the broadest possible sense of these terms). It is not immediately obvious that or even how any sort of critical art could then be possible, since what's taken to be art may simply be just an uncritical extension of the status quo.

In *Aesthetic Theory*, Adorno writes that "the unresolved antagonisms of reality return in artworks as immanent problems of form." Adorno also stresses that form must be understood as "sedimented content." In his lectures on *Aesthetics*, Adorno makes the claim even more extreme for rhetorical purposes, in order to formulate things as "dogmatically" and "as starkly" as possible. He thus claims simply that there are in fact "no so-called formal aspects in art which are not themselves sedimented content." He uses the image of ornamentations on ordinary objects as a means to illustrate the claim. The claim is that the ornament on, say, a vase is there as a reminder, a "scar that appeared on a vase at the point where it could not be made at the potter's wheel without such an interruption." Art is the expression of objective conditions, especially around injustice, needless suffering, and lack, which are transfigured in aesthetics. Such expression necessitates the development or refinement of form, since without such a refinement, art would not be other than an extension of present society, would be merely another version of the status quo. In the lectures, Adorno points out that, "following this analogy, it should be the case for all so-called artistic forms that they were once content, and through a process of … artistic development … took on that peculiar independence." Such a relationship between form and content can carry great nuance. For example, in his decades-long study of Beethoven (which was never completed), Adorno diagnoses relationships between musical forms in Beethoven as relations also between "sedimented *content*," where "in this case" one form is "mockery, parody" of the other.

Every work of art bears, if investigated properly (and thereby not immediately or explicitly), the stamp of its historical moment. To get at the full import of a work of art, then, it is never sufficient to understand what its creator(s) intended (such intentions may be useful or they may not, they alone will never settle matters). Adorno would thereby agree with the philosopher Arthur Danto (1924–2013) who writes in *The Transfiguration of the Commonplace* (1981) that a work of art is a means of "externalizing a way of viewing the world, expressing the interior of a cultural period, offering itself as a mirror to catch the conscience of our kings." The way in which works of art do this is not solely or exclusively through what they are about. Every art work says more than what it says explicitly. Furthermore, the forms by which works of art do what they do— be it a style of painting, writing, or music, just to name a few— are also sedimented content, in the sense that such content at some prior point *explicitly responded* to reality as it was organized.

This response, though, became sedimented into a stylistic fixture, a formal quality of how something comes to be done in and with art. (To get a sense of this, just think of Cavell's claim above that forms of art are like forms of speech, but inflect this idea now with Adorno's story about the importance of needless suffering in this context.) A serious or successful work of art always expresses reality as it presently stands. To the extent that society instantiates needless suffering and brutality, the work of art expresses something that both acknowledges this situation and pushes against this. Doing this requires the discovery of a form that would allow such expression to stand outside the broader social order that produces the suffering and brutality. A work of art then may be said to offer resistance to reality even as it exactly is an expression of that reality. Adorno writes in *Aesthetic Theory* that in works of art,

> [T]he criterion of success is twofold: whether they succeed in integrating thematic strata and details into their immanent law of form and in this integration at the same time maintain what resists it and the fissures that occur in the process of integration.

The reason that such procedures emerge as "immanent problems of form" is because the "unresolved antagonisms of reality" demand an alternative reality, one where these antagonisms don't exist. Woe says go. *Things could be different.* The exhibition of such an alternative, however, always runs the danger of being a mere extension of the status quo, of merely acquiescing to current society. There exist a range of practices that already count as artistic forms, but these are already always implicated with present society in various ways (from explicit appropriation as with the culture industry to forms of expression that present resistance only to result in betrayal of that resistance, even if inadvertently). The problem, so to speak, is to find an artistic form that is able to accomplish such resistance, to cut through the sedimentation of society, to present, however briefly, a path of resistance, or an alternative picture. As Adorno puts it in "Those Twenties" (1962), "no artistic form is conceivable any longer that is not a protest."

Questions around form, of how to find the right aesthetic form, will continue to persist and multiply as long as a wrong society persists. In *Negative Dialectics*, Adorno claims that philosophy "lives on because the moment to realize it was missed." Elsewhere in the text, he claims that, "dialectics is the ontology of the wrong state of things." Philosophy as a critical theoretical pursuit persists because the world contains needless suffering that demands the procedures of philosophy. The same is true of art and its problems of form. In *Aesthetic Theory* Adorno claims that "art keeps itself alive through its social force of resistance." Because of this, though, it is not "possible to sketch the form of art in a changed society." Marcuse similarly notes in *The Aesthetic Dimension* that "in a free society" such forms of art would "become aspects of the real." A serious or successful work of art is thereby doubly difficult, for it must both capture or diagnose the needless suffering of the present social order even as it institutes an aesthetic form that points beyond that order. As Adorno puts it in *Aesthetic Theory*: a work of art is ultimately "a social product that has rejected every semblance of existing for society."

5. TWO EXAMPLES: SCHOENBERG AND BECKETT

While the Frankfurt School wrote extensively about a range of artists, for the purposes of space and exigency, let me focus on two of Adorno's heroes, the composer Arnold Schoenberg (1874–1951) and the writer Samuel Beckett (1906–1989), who was also much admired by Marcuse (so much so that in the late 1970s, Marcuse and Beckett exchange letters, with the latter even writing a poem for Marcuse's eightieth birthday). The pairing of Schoenberg and Beckett is also not artificial since Adorno himself frequently invokes the two together. While both writers have an extensive and complex oeuvre that makes it difficult to discuss their work in any compact way, it is striking that the two are unified in introducing novel aesthetic forms. Schoenberg explicitly sought "the emancipation of dissonance" (his phrase) in his works, while Beckett claimed that he could not imagine "a higher goal for today's writer" than to "drill one hole after another" into language. Both ultimately aimed to avoid reconciliation, with the aesthetic forms of the past, or with the present by means of their artistic output. Nonetheless, each of them prioritized the present historical moment, and the kind of meaning it did or did not make available, all while acknowledging prior aesthetic forms, even as they aimed to move beyond them. It is striking that both of their aesthetic creations culminate in the exhibition of limits, dissonances, continual repetitions, incompletions, and, it may be said, even failure.

This is why Adorno claims in *Aesthetic Theory* that in Beckett "aesthetic transcendence and disenchantment converge in the moment of falling mute," which may be classified as "a language remote from all meaning," which is thereby "not a speaking" and so "this is its affinity to muteness." Adorno wrote extensively about Beckett's *Endgame* (1957) and some of his remarks on that play may be fruitful in this context. In the play, Hamm and Clov are two characters seemingly trapped in some sort of bunker that appears to have no life outside its walls. Giving us a glimpse into their life in such a state of affairs, where Clov is servant to a Hamm who appears to be dying, Beckett's characters pursue dialogue, yet the play ultimately offers no plot, no narrative, and no discernible meaning. Beckett appears, then, to disenchant the capitalist society that gave rise to *Endgame*: there is no meaning because the structure of commodification has become universal, a feature expressed equally in the destruction of almost all human life and the world. By nonetheless producing a work of art amidst a society that harbors this as an ever-present possibility, Beckett equally expresses that society. Beckett's play, like the rest of his writings, then, is not "about" his society or the late capitalist moment; the play and his writings *are* that moment expressed in art. He has transformed the content of the moment into a form that could get us properly to experience that content in aesthetic terms. Beckett's plays are oftentimes understood as "absurd," thereby somehow commenting on the human condition as such, but Adorno's reading of the writer is that Beckett depicts late capitalist "prototypes," which are fundamentally "historical in that they hold up as typical of human beings only the deformations inflicted upon them by the form of their society." (Think here of the way in which Lukács used "prototype" in his thought, as outlined in the last chapter.) Beckett says the only thing that can be "meaningfully" said at that moment, and in so saying it, he immediately points beyond it, for it is said in artistic terms that push against the present moment. Such art is thereby a sort of freedom or autonomy, since it perfectly responds to the moment at hand, even as it refuses to acquiesce to it. Notably, Adorno stresses that it is impossible to say anything about the *beyond to which* Beckett points, since it would mean either purposively invoking the categories of present society (themselves already compromised) or invoking artistic forms that follow in the wake of Beckett's (but these cannot be predicted in advance, for, in addition to Beckett, they would have equally to take stock of the perpetually changing social situation).

In *Aesthetic Theory*, Adorno presents Schoenberg's significance in a similar fashion, where "undisguised, corporeal impulses of the unconscious, shocks, and traumas are registered in the medium of music ... the first atonal works are depositions, in the sense of psychoanalytic dream depositions." Akin to Beckett, Schoenberg sonically presents the present moment, with its brutality. Adorno's favorite period of Schoenberg's is his free atonal period, where he sloughs off the necessity of compositions being written in a major-minor key system in which a tonal chord might assert dominance over other possible notes. Schoenberg aims to proceed musically without these conventions since these very conventions may be understood as aiming towards harmony and reconciliation, which must be rejected on any sober expression of present society. Schoenberg is not wholly singular, for Adorno registers sonic precursors to Shoenberg who pursued similar moves during their own period, most notable among them being Beethoven with his late works. Adorno remarks in *Aesthetic Theory* that in such music, "the dissonances that frighten" audiences do so exactly because they "speak of their own situation." (The comedian and actor Martin Mull is alleged to have claimed that "writing about music is like dancing about architecture." Taking the thought to heart, I am eschewing the idea of writing about the experience of listening to such music and invite the reader instead to listen to a prominent piece from this period—for example Schoenberg's "5 Orchestral Pieces" [Op. 16]," which was composed in 1909.) Schoenberg himself moved on from this period, developing a "twelve-tone system," which he notes in his essay, "Composition with Twelve Tones" (1941/1948) as having "laid the foundation for a new procedure in musical construction, which seemed fitted to replace those structural differentiations provided formerly by tonal harmonies." The development of such a standardized procedure is what makes Adorno hesitant and critical of this development in Schoenberg (although here Adorno notes that Schoenberg also evinces a sort of late style where he stands in a critical relation to the very tradition that he develops). In *Philosophy of New Music* (1949), though, Adorno terms this development in Schoenberg a "reversal into unfreedom," where "the subject rules over the music by means of a rational system in order to succumb to this rational system itself." Adorno ultimately stresses in "Individual and Organization" (1954) that "if hope remains in the administered world, then it does not lie in mediation, but at the extremes."

In the planned book on Beethoven, Adorno muses that "art-works of the highest rank are distinguished from the other not through their success—for in what have they succeeded?—but through the manner of their failure." We may make explicit that the failure here is overdetermined: a work of art must point beyond the present moment and present society, but can do so only negatively, only by remarking on what shouldn't be there. Making positive claims runs the risk of immediately being subsumed to the present state of affairs. Adorno stresses that this is because the problems posed in such works of art—especially to the extent they reflect non-administered responses to the present moment—are "so posed that the attempt to solve them must fail." Works of art become great when they are able to register "a failed attempt to reconcile objective antinomies." Such a work of art ultimately "succeeds" (and Adorno himself has this word in quotes to note that he doesn't intend it fully), exactly because it has "come up against its own limit." Another way to understand this failure is to see Adorno as stressing a peculiar formal feature of any such art: prior to its emergence, such art was not predictable according to present-day norms, but once it emerges, then it can of course be understood as having emerged from those norms exactly because it has itself established a new norm, one that stands in relation to earlier ones. There is then here both the failure of present norms to capture the current needless suffering society produces and the failure of the new norm conclusively to change that society so that it no longer produces such needless suffering.

While Marcuse's and Adorno's sympathies are generally with a range of "high-culture" works and artists, this theory of form can in fact be useful for situating many kinds of art. For example, in music, genres like punk, industrial, hip-hop, or noise—just to name a few—can be understood as initially pursuing a related vision of art. Of course, such attempts, as soon as they are taken up and commodified by the culture industry, ultimately morph into something else, but they do so no less tragically than the works of high modernist culture do. (For better and for worse, "Kafkaesque" is now a well-worn word in ordinary parlance and thereby different only in degree rather than kind from the way in which The Clash's "Should I Stay or Should I Go" is used to peddle everything from jeans to computers.) Despite this, for example, in the words of philosopher Samir Gandesha in "Punk Multiculturalism" (1999), "punk offered, if only for a moment, like a firecracker in a darkened sky, the possibility of a future beyond demographic categories and control groups, beyond monolithic radio station formats and marketing strategies." He continues, stressing that what punk first presented was "a utopic moment ... the shock of the new, of coming face to face with the real otherness of experience as opposed to the tired cliches of popular culture." In this vein, take, for example, the way in which the band Gang of Four recorded a song called "Anthrax" (1979) which reflects on the form the popular love song even as it harnesses the form to reflect on the form itself. Making use of a technique where the left and right channels present vocals at the same time, one channel has a member of the band explicitly musing on the form of love songs even as the other channel plays a sort of love song:

> Love comes up quite a lot and it's something to sing about
> 'cause most groups make most of their songs about falling in love
> or how happy they are to be in love
> You occasionally wonder why these groups sing about this all the time
> It's because there's something very special about it
> Either that or it's because everybody else sings about it, always has

One finds similar sentiments, for example, in early industrial music. Here is how Genesis P-Orridge (1950–2020), the lead vocalist of the industrial group Throbbing Gristle, described their aspirations as fundamentally trying to "decondition people's ... responses, demystify creative, musical activity and life too, and most of all it's ... trying to make people think for themselves, decide for themselves and direct their own lives" (as quoted in Simon Ford's *Wreckers of Civilization*

[1999]). In *Aesthetic Theory*, Adorno sees autonomous art "crystallizing in itself as something unique to itself, rather than complying with existing social norms and qualifying as 'socially useful.'" He continues, noting that art "criticizes society merely by existing." Such distinct existence, though, depends on "its opposition to society." Importantly, though, this opposition is not to be found in its content but rather its form: it must be unique in a way that pushes the boundaries of what ultimately counts as art. Such opposition, then, may be found in a variety of styles and genres. The stress on historical specificity requires, it seems to me, a fresh analysis in every case, with the possibility that matters about what can and cannot be a serious work of art are incapable of being settled in advance. (Of course, as Adorno also stresses, the very constitution of form in particular media is a lineage of technical problems that require increasing complexity and sometimes even austerity to "solve"—I can note that such a position is admittedly in tension with the way in which I've suggested popular works may be understood as serious works of art.)

6. SOCIETY AND THE EVERYDAY

The relationship between art and society that's emerged raises questions about art and the everyday. Equally, the invocation of an autonomy of art appears to trade on certain assumptions about the category of art as an institution within society, a point that art critic Peter Bürger (1936–2017) pursues against Adorno in *Theory of the Avant-Garde* (1984). To bring this into focus, think of artistic practices that aim to dissolve the boundaries between art and the everyday. We may think here of the art movement known as Dada—take for example the by now well-known "readymades" of the artist Marcel Duchamp (1887–1968) or think of later musical developments like those pursued by John Cage (1912–1992) who had a famous piece now called 4'33" (1947/1948). The piece demanded that the musician or musicians not play their instrument for the duration of the piece through three movements. It is because the first public performance was for four minutes and thirty-three seconds that its length became codified as its name (as Adorno might put it: unpredictability codified into sameness). Such pieces may be characterized as antiart, in the sense that they appear to reject traditional artistic categories. Nonetheless, they at the same time remain parasitic or dependent upon those practices. (Even the Dada Manifesto [1918] by the artist Tristan Tarza [1896–1963] claims "we must sweep and clean," implying the presence of something there to be swept and cleaned.)

While such art also potentially offers a critique of society (and especially of the sort of art that it can or cannot produce), the Frankfurt School is hesitant about its possibilities. For example, Marcuse finds it ultimately self-defeating. In *The Aesthetic Dimension*, he notes that it expresses a false immediacy, where what results from it is "a mere abstraction from the real-life context which establishes this immediacy." Marcuse's claim is that the immediate nature of such art ultimately mystifies our everyday existence since such ordinary existence "does not appear as what it is and does—it is a synthetic, artistic immediacy." Adorno is sometimes more sympathetic, noting in "Vers une musique informelle" (1961) that such music hurls "culture into people's faces" as "a joke," which is "a fate which both culture and people richly deserve." In his *Aesthetics* lectures, Adorno sees such movements as limited in their possibilities. He claims that while Dada is in a way "rigorous," it can only do exactly what its name suggests, namely to say "Da," which in Adorno's German means "there," i.e., that Dada and related art "seeks to the present the pure 'this-here,' the pure moment of expression … this art approaches in an almost literal sense … the threshold of silence." This is very little, almost nothing, though, and as a piece of art seems only to work once, or at best to fail exactly at the instant that it succeeds.

This leads Adorno to two considerations. On one hand, Adorno takes it that the "joke" of music like Cage's and related artistic practices ultimately falls flat because such a move is "neutralized in contemporary society," for "the latter defends itself" simply "by swallowing everything." In other words, society in fact deeply appreciates such art, for it is incapable of generating distance from the very status quo that it so brazenly flings in the face of the audience. Another way to put this point is that the joke only works if you're already primed to find it funny (i.e., only if you already have a critical stance towards society). (It should be noted that Adorno is more approving of compositions by Cage that are less akin to simple performance art, as when he approvingly writes about Cage's "Concert for Piano and Orchestra" [1957/1958], which is a piece that presents the performer with a score that can be played in its entirety or piecemeal, in any sequence, using a wide array of types, techniques, and operations. Chance thereby enters but does not wholly dominate every performance. Adorno speaks of this piece in approving terms as when he notes, for example, in "Difficulties" [1964/1966] that the piece emits "an extraordinary shock that stubbornly resists all neutralization.") On the other hand, Adorno also glorifies the very impulses that animate such traditions in art. He writes in *Aesthetic Theory* that "art must go beyond its own concept in order to remain faithful to that concept. The idea of its abolition does it homage by honoring its claim to truth." Moments of the negation of tradition within the varied practices and sites of art is a crucial element of the continuing persistence and existence of art. They are thus not to be rejected or expelled, but, by the same token, they cannot be glorified or taken as final. For "the neediness of the world" reveals the "objective need" for art. In "On Tradition" (1966) Adorno may be taken to be speaking to this oscillation between art and antiart as follows: "Whoever seeks to avoid betraying the bliss which tradition still promises in some of its images and the possibilities buried beneath its ruins must abandon that tradition which turns possibilities and meanings into lies. Only that which inexorably denies tradition may once again retrieve it."

7. NEGATIVITY AND SOCIETY

Questions about art and the everyday can also be raised in a slightly different register. With regard to society, the strength of the culture industry, and the sort of integration and homogenization of society that it pursues, has only gotten stronger and more extreme since the first generation of the Frankfurt School, especially with the rise of social media and big data. One byproduct of this is that it has in many ways never been easier to criticize anything. Made only more extreme and forceful by the internet, contemporary aesthetic practice also equally seems to allow everything. Everything is permitted, and thereby the critical potential of art seems already to be neutralized, having, in a way, its feet cut out from it. Marcuse termed such a state of affairs "repressive desublimation." Sublimation was a technical term that Freud introduced; its contours should be readily apparent from our discussion of Freud earlier in this book. Introduced in order to capture how human drives evince a "plasticity," that as he put it in the *New Introductory Lectures on Psychoanalysis* (1932), pointed above all to "their capacity for altering their aims," where "one instinctual satisfaction" could be "replaced by another." In his lectures on *Aesthetics*, Adorno unpacks sublimation with the idea that "something desired" may be transformed into "something that is merely imagined," and that exactly through this "altered form" such a transformation "brings happiness." Freud himself notes that sublimation is the source "of the noblest cultural achievements." When a particular desire is incapable of being satisfied—imagine here everything from the inability to be with someone you desire to the inability to live or work or exist in a way that is socially acceptable or to find modern life as somehow intrinsically meaningful—then such pain may be sublimated into works of art, which allow for a sort of coping with existence. As already noted, in his *Aesthetics* lectures and elsewhere, Adorno stresses that "a process of sublimation, of spiritualization" is in fact "the process of artistic development as such." Marcuse also tells the entire history of Western art as such a process in the "Affirmative Character of Culture" (1937).

Here the psychoanalytic dynamics around art are similar to what we saw earlier in the discussion around human subjectivity: just as resistance to society in the form of a conflict with a domineering superego provides an opportunity for the ego to develop, so in the realm of aesthetics, restrictions on what's permissible allows for the development of aesthetic form by means of sublimation. In *One-Dimensional Man* (1964), however, Marcuse diagnoses in modern society an increasing, "harmonizing pluralism, where the most contradictory works and truths peacefully coexist in indifference." The sort of alienation or friction between artist and society that allowed for the development of aesthetic form now appears to be shrinking or even closed. And so the gap necessary for serious art increasingly appears closed, since, in Marcuse's words, "works of alienation are themselves incorporated into this society and circulate as part and parcel of the equipment which adorns and psychoanalyzes the prevailing state of affairs." These works of alienation or estrangement are now "commercials—they sell, comfort, or excite." Even so-called protest music or music that shocks (think here of everything from Joan Baez to Rage Against the Machine to Nine Inch

Nails to Marilyn Manson to Cradle of Filth to whatever else) simply props up the status quo by selling more material (a point captured quite well by the "15 Million Merits" episode of Charlie Brooker's television show, *Black Mirror* [2011–2019]). Marcuse highlights that all of "this imagery is invalidated. Its incorporation into the kitchen, the office, the shop; its commercial release for business and fun is, in a sense, desublimation." Marcuse stresses that there are multiple dimensions to this situation. Society itself is in many ways more tolerant; there is thereby less to sublimate or to be alienated from (this, in and of itself, is not a problem). Such tolerance occurs largely by means of the appropriation of all forms of rebellion or aesthetic alienation, so that all forms of extremism in relation to society are increasingly permitted exactly because they are commodified so as to be managed and administered (and thereby defanged of any critical potential). Marcuse in fact notes that extreme art is encouraged, since "what happens is surely wild and obscene, virile and tasty, and quite immoral—and, precisely because of that, perfectly harmless." When the possibilities for sublimation shrink—while the needless suffering that exists in society does not or does not in the same proportion—then what's happening is exactly a desublimation that turns out to be repressive, since it exactly closes off possibilities for resistance. As Marcuse puts it in "Repressive Tolerance" (1965), such tolerance may in fact "minimize or even absolve prevailing intolerance or suppression." We are once again circling around the issue and possibility of maturity, but this time in the register of aesthetics, where the permissibility of all sorts of extreme production in no way necessarily leads to a critique of the whole. Quite the opposite, in fact—such permissibility only gives the illusion of true maturity because it in fact eludes or intentionally covers over the full scope of the horror, thereby eliding the sort of expression and art that the historical moment demands.

In *Aesthetic Theory*, Adorno speaks to this situation when he points out that:

> [E]verything depends on this: whether meaning inheres in the negation of meaning in the artwork or if the negation conforms to the status quo; whether the crisis of meaning is reflected in the works or whether it remains immediate and therefore alien to the subject.

Art that has a hope of accomplishing what Marcuse and Adorno think art has a potential to do in its opposition to society must do many things at once: (1) acknowledge the extent to which any sort of meaningful human activity (of which art is a subset) has become nearly impossible given that all human activities are increasingly subject to commodification and administration, (2) refuse thereby any retreat into cynicism, irony, the status quo, or other kinds of defeatism, and (3) point—even if briefly or fleetingly—beyond present society from current society. This third criterion unifies the others. As Adorno puts it in *Aesthetic Theory*: "insofar as a social function can be predicated for artworks, it is their functionlessness." A work of art serves no purpose beyond itself; it exists primarily neither for pleasure nor for politics, even as it may contribute to both. In *Aesthetic Theory*, Adorno memorably puts the idea as the thought that at any given moment, there is a "negative canon" for art, "a set of prohibitions" against what has been "disavowed in experience and technique." Adorno claims that such a negative canon is "virtually the canon of what is to be done." Such a canon is historically determined at any particular moment, "it is not just the yearning of a rebellious attitude." Every moment proposes to the artist "what needs to be done." In this way, as Marcuse puts it in *The Aesthetic Dimension*, art may thereby contain "more truth than does everyday reality," for everyday reality is "mystified in its institutions and relationships." This is why Adorno stresses in *Aesthetic Theory* that works of art, "provided they go deeply enough," ultimately "touch on historical constellations back of the facades of reality and psychology." In his autobiographical reflections, *An Unmastered Past* (1987), Leo Lowenthal sums things up with the idea that, "art is in fact the great reservoir of creative protest against social misery, which allows the prospect of social happiness dimly to shine through."

8. SENSIBILITY, SUBJECTIVITY, AND THE SHUDDER

Works of art thereby have an affective and critical dimension. In his *Aesthetic Theory* and *Aesthetics* lectures Adorno introduces the technical term "shudder" for what the subject may experience in the face of a work of art. Adorno's suggestion is not, as so much contemporary writing about art suggests, that art's power lies exclusively in its affective or emotional dimension (although, of course, he does not deny it has this power). What the shudder does is to force upon the subject an experience that entirely annihilates that subject, forces the subject to see itself as entirely contingent. In *Aesthetic Theory*, Adorno's image is that of a subject that's been liquidated, "which, shaken, perceives its own limitedness and finitude." In the *Aesthetics* lectures he frames the experience as "of being overwhelmed, of forgetting oneself, really the annihilation of the subject." What Adorno is attempting to capture is the experience, allegedly possible with serious or successful works of art, where a subject is removed from the immediacy of present society (recognizing its fundamental wrongness) and where that same subject is shaken to their core, so that the fundamental contingency of whatever fixed nature they took themselves to have is exactly put into question. As Adorno puts it in *Aesthetic Theory*, "the subject, convulsed by art, has real experiences; by the strength of insight into the artwork as artwork, these experiences are those in which the subject's petrification in his own subjectivity dissolves and the narrowness of his self-positedness is revealed." Adorno equally stresses that this is quite different from the weakening of the ego that "the culture industry manipulates." This is because the sort of aesthetic experience—shudder—that Adorno is describing is not entertainment or distraction, but rather requires great effort ("insight into the artwork as artwork"). Adorno thereby notes that, "to catch even the slightest glimpse beyond the prison that it itself is, the I requires not distraction but rather the utmost tension." Such a shudder, may, in short, be a sort of conversion experience, where both self and world are open to radically novel possibilities, kinds of experience, and affective comportments. This is why Adorno muses in *Aesthetic Theory* that "goose bumps" might be seen as a sort of stand-in for the "first aesthetic experience."

It is worth pausing now to reflect on the complex strands of thinking that come together here for Adorno. On one hand, there is the general story about form pursued throughout this chapter, that art offers the possibility of glimpsing more than present reality. In one of his final essays, "Is Art Lighthearted?" (1967), Adorno reflects on the question of the title and suggests that "what is lighthearted in art is, if you like, the opposite of what one might easily assume it to be: not its content but its demeanor, the abstract fact that it is art at all, that it opens out over the reality to whose violence it bears witness at the same time." He concludes his thoughts by noting that "art is a critique of the brute seriousness that reality imposes upon human beings." On the other hand, there is implicit to Adorno's notion of the shudder also a whole story about the potential unfolding of human subjectivity and what such a shudder reveals about the historical features of that subjectivity. In *Dialectic of Enlightenment*, Horkheimer and Adorno suggest that mimesis—imitation—was a way in which early humans related to reality. In his *Aesthetics* lectures, Adorno summarizes the story of *Dialectic of Enlightenment* in a usefully compact way as follows:

> There was a time in the history of mankind [sic] when mimetic behaviour—that is to say, direct imitation in general—was one of the primary behaviours. We know how decisive a part mimesis or mimicry plays in the survival of primitive creatures; without a doubt, it played an equally central part in the lives of primitive humans, ultimately leading to the practice of magic, whose underlying idea is essentially that one can gain control of nature by imitating some natural phenomenon or other.

Adorno continues, now summarizing the story that he and Horkheimer pursued in *Dialectic of Enlightenment*, about how such mimetic behavior eventually gives rise to the sort of conceptual activity that culminates in the human rational manipulation of nature (there is here again the idea discussed in Chapter 2 of concepts as rules or tools). For Horkheimer and Adorno, both this early mimetic orientation towards nature and the later human possibility of the conceptual organization of nature, share a common impulse that aims to subject nature to self-conscious human control. As they put it in *Dialectic of Enlightenment*, one approach (conceptual cognition) resigns "itself to being calculation and, to know nature, must renounce the claim to resemble it," while the other approach (mimesis) resigns "itself to being a likeness and, to be entirely nature, must renounce the claim to know it." Each is equally an instantiation of human subjectivity in relation to nature, a relation between subject and object, albeit in the different registers of "images" (a mimetic relation to reality) and "signs" (a conceptual relation to reality).

Adorno notes in the *Aesthetics* lectures that art clings "to the mimetic process, to this archaic, older phenomenon rather than the rational one." He continues, pointing out that, in this way, "all art is childlike, infantile, because it truly still has the notion that it can take full control of reality through the image, not by intervening in reality with thought and action." Art thereby always somehow tries "to do justice to that element of suppressed nature." The shudder instantiates the possibility of a sincere and serious otherness in the face of human subjectivity. This is unlike the normal course of things, where human subjectivity manipulates and conceptually organizes anything that comes before it (in the words used in *Dialectic of Enlightenment,* "the distance of subject from object, the presupposition of abstraction, is founded on the distance from things which the ruler attains by means of the ruled"). Equally, they compare such a rational conceptual relation "to things" as one of the "dictator to human beings," objects known to the extent that they can be manipulated. Even as the mimesis of rites of magic aims also at manipulation, it is oriented entirely differently, acknowledging from the very beginning the radical otherness of the object of imitation. Not so for the object of rational calculable manipulation, which through the processes of abstraction ultimately leads to a "liquidation" of its otherness, its alterity. Art points to the possibility of an alternative relationship between subject and object, where the genuine otherness of what is not the subject can appear. In "Notes on Philosophical Thinking" (1964/1965), Adorno speaks of a thought that will "snuggle up to an object," implying a sensibility and subjectivity that makes room for the particularity and otherness of its object, giving itself over to the genuine novelty and unpredictability of such an experience.

The aforementioned shudder thereby reveals as much about a genuinely novel object as it does about the possibility of a genuinely novel subject (one that does not dominate or abstract or determine its object, conceptually, economically, or otherwise). As Adorno puts it in *Aesthetic Theory,* "that shudder in which subjectivity stirs without yet being subjectivity is the act of being touched by the other. Aesthetic comportment assimilates itself to that other rather than subordinating it." Implied here is an ethically tinged aesthetics, where, as Adorno puts it in his *Aesthetics* lectures, "what calls out from works of art is in fact always the voice of the victim, and that there is no art which cannot truly do this. So, because of its very principle, it is primarily on the side of whatever is suppressed."

Maturity, or autonomy, of the sort stressed by Adorno and the Frankfurt School, is at least in part made possible by aesthetics. As Adorno points out in *Aesthetic Theory*, "consciousness without shudder is reified consciousness."

9. THE AUTONOMY OF ART

Autonomous works of art thereby offer a glimpse beyond the status quo. They may work upon our very sensibility as much as on our imaginative capacities, thereby potentially opening possibilities for a range of critical and political projects. If not that, then it may be the case that art at least offers an antidote to the way in which the status quo would warp our imaginative capacities. These are all aftereffects, though, and cannot be the purpose of autonomous art, which can, if it is to be successful, have only itself as its purpose. Nonetheless, as Marcuse puts it, art may allow people to "unlearn the language, concepts, and images of this administration." It may thereby lead to "qualitative change," where possibilities for subjectivity are created. As the American critic Robert Warshow (1917–1955) put it in *The Immediate Experience* (2001), we are all "self-made" in what aesthetic objects we interact with; it matters whether it is the culture industry or art that we encounter, and how. This also means, however, that art cannot itself be directly political. As Marcuse puts it in "Society as a Work of Art" (1967): "art itself can never become political without destroying itself, without violating its own essence, without abdicating itself." So, while art is not thereby itself political, it may open up political possibilities, it may change even our very needs, shifting them towards, in Marcuse's words, "a sensibility, imagination and reason emancipated from the rule of exploitation." Or, as Marcuse puts it, "art cannot change the world, but it can contribute to changing the consciousness and drives of the men and women who could change the world."

There is a puzzle here, though. Marcuse notes in "Art in the One-Dimensional Society" (1967), to the extent that art depends on the sublimation of impulses that cannot be satisfied, then any sort of utopian possibility would ultimately mean "the construction of a new reality, a prospect which would mean the cancellation *and* the transcendence of art in the fulfilment of its own end." Marcuse pursues aspects of exactly such a picture in *Eros and Civilization* and

One-Dimensional Man. In the latter he posits the existence of technological advancement that would allow humans to satisfy all of
their basic needs. As he puts it, "complete automation in the realm
of necessity would open the dimension of … historical transcendence toward a new civilization." It would "revolutionize the
whole society." In *Eros and Civilization*, he notes that in such a situation, there would be a wholesale transformation of human sexuality and subjectivity:

> No longer used as a full-time instrument of labor, the body would be
> resexualized. The regression involved in this spread of the libido would
> first manifest itself in a reactivation of all erotogenic zones and, conse-
> quently, in a resurgence of pregenital polyamorphous sexuality and in a
> decline of genital supremacy. The body in its entirety would become an
> object of cathexis, a thing to be enjoyed—an instrument of pleasure. This
> change in the value and scope of libidinal relations would lead to a disin-
> tegration of the institutions in which the private interpersonal relations
> have been organized, particularly the monogamic and patriarchal family.

This is a striking image, but it is hard to know what to make of it.
Apart from worries about whether Marcuse has correctly assessed
the technological moment and its possibilities (the idea of "basic
needs," as Horkheimer and Adorno had stressed in their "Theses on
Need," is itself perhaps a dubious notion, or at least one historically
indexed), there is also the question, already raised in the last chapter, of whether the sort of infantile narcissism that Marcuse glorifies
even makes sense as a picture of human *subjectivity* (as opposed to
human existence or organic existence). Marcuse's picture of subjectivity here appears as a sort of inversion of Nietzsche's picture of
"last humans" in *Thus Spoke Zarathustra* (1883). Intended as a criticism of the kind of subjectivity that modernity produces, Nietzsche
imagines a group of "last humans" who carry on an atomistic existence of sameness and utility, occasionally rubbing elbows with
each just for warmth. Marcuse's proposed new humans exist as a
sort of blob, already always perpetually together for warmth, but in
other ways comparable to Nietzsche's last humans. As Marcuse suggests, work should now become play, while analogously Nietzsche's
last humans conceive of work as entertainment. In neither case
should there be too much exertion (in this context, recall Adorno's

discussion of the possibility of difficult work during free time in the previous chapter).

None of the above is exactly an argument against Marcuse's suggestion (what might that even mean—are Marcuse's new humans responsive to arguments?), for it may be that such a form of life eventually emerges. But it is impossible to speak in any meaningful fashion about it from our perspective, since it, as Marcuse notes in "Art in the One-Dimensional Society," exactly requires the "construction of a *qualitatively new environment*, technical and natural, by an *essentially new type of human being*" (emphases added). Perhaps the limitations of my perspective will fade away as developments in aesthetics and/or philosophy and/or critical theory alter human consciousness, leading also somehow to changes in political structure. Or it may be that neither these changes nor the changes in political structure nor the eventual emergence of a world without needless suffering are possible without more traditional conceptions of human subjectivity. (Another way to put this point is simply to ask whether a world without the sort of needless suffering highlighted in this book *requires* a regression to infantile narcissism). In either case, it seems that art requires, as Adorno puts in *Aesthetic Theory*, that "every specific form idea must be driven to its extreme," for as he notes in an interview with *Der Spiegel* in 1969, the idea "if you only change little things here and there, then perhaps everything will be better" simply cannot be accepted. And elsewhere Marcuse seems to frame things in such a way that traditional subjectivity could stand, as when he stresses in an unpublished text, "Cultural Revolution" (1970), that:

only if the vast capabilities of science and technology, of the scientific and artistic imagination direct the construction of a sensuous environment, only if the work world loses its alienating features and becomes a world of human relationships, only if productivity becomes creativity, are the roots of domination dried up in the individuals.

In conclusion, note that the question of maturity and autonomy amidst a consideration of art makes recourse to notions of transforming or transfiguring the human being and/or human sensibility (this can be seen in Marcuse and Adorno's thoughts in the last paragraph as much as in the promise of Kant's very notion of reflective judgment and its stress on a common humanity). Given the throughline of maturity or autonomy pursued throughout this book, this is not surprising—it is just one more feature of what any such maturity or autonomy might ultimately come to be. Understanding the possibilities and parameters of what a transformation of the human being might be, thereby, especially in the face of a society that deforms through direct and indirect sites of needless suffering, remains crucial. Such an understanding, both of what it means to be human and of what it might mean to have a transfiguration or conversion in our understanding of the same, however, suggests at the very least a formal if not a more substantive analogy with or reference to religion and its history.

SUGGESTED READING

THE FRANKFURT SCHOOL AND ART (INCLUDING PARTICULAR FIGURES)

Berman, Russell A. *Modern Culture and Critical Theory: Art, Politics, and the Legacy of the Frankfurt School.* Madison: University of Wisconsin Press, 1989.

Bernstein, J.M. *The Fate of Art: Aesthetic Alienation from Kant to Derrida and Adorno.* University Park: Penn State Press, 1992.

Berry, David. *Revisiting the Frankfurt School: Essays on Culture, Media and Theory.* Farnham: Ashgate, 2013.

Huhn, Tom, and Lambert Zuidervaart. *The Semblance of Subjectivity: Essays in Adorno's Aesthetic Theory.* Cambridge: MIT Press, 1997.

Kellner, Douglas. "Herbert Marcuse and the Art of Liberation." *Telos* 1983, no. 56 (1983): 223–29.

Leonard, Craig. *Uncommon Sense: Aesthetics after Marcuse.* Cambridge: MIT Press, 2022.

Menke, Christoph. *The Sovereignty of Art: Aesthetic Negativity in Adorno and Derrida.* Cambridge: MIT Press, 1998.

Miller, Tyrus. *Modernism and the Frankfurt School.* Edinburgh: Edinburgh University Press, 2014.

Reitz, Charles. *Art, Alienation, and the Humanities: A Critical Engagement with Herbert Marcuse.* Buffalo: State University of New York Press, 2000.

Roberts, David. *Art and Enlightenment: Aesthetic Theory after Adorno.* Lincoln: University of Nebraska Press, 2006.

Ross, Nathan. *The Aesthetic Ground of Critical Theory: New Readings of Benjamin and Adorno.* Lanham: Rowman & Littlefield, 2015.

Zuidervaart, Lambert. *Adorno's Aesthetic Theory: The Redemption of Illusion.* Cambridge: MIT Press, 1993.

KANT, GERMAN IDEALISM, AESTHETICS, AND AUTONOMY

Bowie, Andrew. *Aesthetic Dimensions of Modern Philosophy*. Oxford: Oxford University Press, 2022.

———. *Aesthetics and Subjectivity*. Manchester: Manchester University Press, 2003.

———. *From Romanticism to Critical Theory: The Philosophy of German Literary Theory*. London: Routledge, 2012.

Gandesha, Samir, and Johan F. Hartle. *Aesthetic Marx*. London: Bloomsbury, 2017.

Haskins, Casey. "Kant and the Autonomy of Art." *The Journal of Aesthetics and Art Criticism* 47, no. 1 (1989): 43–54.

Hulatt, Owen. *Aesthetic and Artistic Autonomy*. London: Bloomsbury, 2013.

Zammito, John H. *The Genesis of Kant's Critique of Judgment*. Chicago: University of Chicago Press, 1992.

Zuckert, Rachel. *Kant on Beauty and Biology: An Interpretation of The Critique of Judgment*. Cambridge: Cambridge University Press, 2007.

ADORNO ON ART, SUFFERING, AND THE SHUDDER

Finlayson, Gordon. "Adorno: Modern Art, Metaphysics and Radical Evil." *Modernism/modernity* 10, no. 1 (2003): 71–95.

Gordon, Peter. "Social Suffering and the Autonomy of Art." *New German Critique* 48, no. 2 (2021): 125–46.

Hammer, Espen. *Adorno's Modernism: Art, Experience, and Catastrophe*. Cambridge: Cambridge University Press, 2015.

Kaushall, Justin Neville. "Natural Spontaneity, or Adorno's Aesthetic Category of the Shudder." *Telos* 2020, no. 192 (2020): 125–44.

Kiloh, Kathy. "Towards an Ethical Politics: T.W. Adorno and Aesthetic Self-Relinquishment." *Philosophy & Social Criticism* 43, no. 6 (2017): 571–98.

Ross, Nathan. *The Aesthetic Ground of Critical Theory: New Readings of Benjamin and Adorno*. Lanham: Rowman & Littlefield, 2015.

Singh, Surti. "The Aesthetic Experience of Shudder: Adorno and the Kantian Sublime." In *The Aesthetic Ground of Critical Theory: New Readings in Benjamin and Adorno*, edited by Nathan Ross, 129–45. Lanham: Rowman & Littlefield, 2015.

ADORNO ON PARTICULAR ARTS AND ARTISTS

Leeder, Natalie. *Freedom and Negativity in Beckett and Adorno: Something or Nothing*. Lanham: Rowman & Littlefield, 2017.

Okiji, Fumi. *Jazz as Critique: Adorno and Black Expression Revisited*. Palo Alto: Stanford University Press, 2018.

Paddison, Max. *Adorno's Aesthetics of Music*. Cambridge: Cambridge University Press, 1997.

Schmidt, James. "Mephistopheles in Hollywood: Adorno, Mann, and Schoenberg." In *Cambridge Companion to Adorno*, edited by Tom Huhn, 148–81. Cambridge: Cambridge University Press, 2004.

Zuidervaart, Lambert. "The Social Significance of Autonomous Art: Adorno and Bürger." *Journal of Aesthetics and Art Criticism* (1990): 61–77.

REPRESSIVE DESUBLIMATION

Bailes, Jon. "'Enjoy Responsibly': The Continuing Relevance of Repressive Desublimation." *Radical Philosophy Review* 19, no. 1 (2016): 239–62.

Bowring, Finn. "Repressive Desublimation and Consumer Culture: Re-Evaluating Herbert Marcuse." *new formations* 75, no. 75 (2012): 8–24.

ADORNO AND AUTONOMY, AND MIMESIS

Bernstein, J.M. "Mimetic Rationality and Material Inference: Adorno and Brandom." *Revue internationale de philosophie*, no. 1 (2004): 7–23.

Hohendahl, Peter Uwe. "Autonomy of Art: Looking Back at Adorno's Ästhetische Theorie." *German Quarterly* (1981): 133–48.

———. *The Fleeting Promise of Art: Adorno's Aesthetic Theory Revisited*. Ithaca: Cornell University Press, 2013.

Hulatt, Owen. "Reason, Mimesis, and Self-Preservation in Adorno." *Journal of the History of Philosophy* 54, no. 1 (2016): 135–51.

Skees, Murray W. "Kant, Adorno and the Work of Art." *Philosophy & Social Criticism* 37, no. 8 (2011): 915–33.

RELIGION

1. ART, RELIGION, SOCIETY, AND NEGATIVE THEOLOGY

In "The Role of Religion in a Changing Society" (1969), Marcuse rehearses the traditional Marxist understanding of religion, stressing, with Marx, how religion allegedly arises because of needless suffering, as a kind of "compensation for the prevailing injustice and inequality" of society, and yet also thereby meets a genuine human need "as long as mental and physical oppression prevail and no effective forces striving for change of these conditions are operating." Marx's sentiment, quoted quite frequently from his never completed *Towards a Critique of Hegel's Philosophy of Right* (1843), is that religion is "the opium of the people." What's less quoted, however, is what precedes that claim, that religion "is the sigh of the oppressed creature, the sentiment of a heartless world, and the soul of soulless conditions." Marx demands the abolition of religion as the displacement of the allegedly "*illusory* happiness" offered by religion with the "*real* happiness" afforded by changed social conditions. As Marx puts it, "the criticism of religion is, therefore, *the embryonic criticism of this vale of tears* of which religion is the *halo*." Marcuse summarizes the idea as the thought that religion is a "mixture" of two elements, a "protesting one" and an "accepting one," a "radical one" and a "tranquilizing one." Like autonomous art, religion thereby potentially expresses a genuine response to the needless suffering that is omnipresent in modern society. This is why Marcuse can claim that religion can be an "indictment, [a] refusal of the established conditions and of the established powers as

DOI: 10.4324/9781003200963-6

a final authority on what is moral, and what is right behavior." He stresses how "religion may indeed help to transform society." Religion, at least formally, then may also have something to offer towards the achievement of maturity. Think here of the ways in which the Hebrew Bible prophetic traditions call for justice, or the visions of utopia they propose, where the wolf will dwell with the lamb or where swords will be turned to ploughshares (both images found in the book of *Isaiah*).

Adorno also draws links and analogies between art and religion in many places in *Aesthetic Theory* and in his lectures on *Aesthetics*:

> Whatever it wills or states, art remains theology; its claim to truth and its affinity to untruth are one and the same.
>
> In their relation to empirical reality, artworks recall the theological statement that in the redeemed world everything would be as it is and yet wholly other.
>
> Art's blemish is that it is bound up with superstition. Art all too happily, and irrationally, revalues this blemish as a merit.
>
> Works of art have certainly preserved enough of their sacred origins that, as Benjamin once put it very aptly, they are not directly intended for an audience. No painting is there for the viewer, no symphony for the listener, nor even any drama for the audience, as they are first of all for their own sake; and only through this aspect, which must be described as a secularized theological one, so only with reference to the absolute, and not in some immediate relationship with humans, do [the works] exist, do they speak at all.

One way to understand these claims is as circling around the idea that there is some possible orientation towards reality that art takes up from religion (a view not implausible given the connection between religion and art for much of its history, as already noted in the previous chapter). On such a view, religion, rather than being delineated by any particular doctrinal belief or faith instead evinces a general relationship with what's absolute, what's beyond currently existing reality. This would be to see religion as at bottom concerned with ultimately reality, with what's not conditioned by or what somehow escapes human categories. Such a view of religion stresses those streams within religious traditions that prioritize the inscrutability of ultimate reality, the fundamentally finite nature of human consciousness, and the utter irreducibility of ultimate reality or the divine to any human estimation. On such a view, what humans can know about ultimate reality is exactly that they cannot know ultimate reality: their relationship to that reality is negative—they can only understand what it is not. Human cognition simply cannot grasp ultimate reality. Such a theological stance is termed in the history of religion as apophatic or negative theology, exactly to acknowledge such a negative orientation. The philosopher Moses Maimonides (1138–1204) was a proponent of such a view, claiming even that the application of the human category of existence to ultimate reality or divinity may in fact be to say too much. For Maimonides, it is, however, equally impossible to say that ultimate reality or divinity does *not* exist (*every* human category is inapplicable). In his book, *The Guide for the Perplexed* (1190), he says that really the only proper linguistic act in the face of ultimate reality is silence.

With Marx, and unlike proponents of even such radical theologies, the first-generation of the Frankfurt School remains suspicious of organized religion, especially to the extent that the latter tends to minimize such negative theological approaches, opting instead for positive expressions of ultimate reality, oftentimes in quite paternalistic or naïve ways. Equally, especially considering the long history of European, Christian antisemitism, the oppressive nature of organized religion is also something that does not escape their view (nor should it escape ours, as fundamentalist and oftentimes violent versions of Christianity, Islam, Judaism, Buddhism, Hinduism, and other such traditions around the world make explicit). As noted earlier with the invocation of theodicy, organized religion generally tends to attribute meaning even to the most horrendous human acts. Adorno frames this thought in his lectures on *Metaphysics* (1965) as the claim that "in the face of the experiences we have had, not only through Auschwitz but through the introduction of torture as a permanent institution and through the atomic bomb—all these things form a kind of coherent, hellish unity." In the face of such experience, claiming that the world ultimately has a meaning becomes "a mockery" and "downright immoral" (of course, denying any meaning—opting for nihilism—is equally regressive and to be rejected, for that also acquiesces to the status quo).

The analogy that the Frankfurt School wants to draw between art and religion thereby depends on prioritizing negative theological motifs in religion (and notably such motifs are found in nearly all religious traditions). This analogy operates by means of the fact that art, like religion, formally repurposes or revives a relationship to consummate otherness. This is why in certain places, like his lectures on *Metaphysics*, Adorno will classify experiences that point beyond the present state of affairs as a "reprise, a resumption of theology." Like negative theology, art points beyond the present world. Prioritizing the stress on form discussed in the last chapter, art does this, again like negative theology, in a way that cannot be captured by present conceptual categories. In his final years of life, Horkheimer makes this even more explicit as when he claims in a letter after Adorno's death (1969) that in fact the entirety of the critical theory that the Frankfurt School developed "has its roots in Judaism," ultimately derived "from the [negative theological] idea that thou shalt make no image of God." Whether this is a plausible assessment of the entirety of critical theory is a point which will have to be discussed in more detail.

2. SUFFERING AND RELIGION

For the moment, though, note that it at least has some plausibility if what's prioritized about such negative theological approaches is exactly how they highlight the insufficiency of the present situation, as if a crucial feature of maturity or human autonomy is understanding the extent to which the present state of affairs falls short of what's possible. This is why Horkheimer, in "Theism and Atheism" (1964), stresses that either theism or atheism can evince "the longing for something other than this world." The pivot for either orientation, the pull of this longing, is in both cases needless suffering. This is why critiques of religion, such as those found, for example, in philosophers like Arthur Schopenhauer (1788–1860) or Friedrich Nietzsche (1844–1900), stress the impossibility of theodicy, and the bankruptcy of the suffering of this world. Thus, Schopenhauer writes in *The World as Will and Representation* (1818) and Nietzsche in *Beyond Good and Evil* (1886):

> The shortness of life, so often lamented, may perhaps be the very best thing about it. If, finally, we were to bring to the sight of everyone the terrible sufferings and afflictions to which his life is constantly exposed, he

would be seized with horror. If we were to conduct the most hardened and callous optimist through hospitals, infirmaries, operating theatres, through prisons, torture-chambers, and slave-hovels, over battlefields and to places of execution; if we were to open to him all the dark abodes of misery, where it shuns the gaze of cold curiosity ... he too would finally see what kind of a world is this *meilleur des mondes possible (best of all possible worlds)*. ... In vain does the tortured person then call on his gods for help; he remains abandoned to his fate without mercy (Schopenhauer).

Why atheism today? God "the Father" has been thoroughly refuted, and so has "the Judge" and "the Reward-giver." ... He doesn't listen, —and even if he did, he wouldn't know how to help anyway (Nietzsche).

Equally, though, religion can itself be the motivation for the criticism of needless suffering. Think here just as easily of critiques of evil as, for example, in the prophetic book of Isaiah ("Woe to the wicked! What their hands have done will be done to them") as of more specific critiques of capitalism found in, for example, Martin Luther King Jr.'s "Where Do We Go from Here?" (1967):

I'm concerned about a better world. ... There are forty million poor people here, and one day we must ask the question, "Why are there forty million poor people in America?" And when you begin to ask that question, you are raising a question about the economic system, about a broader distribution of wealth. When you ask that question, you begin to question the capitalistic economy. And I'm simply saying that more and more, we've got to begin to ask questions about the whole society. We are called upon to help the discouraged beggars in life's marketplace. But one day we must come to see that an edifice which produces beggars needs restructuring. It means that questions must be raised.

The theologian Abraham Joshua Heschel (1907–1972)—someone who marched with King—thereby claims in *The Prophets* (1962) that the prophet may in fact have no language in common with the rest of society, for to "society, for all its stains and spots," things seem "fair and trim," while to the prophet they are "dreadful." Taking seriously the analogy to ordinary language philosophy proposed in Chapter 1 would be to stress here an orientation akin to the practice of critical theory: the right words (critique of present society) must be found and cannot simply emerge from current vocabulary (and, in this vein, as the last chapter demonstrates, art may help such a process along).

Religious critiques of this sort and the criticisms of critical theory thereby share a common impulse. This is why in "Critique" (1965), Adorno can invoke the religious philosopher Baruch Spinoza (1632–1677) who claimed that, "truth is the index of itself and of the false." Adorno reverses this claim, suggesting that the "the false is the index of itself and the true," taking this to mean "that the true thing determines itself via the false thing, or via that which makes itself falsely known." Needless suffering becomes "already an index of what is right and better." What makes this a shared impulse as opposed to a shared project is exactly that the Frankfurt School, following Marx, generally rejects the positive claims of religion towards knowledge, including knowing that God exists, or that ultimate reality is this way or that—again, negative theology.

3. SCHOLEM, BENJAMIN, AND THE FRANKFURT SCHOOL

While almost all the early members of the Frankfurt School were Jewish, and while some, like Lowenthal and Fromm, were raised in a traditional Jewish household, such (Jewish) theological motifs and invocations chiefly make their way into the Frankfurt School through sometime associate of the school, Walter Benjamin. Benjamin was a close friend of both Adorno and of the scholar of Jewish mysticism, Gershom Scholem (1897–1982). From 1915 until his death in 1940, Benjamin and Scholem maintained a close friendship and correspondence. In *Walter Benjamin: The Story of a Friendship* (1981), Scholem recounts this friendship, oftentimes referring to Benjamin's "genius." Adorno met Benjamin in 1923 (the year that Scholem migrated to Palestine) and also maintained a friendship and correspondence with him. Via Benjamin then, there was a cross-pollination between critical theory and Jewish mysticism. While their approaches, methods, and contexts were quite different, Scholem and the Frankfurt School evince certain interesting points of overlap (and, in turn, Adorno and Scholem maintain a lengthy correspondence, each being profoundly affected by Benjamin's death).

To register some sense of why Scholem's approach to Jewish thought could find resonances in critical theory through Benjamin, it is worth noting Scholem's own claim in "Walter Benjamin and His Angel" (1972) that "many oversimplifying minds" evince a deep misunderstanding of "the mystical tradition and of mystical experience." Scholem notes that ordinary understandings of these matters oftentimes imagine God in mechanical terms, as almost a sort of slot machine (my term). Opposed to such a view, Scholem instead finds in the Jewish mystical tradition a God who is qualitatively distinct, so that mystical experience itself is, as he puts it in *The Messianic Idea in Judaism* (1971), "many-layered," equally bound up with "elements of dread." Scholem traces this mystical tradition to the centuries preceding the common era, operative first in texts like the Biblical book of *Ezekiel* and the apocryphal *1 Enoch*. Like critical theory, for Scholem, mysticism is intimately concerned with concrete history. History becomes a potential site for constant revelation. Scholem writes in *Major Trends in Jewish Mysticism* that "instead of one act of Revelation, there is a constant repetition of this act." Just as with critical theory, the most minute details of human life can become a site for critical understanding. Kabbalah (literally "tradition" in Hebrew) is a further extension of this mystical tradition. In *Origins of the Kabbalah* (1962), Scholem traces the origins of Kabbalah to the 12th century, noting that with the expulsion from Spain in 1492 (and the milieu of needless suffering that follows from it), Kabbalah becomes the dominant Jewish theological position until modernity.

A striking example of how themes in critical theory and Jewish thought find common purchase (and an additional confirmation of the potential connections between art and religion) can be found in a shared interest in the work of writer Franz Kafka (1883–1924) by Scholem, Benjamin, and Adorno. For each of them, Kafka's stories speak in powerful ways to the present moment (a point no less true now). In Kafka's stories, one encounters rich descriptions of fantastical situations that nonetheless address the everyday in modernity—to name a few: a traveling salesman awakens after having been transformed into dung-beetle ("The Metamorphosis"), a man is persecuted by an inaccessible authority for a crime that is never revealed ("The Trial"), an artist whose craft is starvation ("A Hunger Artist"), or a story about a torture device that executes the guilty by carving the law they broke onto their body ("In the Penal Colony"). Anyone even cursorily familiar with Kafka's writings will recognize in them a keen sense for the kinds of suffering the modern world engenders: alienation, unreason, pain, crisis, meaninglessness, and of, course, the theme of this book—needless suffering.

For Scholem, Kafka is closely associated with Jewish mysticism. As recounted in *Walter Benjamin: The Story of a Friendship*, Scholem recounts how Kafka was "decisive" for his "entire life," through whom he finally stumbled upon a tradition that walks "the fine line between religion and nihilism." For Scholem, religion could never be separated from unfulfilled longing and antinomianism. In Kafka he finds "the most perfect unsurpassed expression of this fine line" and "a secular statement of the Kabbalistic world-feeling in a modern spirit." The writings must be understood as wrapped "in the halo of the canonical" and if one desires to "understand the Kabbalah nowadays, one has to read Franz Kafka's writings." Scholem's understanding of Kabbalah and Jewish mysticism maps quite easily onto Kafka's thought. For Scholem, central features of this Jewish tradition is (1) a rejection of any essentialist understanding of Judaism, (2) an understanding of Judaism as evolving over the course of history, with developments in Judaism being a byproduct of the interaction between concrete historical experience and theology (itself a mediated and pluralistic phenomenon), (3) the fundamental inaccessibility of ultimate reality, it being instead perpetually subject to (4) the infinity of human interpretation, all tempered by (5) the possibility of messianic redemption.

4. SCHOLEM ON JEWISH THEOLOGY

Before turning in more detail to the connections between the Frankfurt School and Scholem's elaborations of Jewish thought, it is worth pausing to make explicit the nature of the connection being drawn. Nothing in what follows should be taken to suggest— even despite Horkheimer's remark quoted above—that the Frankfurt School is somehow just an extension of Jewish thought (a thought sometimes suggested by a comical bowdlerization of the School as the Jewish inventors of "Cultural Marxism," whatever that term may mean). What's being drawn here are some formal analogies and contextual connections. To really make this clear, note that Scholem himself continually stressed that Jewish thought had no essence; rather it was a reservoir of oftentimes contradictory currents. Concrete historical situations could bring to the fore—activate—dormant theological positions. This stress on theology is obviously an important difference from critical theory—the form of the two projects, of activating dormant conceptual resources, however, is analogous. Equally, a strong thematic connection between the two is a focus on needless suffering. Scholem, for example, locates the expulsion of the Jews from Spain in 1492 as a central event, one that continues to resonate for centuries after, including in Europe's long history of antisemitism and the Nazi genocide. This expulsion leads to a particular Kabbalistic theology. In *On the Kabbalah and its Symbolism* (1965), Scholem notes that this theology, as developed by mystic Isaac Luria (1534–1572), revolves around three great symbols: the "self-limitation of God," the "breaking of the vessels," and the eventual "harmonious correction and mending of the flaw which came into the world."

Underwriting these claims is a conceptualization of the divine essence as infinite. This essence contracts to allow possibility to emerge. Such pure possibility requires form for its actuality (in Kabbalistic lingo it must be contained in vessels). Due to the infinite nature of the divine, though, such vessels cannot contain this possibility. They shatter, and this sundering creates a world of chaos. Generally devoid of the divine, there nonetheless exist divine fragments that occasionally allow divine light to shine through. Scholem writes in "The Messianic Idea in Kabbalism" (1958) that "there is nothing that was not damaged by the breaking." History unfolds in a fundamentally damaged state, where the moral imperative is repair. Equally, everything is potentially of interest to the extent that nothing is not affected. Participation in Jewish religious and moral life, with its own stress on all facets of life, becomes a means of pursuing such repair. In "Toward an Understanding of the Messianic Idea in Judaism" (1959), Scholem points out that "by amending themselves, the Jewish people can also amend the world, in its visible and invisible aspects alike." At a high-altitude view, there are connections here to what's termed by scholars as Gnosticism, a worldview that rose to prominence at the dawn of the common era, a point Scholem pursued in *Jewish Gnosticism, Merkabah Mysticism, and Talmudic Tradition* (1960). I mention this to note other sites of connection between the Frankfurt School and Jewish thought, acknowledged, for example, by the Jewish antinomian Jacob Taubes (1923–1987), who had encountered Scholem and the Frankfurt School (and many others besides—Taubes's recent biography by Jerry Muller, *Professor of Apocalypse*, is striking in revealing how Taubes seemed to have met everyone).

Scholem stresses how this basic picture connects to other themes in Jewish thought, especially to the idea of a messiah and messianic redemption. True to Scholem's earlier point, though, there were conflicting accounts of the messianic moment in Jewish thought. On one hand, there is the idea of a messiah who restores some prior, lost state. On the other hand, there is also the idea of a messiah that ushers a novel, utopian state. The former idea is conservative, while the latter idea is radical. Scholem notes regarding this contradiction in "Toward an Understanding of the Messianic Idea in Judaism" that as long as historical circumstances were such that the messianic idea remained "abstract, not yet concretized in people's experience or demanding of concrete decisions, it was possible for it to embody even what was contradictory." Eventually, though, historical circumstances shift in such a way that "the energies that lay dormant in these two elements" emerged "into conflict with each other." Such moments revealed themselves in early Christianity (which ought to be seen as a Jewish development) and in the modern sectarianism of Sabbatai Zevi (1626–1726). Scholem points out that "in Sabbatianism as well as in early Christianity the sudden appearance of the redemption, which is experienced as real and full of meaning, creates the element that releases the crisis of tradition." This release is, in Scholem's words, a sort of "anarchic breeze" that forces theology to adapt, culminating, he argues, in a notion of redemption through sin.

This notion suggests that the messiah pursue sin, doing what is contrary to religious life, exactly, as Scholem argues in "Redemption through Sin" (1937), in order "to accomplish what not even the most righteous souls in the past have been able to do: to descend through the gates of impurity" and "rescue the divine sparks still imprisoned there." In such a case, "the Kingdom of Evil collapses of itself, for its existence is made possible only by the divine sparks in its midst." There is here, then, a sort of reversibility of even the most basic or sacred religious concepts. While the contexts are quite different, such reversibility equally animates the dialectical structure that Horkheimer, Adorno, and Benjamin each diagnose within history: whether it is the way in which Horkheimer shows how the rise of bourgeois individuality first serves a progressive function but then in different historical circumstances leads to regressive outcomes (Chapter 2), the way in which enlightening practices of abstraction eventually give way to authoritarian and genocidal modes of relating to the world (Chapter 3), or the way in which Benjamin shows how progressive notions of historical progress in fact carry barbarism and brutality (Introduction).

5. KAFKA AS LOCUS

Kafka's writings allegedly evince a similar orientation: history has reached a moment where religious concepts appear to linger on even as various actualizations of them have failed, where vaunted concepts produce anticipated or opposite effects, and where needless suffering lurks at every step. Writing to Benjamin, Scholem describes Kafka's world as a place where "for once, a world is expressed in which redemption cannot be anticipated." Because even the most vaunted concepts may lead to catastrophe, there is no way to suggest redemption is forthcoming. Or, as Adorno put it in *Negative Dialectics*, "there is no word tinged from on high, not even a theological one, that has any right." In the same aforementioned letter, though, Scholem continues that nonetheless, "the light of revelation never burned as unmercifully" as it does in Kafka. Scholem sees this as the "theological secret of perfect prose." Compare this to Adorno's claim in *Minima Moralia* that a thought of redemption must continue to animate thinking ("woe says go"), and so the critical theorist must "contemplate all things as they would present themselves from the standpoint of redemption." Scholem writes another letter to Benjamin, putting a related thought in poetic form, claiming that Kafka shows how "no life can unfold / that doesn't sink into itself" yet "from the center of destruction / a ray breaks through at times / but none shows the direction / the law ordered us to take."

In a letter to Scholem in 1938, Benjamin develops a related reading of Kafka that takes a broader view of the issues. He argues that Kafka's works evince a tension between modernity and the mystical tradition. Benjamin frames the idea as the thought that "Kafka's work represents tradition falling ill." There exists no longer any "doctrine that one could learn and no knowledge that one could preserve." Tradition nonetheless continues, so even though "we can no longer speak of wisdom," we must realize that "the products of its decay remain." Benjamin cites Kafka's dictum (as does Adorno) that "there is an infinite amount of hope, but not for us." To register the force or character of this point, think of the possibility of planetary destruction (suggested to these thinkers by the world wars that wreaked havoc in their world, but available to us just as easily through meditation on the possibility of wholesale environmental collapse). Benjamin ominously claims that Kafka's worlds will become truly accessible "to the masses at such time as they are about to be annihilated" (it is in this context that the emergence of "Kafkaesque" as an established concept with a dictionary meaning should be placed). As in critical theory, every detail becomes potentially ripe for reflection, for meaning and tradition are everywhere equally potentially a problem. As Benjamin puts it in "Franz Kafka" (1934), "even the most everyday things have their weight." In Kafka, meaning and tradition are potentially everywhere absent, so, just as in Scholem's account of Kabbalah, the everyday becomes a site for deep critical reflection. Kafka's stories are "not parables" (for they have no explicit teaching), yet they also "do not want to be taken at their face value." Just as in Beckett's work (as recounted in the last chapter), Kafka's stories are not "about" society but express that society in art, requiring a critical procedure for grasping what's happening just as the world itself may require the procedures of critical theory.

Adorno also pursues Kafka's writings as important, sharing features of Benjamin's and Scholem's readings. In his "Notes on Kafka" (1953), Adorno writes that Kafka "feigns a standpoint from which creation appears as lacerated and mutilated as it itself conceives hell to be." To Scholem, he writes affirming Kafka's remark about his own writings, that they are all "symbolic, but only in the sense that they should be interpreted through ever new symbols in an endless series of steps." Earlier, in 1934, Adorno writes to Benjamin praising Benjamin's Kafka essay, noting that in Kafka there is an "inverse theology." To explain the claim, Adorno invokes the image of an at that time standard view camera, where a front and rear standard are separated by a bellows. The front standard holds a

lens and shutter, while the rear standard has a glass that allows someone to focus the camera before opening the front shutter (all of this
would be performed before film is put in the front). Such a camera
would generally have a black cloth attached to the back glass, so
that it could be used to prevent any excess light entering through
this back glass, guaranteeing a sharper image in the front. Adorno
writes in his letter that Kafka's writings present "a photograph of
our earthly life from the perspective of a redeemed life." The catch,
though, is that this perspective is nothing more than "an edge of
black cloth," evincing "the terrifying distance optics" of "the
obliquely angled camera itself." There is then no picture of
redemption—all that's captured is the deficiency of any attempt to
capture its picture (the black cloth). Note the resonances to negative theology. Adorno in this letter terms it an inverse theology
only because just as throughout the long history of European
antisemitism, "Jews were tortured and executed 'perversely'—i.e.,
inversely," where "offenders were hung head down," so does Kafka
in his writings photograph "the earth's surface just as it must have
appeared to these victims during the endless hours of their dying."

6. REDEMPTION, CRITICAL THEORY, AND THEOLOGY

Adorno expands these themes in various places, most notably in the
already cited conclusion to *Minima Moralia*, where he muses that
"the only philosophy which can be responsibly practiced in the face
of despair is the attempt to contemplate all things as they would
present themselves from the standpoint of redemption." Formally
analogous to negative theology, there is no picture of redemption;
rather standpoints must be fashioned that "displace and estrange the
world, reveal it to be, with its rifts and crevices, as indigent and
distorted as it will appear one day in the messianic light." Adorno
acknowledges the difficulty, if not outright impossibility of such a
procedure, noting that it is "the utterly impossible thing, because it
presupposes a standpoint removed, even though by hair's breadth,
from the scope of existence." Nonetheless, the needless suffering
that permeates the world requires that the impossibility of the task
"must at least be comprehended for the sake of the possible." Given
such an approach, Adorno stresses that "the question of the reality

or unreality of redemption itself hardly matters." After reading *Minima Moralia*, Scholem wrote to Adorno claiming that he perceived in it, "one of the most remarkable documents of negative theology." Adorno responded to Scholem's letter with the rejoinder that this could only be true if one does not translate the book "straightforwardly into theological categories," for otherwise things do not "feel at ease."

This thought can serve as a sort of shorthand for the way in which the Frankfurt School relates more generally to religion, especially Judaism. Horkheimer's suggestion that the School's basic picture "derives from the idea that thou shalt make no image of God" has some plausibility, albeit with serious caveats and from an incredibly high-altitude view (indeed, the meaning of Horkheimer's claim continues to be debated by scholars—Yael Kupferberg just last year published a book in German on Horkheimer's late thought called *On the Ban of Images* [2022]). What's indisputable is that the Frankfurt School explores religion in many different contexts, positive and negative, seeing it, especially in the midst of needless suffering, just as Marx did, as a feature of human life that cannot be ignored, for better or for worse. Thus, in addition to the ways in which there are formal analogies to religious motifs in some of the School's work, there are also moments where religion is an explicit topic of inquiry. For example, Fromm's aforementioned "The Dogma of Christ" (see Chapter 2) argues that the original Christian impulse was a response to the socio-economic conditions of Roman rule, becoming defanged exactly when standardized into dogma. Despite Fromm's break from the Frankfurt School, this early essay was crucial to the development of critical theory, serving as a sort of proof text for Horkheimer's claim in "Materialism and Morality" (1933) that "human impulses which demand something better take different forms according to the historical material with which they have work."

Given this reference to human impulses, it is possible to find deep resonances to theological traditions that stress a response to needless suffering, for example the kinds of liberation theologies developed in South America and the sort of Black theology that emerged in the United States. Thus, for example, there's a thought that has some similarity to Fromm's claims in James Cone's (1938–2018) declaration in *A Black Theology of Liberation* (1970) that "Christianity is essentially a religion of liberation." In that work

Cone notes that, "if the basic truth of the gospel is that the Bible is the infallible word of God, then it is inevitable that more emphasis will be placed upon 'true' propositions about God than upon God as active in the liberation of the oppressed of the land." Cone rejects any such understanding of truth divorced from a project of liberation from oppression. In this way, he is echoing Adorno's thought in *Negative Dialectics* that "the need to give voice to suffering is a condition for all truth."

Seeing these connections between the Frankfurt School and certain traditions of theology, though, raises broader questions about status of religion in critical theory. As already noted, there cannot be any sort of *straightforward* translation between theology and critical theory. As Adorno suggests in the conclusion to *Minima Moralia*, any direct translation risks abandoning an acknowledgment of the needless suffering that animates the critique in the first place. In the parlance of the Frankfurt School, a negativity is required towards concrete existence (i.e., needless suffering emerges from concrete historical conditions). Such negativity cannot simply be translated into the positive categories of traditional or institutional religion. Once again, an analogous impulse can be seen as emerging internally to the development of, for example, Black theology in the United States. Following *A Black Theology of Liberation*, James Cone writes in "Black Theology in American Religion" (1985) that "because black theology is to be created only in the struggles of the poor, we have adopted social analysis, especially of racism, *and more recently* of classism and sexism" (emphasis added). Cone notes that additional sites of needless suffering have emerged, necessitating additional critical resources (negativity). More specifically, Black theology recognized that it had neglected the distinct kinds of needless suffering experienced by, say, Black women (this is one way to understand the aims and emergence of Womanist theology). Theologian Kelly Brown Douglas thus makes explicit how a certain positive conception of the divine had to be negated so as to be revised. As she writes in *The Black Christ* (1994): "the black church's inability to respect the complex issues of class, gender, and sexuality is tied to the way in which Christ's blackness has been defined." Tracking this development shows how even with intentions towards liberation, institutionalized forms of religion can oftentimes find themselves incapable of entirely divorcing themselves from broader social problems and currents. Institutionalization can often be in tension with the sort of critical stance required to address the broad range of needless suffering that emerges in society. In a different context, Adorno will say in *Negative Dialectics* that without changed empirical conditions, religious theological trends may end up serving as "ideological passports for conformism."

In "Reason and Revelation" (1957), Adorno writes that, "nothing of theological content will persist without being transformed; every content will have to put itself to the test of migrating into the realm of the secular, the profane." These claims are not meant to champion some kind of abstract universalism, where religion is entirely barred from society. Adorno's point is instead about society itself: that the kinds of needless suffering it produces calls into question religious viewpoints since they themselves may be intimately involved with the very social whole that produces this suffering. This is why, as noted already, Adorno writes in *Negative Dialectics*, that after the brutality of the last century, "there is no word tinged from on high, not even a theological one, that has any right unless it underwent a transformation." Society, secular and religious alike, is implicated. Neither is the image of migration accidental here: migration is exactly a response to an oppressive society, and involved in it is a mixture of desperation and hope. Relatedly, no immigrant arrives untransformed. In the context of these thoughts on religion, the notion of migration highlights how even what counts as theological versus what is profane may itself come to be blurred, subjected to shifts as historical circumstances themselves shift (inviting again a comparison to the way in which Scholem understands antinomian currents, for example in his elaboration of redemption through sin). Such possible variability is why in a letter to Scholem, Adorno stresses that his understanding of the materialism that underwrites critical theory "is not conclusive; it is neither a worldview, nor something fixed." While it warrants an "affinity with metaphysics (I would have almost said theology)," this materialism equally opposes "official doctrines" and is "heretical through and through." Akin to all kinds of religious and theological streams, any detail of human life may come to be relevant since any could be revelatory of needless suffering (Adorno's materialism). Contrary to most religious and theological streams (except for negative theological ones), though, there just is no fixed picture of the world beyond this one, for the contours of that picture shift constantly in response to concrete historical events (Adorno's metaphysics). Adorno summarizes this position in "Reason and Revelation" as an "extreme ascesis toward any type of revealed faith" but nonetheless "an extreme loyalty to the prohibition of images far beyond what this once originally meant." In 1968 Horkheimer pens an essay on *Psalm 91* that evinces a related thought. (And Psalm 91:2: "In you God, I trust" is inscribed on his gravestone and the psalm was also a favorite of his mother, its first line inscribed also on the gravestone of his parents.) In the essay, he elaborates that the sentiment of the psalm must be understood as "being different from the categorical principles that are ascribed to reason," so that "the thought of refuge as it expresses itself in Psalm 91 awakens not merely obedience but the love for that which is other than the world and which gives meaning to life and the suffering in it. Despite everything." The negative theological motifs are apparent in Horkheimer's remarks, but the "ascesis" Adorno urges certainly seems to be relaxed.

7. CRITICAL THEORY AND THE ARCHIVE OF RELIGION

Reflections on religion more generally do not stop with the first-generation of the Frankfurt School, and it is worth straying here a bit beyond this book's general focus on the early Frankfurt School. Habermas writes extensively and variously on religion, especially in works like *Postmetaphysical Thinking* (1988, *II* in 1992), *Between Naturalism and Religion* (2005), and *This Too a History of Philosophy* (2019). While it is impossible to summarize in any compact way the variety of Habermas's engagements, it is interesting that over time, Habermas abandons his initial position that religion cannot play any significant role in the unfolding of modern society oriented around communicative rationality. Perhaps religion may be existentially unavoidable for human beings, or perhaps religion may be useful for refining the moral intuitions of modern agents (a version of the position suggested by Marcuse in the opening of this chapter). In each case, everything hinges on the full valence of "may" in these claims. There are scholars who see in Habermas a sharp analytic break from his earlier work, so that now religion must have a part to play in the construction of modern society.

Other scholars see Habermas as making a historical acknowledgment that indeed religion continues to play a part, and thereby theoretical resources need to be activated to take stock of this fact. Everything hinges perhaps on how to understand Habermas's claim in *Postmetaphysical Thinking*, that religion is the bearer of "semantic content that is inspiring and even indispensable."

Whether "indispensable" above is an empirical claim or some other kind of claim is a question that invites deeper reflection on the contours, parameters, and scope of what might be termed the religious archive altogether. While Habermas has acknowledged in "The Political" (2009/2011) that "philosophy continuously appropriates semantic contents from the Judeo-Christian tradition," it remains an open question whether talk of appropriation is the best image of the relationship to the archive of religion. On one hand, of course, it is in fact plausible to speak of appropriation in certain cases, as in the way in which, say, certain kinds of secular universalist views or state institutional structures have their origins in religious views or practices. On the other hand, many of the central terms around this entire realm ("Judeo-Christian" and "philosophy" here and "semantic content," "inspiring," "indispensable" earlier) are themselves historically shifting, always in the process of migration, capable of being thought of quite easily as profane as much as sacred and vice versa (if they are not entirely denied or rejected). When Habermas notes, following his claim about appropriation, that "it is an open question whether this centuries-long learning process can be continued or even remains unfinished," it is just as plausible to ask here also whether "learning process" is the right image of how things have been unfolding. To put all this another way, moving in and out of a religious archive is not a merely neutral procedure: as with any archive, traces are left behind in the archive just as the archive itself leaves traces upon those who enter it. Equally, reports of the archive determine how future visitors navigate the archive and so forth. (These are points that I take the philosopher Hent de Vries to raise against Habermas in a different vernacular in *Minimal Theologies* [2005] and subsequent works.) The first-generation of the Frankfurt School then shares—perhaps more accurate is to say inspires— Habermas's implicit suggestion, in the terms of this book, that the religious archive remains crucial to the development of autonomy and maturity. Where the first-generation remains less optimistic than Habermas is in the prospect of drawing a sharp distinction between religion and reason (and their actualizations), seeing the two as in fact much more intimately related, their relationship and parameters at every moment dependent on the kinds of needless suffering produced by history.

This way of putting things suggests an interest in the mechanics of how the religious archive comes to be constructed (as does the general analogy with art). For the first-generation of the Frankfurt School, Freud is a central figure for thinking about this question to the extent that Freud stresses that instinctual renunciation is a central feature of religion as much as of art. Freud reflects on sublimation in *Civilization and Its Discontents*, noting its twofold character. On one hand, sublimation "is what makes it possible for higher psychical activities, scientific, artistic or ideological, to play such an important part of civilized life." Religion should be understood in this vein. (Freud in a letter, for example, suggests that religion and the religious is "sublimation in its most comfortable form.") On the other hand, Freud reflects on the dark underside to such sublimation. So while it is "impossible to overlook the extent to which civilization is built up upon a renunciation of instinct," such renunciation comes with a price. Freud poses an ominous thought (already quoted earlier in Chapter 2): "It is not easy to understand how it can become possible to deprive an instinct of satisfaction. Nor is doing so without danger. If the loss is not compensated for economically, one can be certain that serious disorders will ensue."

8. ANTISEMITISM AND CRITICAL THEORY

Freud returns to this point in his last work, *Moses and Monotheism* (1939), where he diagnoses antisemitism as exactly one such disorder. Freud stresses that Judaism, "which began with the prohibition against making an image of God develops more and more in the course of centuries into a religion of instinctual renunciations." In a way that circles around many of the issues discussed in this chapter, Freud elaborates how this ban exceeds the bounds of Judaism, coming also to animate the rise of the core enlightenment program animating the modern world. In such a context, then, critical theory must itself be understood as another such renunciation (the Frankfurt School's own understanding of the relationship between critical theory and the drives that serve as motor to critique would be central here). When put this way, though, a new perspective emerges about *resistance* to the claims and procedures of critical theory: antisemitism may be seen exactly as a species of such resistance, and thereby as a sort of disorder arising from a rejection of the instinctual renunciations necessary for the development of our human capacities. As Shane Burley puts it in "The Continuing Appeal of Antisemitism" (2021), "at the heart of antisemitism is a story that makes no *sense*, and for the antisemites it is the decision to reject the search for meaning in favor of the heart and the fist."

Freud explains such a decision in *Moses and Monotheism* with a particular psychoanalytic story about antisemitism. He suggests that "among the custom by which the Jews made themselves separate, that of circumcision has made a disagreeable, uncanny impression, which is to be explained, no doubt, by its recalling ... castration." Jews allegedly serve somehow as the very reminder of instinctual renunciation (represented most prominently by circumcision). Freud then concludes that "the deeper motives for hatred of the Jews are rooted in the remotest past ages; they operate from the unconscious of the peoples." He adds then that there is a sort of self-loathing involved in hatred of the Jews, for "hatred of Jews is at bottom a hatred of Christians." Freud is claiming that antisemitism is at bottom what he in "Repression" (1915) termed the "return of the repressed," i.e., the return of unsatisfied drives. Freud's suggestion is that the drives curbed by Western (dominantly Christian) culture now come to be unleashed as aggression, hatred, and violence exactly against the people who symbolize the glorification of the sublimation of drives. Antisemitism is at bottom a species of the rejection of what it means to be truly human, a rejection of the necessary movement away from mere instinctual satisfaction.

While the Frankfurt School pursues a complex analysis of antisemitism, arguing that it is by no means a univocal phenomenon, but rather one that admits of several oftentimes contradictory features (which the School traces in remarkable detail in various writings). Horkheimer nonetheless stresses a general orientation akin to Freud's when he notes in a 1943 reflection on a burgeoning project on antisemitism that all forms of antisemitism "share one thing in common: secret hate of civilization." In "Elements of Anti-Semitism" (1947), Horkheimer, Adorno, and Lowenthal propose several specific ways in which this is the case. For example, they suggest that antisemitism is a sort of secret hate available to anyone who profits from the capitalist order, of which Jews—because of their historical circumstances in the rise of that order—are symbolic. Antisemitism is thereby "what they secretly despise in themselves: their anti-Semitism is self-hate, the bad conscience of the parasite." Elsewhere, akin to Freud, they stress the extent to which the antisemite projects onto the Jew all of the repressed impulses they wish to carry out: "the popular nationalist fantasies of Jewish crimes, of infanticide and sadistic excesses" are precisely what "define the anti-Semitic dream." There are other alternatives they suggest, with the common feature being that antisemitism is a sort of "release valve" (their term), where the psychoanalytic pressures associated with the construction of culture by means of instinctual renunciation require a violent outlet (which the antisemite actualizes through the figure of the Jew). This is how Adorno can claim in a memo in 1948 around a proposed project on antisemitism that the cause of antisemitism is "due to the total structure of our society or, to put it more sweepingly, to every basically coercive society."

This is not the place to rehearse the entire complex analysis of antisemitism that the Frankfurt School undertakes, nor, for that matter, is their account sufficient to understand concrete historical instances of antisemitic discourse or activity. Instead, note the *role* that antisemitism plays in their account. In a letter to Horkheimer in 1941, Adorno claims that antisemitism "is today really the central injustice, and our form of physiognomy must attend to the world where it shows its face at its most gruesome." This was in many respects quite true in 1941, but only with the caveat that antisemitism was in many respects intimately related to other kinds of racialization (certainly in Nazi Germany, but also elsewhere and at different times, including pre-modern European history). Nowadays, the picture is more elaborate to the extent that the world is more interlocked and its ills even more complex, and so an understanding of the function of antisemitism can now be more intimately theorized in conjunction with the functioning of other kinds of historical exclusion, including importantly those that flow from colonialism and imperialism. Developing this point is of course beyond the confines of this book, but it is useful for framing a particular way of relating, for example, forms of antisemitism and racism. Here's how Frantz Fanon frames this issue in his *Black Skin, White Masks* (1952), where he draws an analogy between the two. Taking up again the basic Freudian picture sketched above, Fanon notes that:

> Every intellectual gain calls for a loss of sexual potential. The civilized white man retains an irrational nostalgia for the extraordinary times of sexual licentiousness, orgiastic scenes, unsanctioned rapes, and unrepressed incest. In a sense, these fantasies correspond to Freud's life instinct. Projecting his desires onto the black man, the white man behaves "as if" the black man actually had them. As for the Jew, the problem is more clear: he is not trusted, because he wants to possess wealth or take up positions of power. The black man is fixated at the genital level, or rather he has been fixated there. Two different spheres: the intellect and the sexual. ... The black man represents the biological danger; the Jew, the intellectual danger.

One finds such a view of things confirmed in contemporary white nationalist movements. As Eric Ward notes in a pamphlet first circulated in *samizdat* form but recently republished as "Skin in the Game" (2017), "antisemitism fuels white nationalism." The Jew is seen by white nationalists as an allegedly super intelligent race that organizes and inspires inferior people of color (also queer sexual degenerates, but that is not part of Fanon's account). Through such a concerted effort Jews work with people of color (and sexual degenerates) to perpetrate a "white genocide" through intermarriage and through various ways of undermining traditional features of society (like the family, the nation, and so forth). Much more may be said here, but it must be noted that the Frankfurt School's account remains incredibly timely to the extent that it allows antisemitism (and racism) to be understood as projections that Western society has marshaled for its development.

Such projections themselves contribute to needless suffering, and so must be opposed and dissolved, but doing so requires keeping a close proximity to the religious archive—as a means for combating such oppression and violence, as a means for understanding the ways in which religion has participated in this oppression and violence, and finally, as a means for tracing the contours of how these two features of the archive can become reversible or isomorphic with each other as human culture itself reacts to changing historical and material conditions. In each case, the archive maintains its importance, being incapable of being closed merely by fiat. Equally, the archive is—for better or for worse—intimately related, even if formally, to the very possibilities of critical theory as the first-generation of the Frankfurt School envisioned it. In short, the sort of maturity or autonomy that's been invoked throughout this book demands that we have an ear to the ground that is religion, whether as warning or as portend.

SUGGESTED READING

MARXISM AND RELIGION

McKown, Delos B. *The Classical Marxist Critiques of Religion: Marx, Engels, Lenin, Kautsky*. The Hague: Martinus Nijhoff, 1975.
Raines, John. *Marx on Religion*. Philadelphia: Temple University Press, 2011.

THE FRANKFURT SCHOOL AND RELIGION (INCLUDING PARTICULAR MEMBERS)

Banks, Robert. "A Neo-Freudian Critique of Religion: Erich Fromm on the Judaeo-Christian Tradition." *Religion* 5, no. 2 (1975): 117–35.
Brittain, Christopher Craig. *Adorno and Theology*. London: Routledge, 2010.
———. "The Frankfurt School on Religion." *Religion Compass* 6, no. 3 (2012): 204–12.
———. "Social Theory and the Premise of All Criticism: Max Horkheimer on Religion." *Critical Sociology* 31, no. 1–2 (2005): 153–68.
Calhoun, Craig, Eduardo Mendieta, and Jonathan VanAntwerpen, eds. *Habermas and Religion*. London: Polity, 2016.
Cook, Deborah. "Through a Glass Darkly: Adorno's Inverse Theology." *Adorno Studies* 1 (2017): 66–78.
Cooke, Maeve. "Critical Theory and Religion." In *Philosophy of Religion in the 21st Century*, edited by D.Z. Phillips and Timothy Tessin, 211–43. London: Palgrave-Macmillan, 2001.
Finlayson, James Gordon. "Adorno on the Ethical and the Ineffable." *European Journal of Philosophy* 10, no. 1 (2002): 1–25.
Gordon, Peter E. *Migrants in the Profane: Critical Theory and the Question of Secularization*. New Haven: Yale University Press, 2020.
Gur-Ze'ev, Ilan. "Adorno and Horkheimer: Diasporic Philosophy, Negative Theology, and Counter-Education." *Educational theory* 55, no. 3 (2005): 343–65.

Kohlenbach, Margarete, and Raymond Geuss. *The Early Frankfurt School and Religion*. London: Palgrave-Macmillan, 2004.

Martins, Ansgar. *The Migration of Metaphysics into the Realm of the Profane*. Translated by Lars Fisher. Leiden: Brill, 2020.

Mendieta, Eduardo. *The Frankfurt School on Religion: Key Writings by the Major Thinkers*. London: Routledge, 2005.

Müller-Doohm, Stefan. "Adorno and Habermas: Two Varieties of Post-Metaphysical Thinking." *European Journal of Social Theory* (2023).

Portier, Philippe. "Religion and Democracy in the Thought of Jürgen Habermas." *Society* 48, no. 5 (2011): 426–32.

Pritchard, Elizabeth A. "Bilderverbot Meets Body in Theodor W. Adorno's Inverse Theology." *Harvard Theological Review* 95, no. 3 (2002): 291–318.

Schimmel, Noam. "Judaism and the Origins of Erich Fromm's Humanistic Psychology: The Religious Reverence of a Heretic." *Journal of Humanistic Psychology* 49, no. 1 (2009): 9–45.

Shuster, Martin. "Adorno and Negative Theology." *Graduate Faculty Philosophy Journal* 37, no. 1 (2016): 97–130.

Siebert, Rudolf J. *The Critical Theory of Religion. The Frankfurt School: From Universal Pragmatic to Political Theology*. Berlin: Walter de Gruyter, 1985.

———. "Fromm's Theory of Religion." *Telos* 1977, no. 34 (1977): 111–20.

Thiem, Yannik. "Beyond Bad Conscience: Marcuse and Affects of Religion after Secularism." *Telos* 2013, no. 165 (2013): 23–48.

Truskolaski, Sebastian. *Adorno and the Ban on Images*. London: Bloomsbury, 2022.

Yates, Melissa. "Rawls and Habermas on Religion in the Public Sphere." *Philosophy & Social Criticism* 33, no. 7 (2007): 880–91.

BENJAMIN, SCHOLEM, ADORNO

Adorno, Theodor W., and Gershom Scholem. *Correspondence, 1939–1969*. Translated by Paula Schwebel and Sebastian Truskolaski. London: Polity, 2021.

Angermann, Asaf. "Adorno and Scholem: The Heretical Redemption of Metaphysics." In *A Companion to Adorno*, edited by Peter Gordon, Espen Hammer and Max Pensky, 531–47. London: Blackwell, 2020.

Jacobson, Eric. *Metaphysics of the Profane: The Political Theology of Walter Benjamin and Gershom Scholem*. New York: Columbia University Press, 2003.

Kaufmann, David. "Beyond Use, within Reason: Adorno, Benjamin and the Question of Theology." *New German Critique*, no. 83 (2001): 151–73.

Moses, Stéphane. *The Angel of History: Rosenzweig, Benjamin, Scholem*. Translated by Barbara Harshav. Palo Alto: Stanford University Press, 2008.

KAFKA

Alter, Robert. *Necessary Angels: Tradition and Modernity in Kafka, Benjamin, and Scholem*. Cambridge: Harvard University Press, 1991.

Foster, Roger. "Adorno on Kafka: Interpreting the Grimace on the Face of Truth." *New German Critique* 40, no. 1 (2013): 175–98.

Hammer, Espen. *Kafka's The Trial: Philosophical Perspectives*. Oxford: Oxford University Press, 2018.

Moses, Stéphane. "Gershom Scholem's Reading of Kafka: Literary Criticism and Kabbalah." *New German Critique*, no. 77 (1999): 149–67.

ANTISEMITISM AND THE FRANKFURT SCHOOL

Braune, Joan. "Who's Afraid of the Frankfurt School? 'Cultural Marxism' as an Antisemitic Conspiracy Theory." *Journal of Social Justice* 9, no. 1 (2019): 1–25.

Jacobs, Jack. *The Frankfurt School, Jewish Lives, and Antisemitism*. Cambridge: Cambridge University Press, 2015.

Jay, Martin. "The Jews and the Frankfurt School: Critical Theory's Analysis of Anti-Semitism." *New German Critique*, no. 19 (1980): 137–49.

Rensmann, Lars. *The Politics of Unreason: The Frankfurt School and the Origins of Modern Antisemitism*. Buffalo: SUNY Press, 2017.

Worrell, Mark. *Dialectic of Solidarity: Labor, Antisemitism, and the Frankfurt School*. Leiden: Brill, 2008.

CONCLUSION

Philosophy, Critical Theory, and the Present

1. THE FRANKFURT SCHOOL: NOW AND THEN

How do we assess the Frankfurt School now? Where do things even stand after our discussion? In the 1960s, especially in the turbulent protests of the late '60s, it was common to find signs at protests with three names: "Marx, Mao, and Marcuse." Thus, the March 1968 issue of *Time* magazine quotes a French protestor explaining this triumvirate with the thought that: "We see Marx as prophet, Marcuse as his interpreter, and Mao as the sword." Whatever this is supposed to mean, compare this remark to comments about the Frankfurt School by the radical scholar and prison abolitionist Ruth Wilson Gilmore in "Public Enemies and Private Intellectuals" (1994):

> I'm not of the Frankfurt School. One must live a life of relative privilege these days to be so dour about domination, so suspicious of resistance, so enchained by commodification, so helpless before the ideological state apparatuses to conclude there's no conceivable end to late capitalism's daily sacrifice of human life to the singular freedom of the market.

If these two dichotomous assessments aren't enough, consider the recent best-selling book written by radio personality Mark Levin. Titled *American Marxism* (2021), Levin's book speaks about the pernicious influence of the "Franklin School" (not a typo since Levin continued to repeat the mistake on subsequent *Fox News* appearances). Add to this the by now well-known clash between Theodor W. Adorno and German radical students in Frankfurt in 1969,

DOI: 10.4324/9781003200963-7

which culminated in what's now known as the "*Busenaktion*" (German for "breast action"), a moment of "planned tenderness" where a group of female students protested Adorno's alleged lack of practical involvement in their movement by circling around him during a packed lecture class with their breasts bared as they showered him with flowers and attempted to kiss him (a few months earlier Adorno had called the police on students who had occupied the Institute for Social Research). Additional data points here may be Horkheimer's refusal to oppose the Vietnam War or his seeming sympathy for the Catholic critique of birth control. There is also Marcuse's involvement with the student movement and the New Left, with the journalist Matt Taibbi recently calling him—in 2021—both "a quack" and someone whose ideas are, in the contemporary landscape, as "ubiquitous as Edison's lightbulbs."

Emerging here, I would suggest, is a complex picture of a group of individuals whose judgments after World War II often differed, sometimes in significant ways. It would also be equally accurate to say that their influence and legacy itself continues to be subject to dispute. My suggestion is that this should not be as surprising as it may seem given that the reality to which they responded was and continues itself to be contradictory. If, as Adorno claimed, "there is no right life in one that is false," then it should at least be plausible— if not even unsurprising—that these different members of the Frankfurt School came to different conclusions. It may be that there were several possible paths forward, each one registering different features of a contradictory world. There may be things to learn from their disagreements, perhaps especially because they disagree.

With that said, it is also striking how much consensus still existed amongst the first-generation of the Frankfurt School (even with the emergence of Horkheimer's apparent late conservatism). They found the world wanting. They understood most fundamentally at their core that: *things could be different.* The needless suffering they registered continues all around us, with no abatement in sight. While they realized that their first critiques of society needed supplementation and additional development, they by no means abandoned these critiques nor found them implausible. Quite the contrary: as they got older, for example, Marcuse's and Adorno's critiques in many ways became even more radical, even as their material conditions so obviously improved. I would suggest we might pursue their approach as a model, recognizing explicitly that even now these critiques should not be abandoned, nor have they been disproved. Quite the contrary.

While our present dangers and ills are not unrelated, there are also new developments: where earlier forms of conservatism at least acknowledged some role for the welfare state (a central feature, as noted earlier, of Pollock's state capitalism thesis), conservative positions, especially in the United States, increasingly reject any notion of a welfare state except for corporations, banks, or the military, prison, or industrial complex (this is one plausible way to understand what contemporary social critics oftentimes refer to with the otherwise ambiguous term "neoliberalism"). In response, apart from precise analyses of these various spheres, the Frankfurt School would invoke arguments showing the extent to which notions of sociality and a common humanity demand curbing the sort of base individualism underwriting such developments. (Equally important here would be the diverse psychoanalytic approaches that reveal in various ways our pre-conscious entanglements with others; Adorno's new categorical imperative; and the sort of common humanity suggested by the possibility of aesthetic experience.) Developments on the left, as almost a sort of exact funhouse mirror, include a sort of pathological stress on identity, as if membership in a particular racial, ethnic, or gender group guarantees or requires certain kinds of thought, action, and/or moral justification. The philosopher Ato Sekyi-Otu writes in *Left Universalism* (2018) that such "perverse ontology" demands for the present moment a re-prioritization and rethinking of the "ideal of individuality," albeit one that is "at once foundationalist and exhortative—of 'a new humanism'" that would vivify "our imagination, demanding to be achieved." These developments in mainstream conservatism and progressivism are in many ways extensions of a certain kind of free market liberalism, one that avoids confronting the economic and material conditions that are intimately intertwined with present day identities of race and gender, not to mention intertwined also with the various sites of needless suffering produced across the globe. My point in making these claims is not to suggest that the focus of critical theory should be entirely on class or material conditions. The idea is rather that the focus cannot be solely on identity markers like race and gender (as the contemporary critical theorist Keeanga Yamahtta-Taylor puts it, it's not enough to have "black faces in high places"). Emerging is thereby a thoroughly dialectical moment, one that calls for deeper analysis and different kinds of action. Relatedly, of course, any serious critical theory that moves forward in this moment must reckon with new technological developments such as the rise of big data, social media, the internet, artificial intelligence, and so forth. Here again, though, the Frankfurt School has powerful resources for doing so (as I argue, for example, about social media in my short piece, "The Monetization of Masochism" [2021]).

2. THEORY AND PRACTICE, REPRISE

To return to the late '60s, it is striking that after Adorno's decision to call the police to clear the student protestors occupying the Institute for Social Research (a move for which he was and continues to be pilloried by many on the left), Marcuse and Adorno in 1969 engage in a correspondence around the merits of Adorno's decision and around the student movement more generally. The question that animates their discussion is the question of praxis, of practical action. Adorno admits to Marcuse that:

> the strongest point that you make is the idea that the situation could be so terrible that one would have to attempt to break out of it, even if one recognizes the objective impossibility. I take that argument seriously. But I think that it is mistaken. We withstood in our time, you no less than me, a much more dreadful situation—that of the murder of the Jews, without proceeding to praxis.

Marcuse responds, claiming that it is exactly around this point that he diagnoses the "deepest divergence" between them. Marcuse exactly focuses on Adorno's claims about their earlier shared context of the Nazi genocide and notes that:

> What is different in the situation is the difference between fascism and bourgeois democracy. Democracy grants us freedoms and rights. But given the degree to which bourgeois democracy ... seals itself off from qualitative change—through the parliamentary democratic process itself—extra-parliamentary opposition becomes the only form of "contestation"; "civil disobedience", direct action. And the forms of this activity no longer follow traditional patterns. I condemn many things about it

> just like you, but I come to terms with it and defend it against opponents,
> simply because the defence and maintenance of the status quo and its
> cost in human life is much more terrible.

There is here a serious debate about how best to assess their situation in addition to a debate about how to respond to it. The debate is no less urgent now, nor is it any more settled. To get some sort of grip on how to assess the debate itself, let me situate the debate between Adorno and Marcuse by means of something Horkheimer writes in one of his letters in 1970; it is notable and striking in this context. He notes that, "in a terrorist state one has a different stance to the idea of revolution than in a state where the society is one that comes as close to what is termed democracy as it is possible to do today given the difficult situation."

As a way into the questions that are emerging here, I cannot but think of how the former Black Panther and American philosopher and activist Angela Davis recounts a meeting with Adorno in Frankfurt (she was then a graduate student studying with Adorno). She relates how in 1966, "after the founding of the Black Panther Party," she felt "very much drawn back" to the United States. Desiring to participate in the political praxis happening there, she finally made the decision to return to the United States, thereby cutting short her studies with Adorno. When she was finally able to schedule a meeting with Adorno, as she recounts in "Marcuse's Legacies" (2008), she describes his response to her decision as follows: "he suggested that my desire to work directly in the radical movements of that period was akin to a media studies scholar deciding to become a radio technician."

One way to read this exchange is to suggest that Adorno is entirely poo-pooing any sort of praxis. In reading things in this way, it might be said that Adorno and Davis exactly fall on opposite sides of the question of to what extent the United States at that moment was a "terrorist state" (an assessment which, if undertaken now, cannot be divorced from an understanding of how the United States dealt with elements of the Black Panther Party—notably in the FBI's involvement in the assassination of Fred Hampton and others, not to mention the politically motivated trial of Davis herself). That is an open question about which members of different communities will surely come to different conclusions now, just as they did then. As

Davis's contemporary and revolutionary, George Jackson (1941–1971), wrote in prison in 1971 (later published in *Blood in My Eye* [1972]), shortly before himself being killed by the police while trying to escape: "all black people, wherever they are [in the United States], whatever their crimes ... are political prisoners because the system has dealt with them differently than with whites."

Another way to read the exchange between Davis and Adorno, however, is to see it as a more sophisticated reflection on critical theory itself. In a *Der Spiegel* interview in 1969 Adorno notes that getting involved in practical affairs would for him "be at the cost of" his "productivity." He explains that, "one can say much against the division of labour, but as is well known, even Marx, who vehemently attacked it in his youth, later declared that without the division of labour nothing would work." On this reading, Adorno might be read—admittedly perhaps counter to some of his other explicit statements—as suggesting that *his* skills are best used in the theoretical register. Perhaps he also thought the same about Davis (a claim that perhaps may seem peculiar in retrospect given her stature as an activist, but perhaps Adorno's claim says more about his estimation of her theoretical abilities than his lack of estimation about her practical ones). All of this would be one way to situate equally Adorno's explicit claim in *Negative Dialectics* that he studiously worked on the book exactly because praxis was "thwarted," but that this development is exactly what "paradoxically" afforded the "breathing-space" for such work, "which it would practically be criminal not to use." This is again perhaps another way to situate his claim, in "Marginalia to Theory and Praxis" (1969), that "despite all of its unfreedom, theory is the guarantor of freedom in the midst of unfreedom."

3. RESISTANCE, MATURITY, AND THE PRESENT

Later in the same essay, Adorno points out that, "whoever thinks, offers resistance" thereby avoiding what's more comfortable, which is "to swim with the current, even when one declares oneself to be against the current." If, as was suggested in Chapter 2, critical theory is itself a kind of practice, one which through its theoretical procedures, already resists the status quo, then once again Adorno's suggestion to Davis may be understood as the thought that Davis's skills, like his own, would have been better used to develop theory rather than to pursue the praxis that she went on to pursue (and, again, such a remark may surely seem odd now with the benefit of hindsight, but, it is almost impossible to judge in any meaningful way such counterfactuals). Surely, though, the *continuing* existence of a brutal penal system offers an important data point. Potentially, it must be noted, in either direction: it both demands additional theoretical work *and* suggests the possible necessity of *far more* of the sort of abolitionist work Davis pursued and continues to pursue (again, especially with an eye to the debate between Adorno and Marcuse, perhaps these questions around praxis and social activity, whether about theory or practice, are nonetheless questions that can only be settled at the level of individual histories and social situations).

Or to put things another way, perhaps it is in fact impossible for me to address the question of what is to be done now in virtue of the account offered in this book. My suggestion is that every reader will have to settle that question for themselves. That, too, is a question of maturity or autonomy. Equally, though, let me be clear that such a question is not settled solely nor entirely nor once and for all at the level of the individual. As suggested in prior chapters, particular social configurations have an important part to play in determining the parameters of how to move forward, and those details may have already shifted significantly from the time I write this to the time you read this. In an essay titled "Theory of Half-Education" (1959) (but oddly translated into English as "Theory of Pseudo-Culture"), Adorno notes that our experience is increasingly replaced "by the selective, disconnected, interchangeable and ephemeral state of being informed which, as one can already observe, will promptly be cancelled by other information." Because there's a dearth of critical theoretical inquiry, examination, and practice, mere commodified and industrially mass-produced facts take hold, not to mention "irrationalisms of every stripe," so that genuine judgment is replaced by "a declarative 'that is,' lacking any judgment, similar to the way passengers on express trains call out the names of ball-bearing or cement factories or the new barracks in every place rapidly disappearing into the distance." What I take Adorno to suggest, then, is that in addition to the work of critical theory, there is also important work to be done in cultivating individual and communal experience, experience which is informed and, in turn, informs critical theory. Each of these stand in intimate proximity (whatever that may mean now and in the future) to needless suffering and its expression (and potentially, thereby, with the contradictions that continue to plague society). The alternative is to be, as Adorno suggests in this same essay, a monadic self with "no immediate relation to anything," being instead "always fixed on its own view of things." In short, properly to express and to acknowledge such needless suffering and the contradictions of contemporary society, already demands a perspective that orients itself by means of a robust sociality.

What I hope this book may offer, then, is a way of orienting one's situation moving forward, of understanding it as needing to arise out of a human judgment both about oneself and who one is, and about the society and historical moment of which one is unavoidably a part, and of what these two can and cannot be, presently or in the future. We must critically assess all these features of our lives to determine whether we presently pursue theory or action, and with whom and when (and this idea may be expanded, as for example in the work of once students of Adorno's, like Alexander Kluge and Oskar Negt, who think explicitly about how a global subject of change might emerge). In either case, though, complete inaction is a surrender to the status quo and all the needless suffering that entails. And here, on this point, if the book offers at least a possible way to see things critically (exactly now with a nod to Marcuse) in more than one dimension, then it will have achieved its purpose. Furthermore, to the extent that it at least makes plausible the relevancy of the deep archive that is the tradition of Frankfurt School critical theory, then the book may have potential effects in the future than cannot be foreseen. As Adorno once put it in "Resignation" (1969):

> Whatever has once been thought can be suppressed, forgotten, can vanish. But it cannot be denied that something of it survives. For thinking has the element of universality. What once was thought cogently must be thought elsewhere, by others: this confidence accompanies even the most solitary and powerless thought.

BIBLIOGRAPHY

Abromeit, John. "Frankfurt School Critical Theory and the Persistence of Authoritarian Populism in the United States." In *Critical Theory and Authoritarian Populism*, edited by Jeremiah Morelock, 3–27. London: University of Westminster Press, 2018.

———. "Genealogy and Critical Historicism: Two Models of Enlightenment in Horkheimer and Adorno's Writings." *Critical Historical Studies* 3, no. 2 (2016): 283–308.

———. "Herbert Marcuse's Critical Encounter with Martin Heidegger 1927–33." In *Herbert Marcuse*, 131–51: London: Routledge, 2014.

———. *Max Horkheimer and the Foundations of the Frankfurt School*. Cambridge: Cambridge University Press, 2011.

———. "The Vicissitudes of the Politics of 'Life': Max Horkheimer and Herbert Marcuse's Reception of Phenomenology and Vitalism in Weimar Germany." *Enrahonar: quaderns de filosofia* 62 (2019): 0039–58.

Adorno, Theodor W. "The Actuality of Philosophy." *Telos* 31 (1977): 120–33.

———. "Adorno's '"Theses on Need."'" Translated by Martin Shuster and Iain Macdonald. *Adorno Studies* 1: 101–04.

———. *Aesthetic Theory*. Translated by Robert Hullot-Kentor. Edited by Gretel Adorno and Rolf Tiedemann. Minneapolis: University of Minnesota Press, 1997.

———. *Aesthetics*. London: Polity, 2017.

———. *Against Epistemology: A Metacritique*. Translated by Willis Domingo. Cambridge: MIT Press, 1983.

———. *The Authoritarian Personality*. London: Verso Books, 2019.

———. *Beethoven: The Philosophy of Music*. Translated by Edmund Jephcott. Stanford: Stanford University Press, 1993.

———. "Commitment." *New Left Review*, no. 87 (1974).

———. *Critical Models: Interventions and Catchwords*. Translated by Henry W. Pickford. New York: Columbia University Press, 1998.

———. "Critique." Translated by Henry W. Pickford. In *Critical Models: Interventions and Catchwords*, 281–89. New York: Columbia University Press, 1998.

———. "Cultural Criticism and Society." Translated by Samuel Weber and Sherry Weber. In *Prisms*, 17–35. Cambridge: MIT Press, 1983.

———. "Culture Industry Reconsidered." *New German Critique*, no. 6 (1975): 12–19.

———. *The Culture Industry: Selected Essays on Mass Culture*. Edited by J.M. Bernstein. London: Routledge, 2001.

———. "Difficulties." In *Essays on Music*, edited by Richard Leppert, 644–81. Berkeley: University of California Press, 2002.

———. "Education after Auschwitz." Translated by Henry W. Pickford. In *Critical Models: Interventions and Catchwords*, 191–204. New York: Columbia University Press, 1998.

———. "Free Time." In *The Culture Industry: Selected Essays on Mass Culture*, edited by J.M. Bernstein, 162–70. London: Routledge, 2001.

———. "Freudian Theory and the Pattern of Fascist Propaganda." In *The Culture Industry: Selected Essays on Mass Culture*, edited by J.M. Bernstein, 107–32. London: Routledge, 2001.

———. *Gesammelte Schriften*. 20 vols. Frankfurt am Main: Suhrkamp Verlag, 1984.

———. *Hegel: Three Studies*. Cambridge: MIT Press, 1993.

———. *History and Freedom*. Translated by Rodney Livingstone. Edited by Rolf Tiedemann. Cambridge: Polity Press, 2006.

———. "The Idea of Natural History." *Telos* 60, no. Summer (1984): 111–24.

———. *Introduction to Sociology*. Translated by Rodney Livingstone. Palo Alto: Stanford University Press, 2002.

———. "Is Art Lighthearted?" In *Notes to Literature*, 247–53. New York: Columbia University Press, 1992.

———. *The Jargon of Authenticity*. Translated by Knut Tarnowski and Frederic Will. Evanston: Northwestern University Press, 1973.

———. *Kant's Critique of Pure Reason*. [Kant's *Kritik der Reinen Vernunft*]. Translated by Rodney Livingstone. Edited by Rolf Tiederman. Cambridge: Polity Press, 2001.

———. "Kultur and Culture." *Social Text* 27, no. 2 (2009): 145–58.

———. "Late Capitalism or Industrial Society?" Translated by Rodney Livingstone. In *Can One Live after Auschwitz? A Philosophical Reader*, edited by Rolf Tiedemann, 111–25. Palo Alto: Stanford University Press, 2003.

———. *Lectures on Negative Dialectics*. Translated by Rodney Livingstone. Edited by Rolf Tiedemann. Cambridge: Polity Press, 2008.

———. "Marginalia to Theory and Praxis." Translated by Henry W. Pickford. In *Critical Models: Interventions and Catchwords*, 259–79. New York: Columbia University Press, 1998.

———. "The Meaning of Working through the Past." Translated by Henry W. Pickford. In *Critical Models: Interventions and Catchwords*, 89–105. New York: Columbia University Press, 1998.

———. *Metaphysics*. Translated by Edmund Jephcott. Edited by Rolf Tiedemann. Stanford: Stanford University Press, 2000.

———. *Minima Moralia*. London: Verso, 2005.

———. *Negative Dialectics*. Translated by E.B. Ashton. New York: The Continuum Publishing Company, 1973.

———. "Notes on Kafka." Translated by Henry W. Pickford. In *Prisms*, 243–72. Cambridge: MIT Press, 1982.

———. *Notes to Literature*. Translated by Rolf Tiedemann. New York: Columbia University Press, 1992.

———. "On Tradition." *Telos* 1992, no. 94 (1992): 75–82.

———. "Opinion Delusion Society." Translated by Henry W. Pickford. In *Critical Models: Interventions and Catchwords*, 105–22. New York: Columbia University Press, 1998.

———. *Philosophical Elements of a Theory of Society*. Translated by Wieland Hoban. London: Polity, 2019.

———. *Philosophy of New Music*. Translated by Robert Hullot-Kentor. Minneapolis: University of Minnesota Press, 2006.

———. *Problems of Moral Philosophy*. Translated by Rodney Livingstone. Stanford: Stanford University Press, 2000.

———. "Progress." Translated by Henry W. Pickford. In *Critical Models: Interventions and Catchwords*, 143–61. New York: Columbia University Press, 1998.

———. *The Psychological Technique of Martin Luther Thomas' Radio Addresses*. Palo Alto: Stanford University Press, 2000.

———. "Reason and Revelation." Translated by Henry W. Pickford. In *Critical Models: Interventions and Catchwords*, 135–43. New York: Columbia University Press, 1998.

———. "Research Project on Antisemitism: Idea of the Project." Translated by Samuel Weber and Sherry Weber. In *The Stars Down to Earth*, edited by Stephen Crook, 181–218. London: Routledge, 1983.

———. "Resignation." Translated by Henry W. Pickford. In *Critical Models: Interventions and Catchwords*, 289–95. New York: Columbia University Press, 1998.

———. "Social Science and Sociological Tendencies in Psychoanalysis." In *Dialektische Psychologie: Adornos Rezeption Der Psychoanalyse*, edited by Wolfgang Bock, 623–42. Wiesbaden: Springer Fachmedien, 2018.

———. "Sociology and Psychology 1." *New Left Review* 46 (1967): 67–80.

———. "Sociology and Psychology 2." *New Left Review* 47 (1967): 79–99.

———. "Theory of Pseudo-Culture (1959)." *Telos* 1993, no. 95 (1993): 15–38.

———. "Theses Upon Art and Religion Today." *The Kenyon Review* 7, no. 4 (1945): 677–82.

———. "Those Twenties." Translated by Henry W. Pickford. In *Critical Models: Interventions and Catchwords*, 41–47. New York: Columbia University Press, 1998.

———. "Vers Une Musique Informelle." Translated by Rodney Livingstone. In *Quasi Una Fantasia: Essays on Modern Music*, 269–323. London: Verso, 1961.

Adorno, Theodor W., Hans Albert, Ralf Dahrendorf, Jürgen Habermas, Harald Pilot, and Karl R. Popper. *The Positivist Dispute in German Sociology*. Translated by Glyn Adey and David Frisby. London: Heinemann, 1976.

Adorno, Theodor W., and Hellmut Becker. "Education for Maturity and Responsibility." *History of the Human Sciences* 12, no. 3 (1999): 21–34.

Adorno, Theodor W., and Max Horkheimer. *Towards a New Manifesto*. London: Verso Books, 2019.

Adorno, Theodor W., and Robert Hullot-Kentor. *Current of Music*. London: Polity, 2009.

Adorno, Theodor W., and Siegfried Kracauer. *Correspondence 1923–1966*. Translated by Susan Reynolds and Michael Winkler. London: Polity, 2019.

Adorno, Theodor W., and Herbert Marcuse. "Correspondence on the German Student Movement." *New Left Review* (1999): 123–36.

Adorno, Theodor W., and Gershom Scholem. *Correspondence, 1939–1969*. Translated by Paula Schwebel and Sebastian Truskolaski. London: Polity, 2021.

Agnoli, Johannes, and Peter Brückner. *Die Transformation Der Demokratie*. Hamburg: Europäische Verlagsanstalt, 1964.

Alexander, Michelle. *The New Jim Crow: Mass Incarceration in the Age of Colorblindness*. New York: The New Press, 2010.

Allen, Amy. *Critique on the Couch: Why Critical Theory Needs Psychoanalysis*. New York: Columbia University Press, 2020.

———. *The End of Progress: Decolonizing the Normative Foundations of Critical Theory*. New York: Columbia University Press, 2016.

———. "Reason, Power and History: Re-Reading the Dialectic of Enlightenment." *Thesis Eleven* 120, no. 1 (2014): 10–25.

Alter, Robert. *Necessary Angels: Tradition and Modernity in Kafka, Benjamin, and Scholem*. Cambridge: Harvard University Press, 1991.

Anderson, Kevin B. *Marx at the Margins: On Nationalism, Ethnicity, and Non-Western Societies*. Chicago: University of Chicago Press, 2020.

Angermann, Asaf. "Adorno and Scholem: The Heretical Redemption of Metaphysics." In *A Companion to Adorno*, edited by Peter Gordon, Espen Hammer, and Max Pensky, 531–47. London: Blackwell, 2020.

Aristotle. *Complete Works of Aristotle*. 2 vols. Princeton: Princeton University Press, 2014.

Aurelius, Marcus. *Meditations.* Translated by Martin Hammond. London: Penguin, 2015.

Austin, John L. "Other Minds." In *Philosophical Papers*, 76–116. Oxford: Oxford University Press, 1961.

———. "A Plea for Excuses." In *Philosophical Papers*, 175–204. Oxford: Oxford University Press, 1961.

Bailes, Jon. "'Enjoy Responsibly': The Continuing Relevance of Repressive Desublimation." *Radical Philosophy Review* 19, no. 1 (2016): 239–62.

Baldwin, James. *Notes of a Native Son.* Boston: Beacon Press, 2012.

Banks, Robert. "A Neo-Freudian Critique of Religion: Erich Fromm on the Judaeo-Christian Tradition." *Religion* 5, no. 2 (1975): 117–35.

Bartlett, Robert. *The Making of Europe: Conquest, Colonization and Cultural Change 950–1350.* London: Penguin, 1994.

Belew, Kathleen. *Bring the War Home: The White Power Movement and Paramilitary America.* Cambridge: Harvard University Press, 2018.

Benjamin, Jessica. "Authority and the Family Revisited: Or, a World without Fathers?" *New German Critique*, no. 13 (1978): 35–57.

———. "The End of Internalization: Adorno's Social Psychology." *Telos* 1977, no. 32 (1977): 42–64.

Benjamin, Walter. *The Arcades Project.* Cambridge: Harvard University Press, 1999.

———. "Franz Kafka: On the Tenth Anniversary of His Death." In *Selected Writings*, edited by Howard Eiland and Michael W. Jennings, 2, 794–818. Cambridge: Harvard University Press, 2002.

———. *Gesammelte Schriften.* Edited by Rolf Tiedemann and Schweppenhäuser. Frankfurt am Main: Suhrkamp, 1977.

———. *Illuminations.* New York: Shocken Books, 1968.

———. "On Some Motifs in Baudelaire." In *Selected Writings*, edited by Howard Eiland and Michael W. Jennings, 4, 313–56. Cambridge: Harvard University Press, 2002.

———. "On the Concept of History." In *Selected Writings*, edited by Howard Eiland and Michael W. Jennings, 4, 389–400. Cambridge: Harvard University Press, 2002.

———. "The Storyteller: Observations on the Works of Nikolai Leskov." In *Selected Writings*, edited by Howard Eiland and Michael W. Jennings, 3, 143–67. Cambridge: Harvard University Press, 2002.

———. "The Work of Art in the Age of Its Technological Reproducibility." In *Selected Writings*, edited by Howard Eiland and Michael W. Jennings, 4, 251–84. Cambridge: Harvard University Press, 2002.

Benjamin, Walter, and Gershom Scholem. *The Correspondence of Walter Benjamin and Gershom Scholem, 1932–1940.* Cambridge: Harvard University Press, 1992.

Berman, Russell A. *Modern Culture and Critical Theory: Art, Politics, and the Legacy of the Frankfurt School.* Madison: University of Wisconsin Press, 1989.

Bernstein, J.M. *Adorno: Disenchantment and Ethics.* Cambridge: Cambridge University Press, 2001.

———. *The Fate of Art: Aesthetic Alienation from Kant to Derrida and Adorno.* State College: Penn State Press, 1992.

———. "Mimetic Rationality and Material Inference: Adorno and Brandom." *Revue internationale de philosophie*, no. 1 (2004): 7–23.

Berry, David. *Revisiting the Frankfurt School: Essays on Culture, Media and Theory.* Farnham: Ashgate, 2013.

Bloxham, Donald. *The Final Solution: A Genocide.* Oxford: Oxford University Press, 2009.

———. *Genocide, the World Wars and the Unweaving of Europe.* Middlesex: Mitchell Vallentine & Company, 2008.

———. "Organized Mass Murder: Structure, Participation, and Motivation in Comparative Perspective." *Holocaust and Genocide Studies* 22, no. 2 (2008): 203–45.

Bloxham, Donald, and Tony Kushner. *The Holocaust: Critical Historical Approaches.* Manchester: Manchester University Press, 2005.

Bonefeld, Werner. *Critical Theory and the Critique of Political Economy: On Subversion and Negative Reason.* London: Bloomsbury, 2014.

Bonefeld, Werner, and Chris O'Kane. *Adorno and Marx: Negative Dialectics and the Critique of Political Economy.* London: Bloomsbury, 2022.

Bowie, Andrew. *Aesthetic Dimensions of Modern Philosophy.* Oxford: Oxford University Press, 2022.

———. *Aesthetics and Subjectivity.* Manchester: Manchester University Press, 2003.

———. *From Romanticism to Critical Theory: The Philosophy of German Literary Theory.* London: Routledge, 2012.

Bowring, Finn. "Repressive Desublimation and Consumer Culture: Re-Evaluating Herbert Marcuse." *new formations* 75, no. 75 (2012): 8–24.

Brandom, Robert. *Tales of the Mighty Dead: Historical Essays in the Metaphysics of Intentionality.* Cambridge: Harvard University Press, 2002.

Braune, Joan. "Who's Afraid of the Frankfurt School? 'Cultural Marxism' as an Antisemitic Conspiracy Theory." *Journal of Social Justice* 9, no. 1 (2019): 1–25.

Braunstein, Dirk. *Adorno's Critique of Political Economy.* Leiden: Brill, 2022.

Brittain, Christopher Craig. *Adorno and Theology.* London: Routledge, 2010.

———. "The Frankfurt School on Religion." *Religion Compass* 6, no. 3 (2012): 204–12.

———. "Social Theory and the Premise of All Criticism: Max Horkheimer on Religion." *Critical Sociology* 31, no. 1–2 (2005): 153–68.

Bronner, Stephen Eric, and Douglas Kellner, eds. *Critical Theory and Society*. London: Routledge, 1989.

Bronner, Stephen Eric. *Critical Theory: A Very Short Introduction*. Oxford: Oxford University Press, 2017.

Buck-Morss, Susan. *Hegel, Haiti, and Universal History*. Pittsburgh: University of Pittsburgh Press, 2009.

Bukharin, Nikolai. *Historical Materialism: A System of Sociology*. London: Routledge, 2013.

Bürger, Peter. *Theory of the Avant-Garde*. Translated by Michael Shaw. Manchester: Manchester University Press, 1984.

Burley, Shane. "The Continuing Appeal of Antisemitism." In *Why We Fight: Essays on Fascism, Resistance, and Surviving the Apocalypse*, 247–89. Chico: AK Press, 2021.

———. *Fascism Today: What It Is and How to End It*. Chico: Ak Press, 2017.

———. *Why We Fight: Essays on Fascism, Resistance, and Surviving the Apocalypse*. Chico: AK Press, 2021.

Butler, Judith. *Precarious Life: The Powers of Mourning and Violence*. London: Verso, 2004.

Butler, Judith, Jürgen Habermas, Charles Taylor, and Cornel West. *The Power of Religion in the Public Sphere*. New York: Columbia University Press, 2011.

Calhoun, Craig, Eduardo Mendieta, and Jonathan VanAntwerpen, eds. *Habermas and Religion*. London: Polity, 2016.

Cavell, Stanley. "Austin at Criticism." *The Philosophical Review* 74, no. 2 (1965): 204–19.

———. "Aethetic Problems of Modern Moral Philosophy." In *Must We Mean What We Say?*, 73–97. Cambridge: Harvard University Press, 2002.

———. "The Availability of Wittgenstein's Later Philosophy." In *Must We Mean What We Say?*, 44–73. Cambridge: Harvard University Press, 2002.

———. *The Claim of Reason: Wittgenstein, Skepticism, Morality, and Tragedy*. Oxford: Oxford University Press, 1979.

———. *Conditions Handsome and Unhandsome*. Chicago: University of Chicago Press, 1990.

———. "Must We Mean What We Say?" In *Must We Mean What We Say?*, 1–43. Cambridge: Harvard University Press, 2002.

———. *Must We Mean What We Say? A Book of Essays*. Cambridge: Cambridge University Press, 2002.

———. *The World Viewed: Reflections on the Ontology of Film: Enlarged Edition*. Cambridge: Harvard University Press, 1979.

Celikates, Robin. "Critical Theory and the Unfinished Project of Mediating Theory and Practice." In *The Routledge Companion to the Frankfurt School*, edited by Peter Gordon, Max Pensky, Espen Hammer and Axel Honneth, 206–20. London: Routledge, 2018.

Césaire, Aimé. *Discourse on Colonialism*. Translated by Joan Pinkham. New York: Monthly Review Press, 2001.

Chitty, Christopher. *Sexual Hegemony: Statecraft, Sodomy, and Capital in the Rise of the World System*. Raleigh: Duke University Press, 2020.

Collective, Combahee River. "The Combahee River Collective Statement." (1977).

Cone, James H. "Black Theology in American Religion." *Journal of the American Academy of Religion* 53, no. 4 (1985): 755–71.

———. *A Black Theology of Liberation*. Ossing: Orbis Books, 2010.

Cook, Deborah. "Adorno on Late Capitalism." *Radical Philosophy* 89 (1998): 16–26.

———. *The Culture Industry Revisited: Theodor W. Adorno on Mass Culture*. Lanham: Rowman & Littlefield, 1996.

———. "Through a Glass Darkly: Adorno's Inverse Theology." *Adorno Studies* 1 (2017): 66–78.

Cooke, Maeve. "Critical Theory and Religion." In *Philosophy of Religion in the 21st Century*, edited by D. Z. Phillips and Timothy Tessin, 211–43. London: Palgrave-Macmillan, 2001.

Crenshaw, Kimberlé. "Demarginalizing the Intersection of Race and Sex: A Black Feminist Critique of Antidiscrimination Doctrine, Feminist Theory and Antiracist Politics." In *Feminist Legal Theories*, 23–51. London: Routledge, 2013.

Crowell, Steven Galt. "Emil Lask: Aletheiology as Ontology." *Kant Studien* 87, no. 1 (1996): 69–88.

———. *Truth and Reflection: The Development of Transcendental Logic in Lask, Husserl, and Heidegger*. New Haven: Yale University, 1981.

Cunningham, David. *There's Something Happening Here: The New Left, the Klan, and FBI Counterintelligence*. Los Angeles: University of California Press, 2004.

Dalla Costa, Mariarosa. *Women and the Subversion of the Community: A Mariarosa Dalla Costa Reader*. Oakland: PM Press, 2019.

Dallmayr, Fred R. "Phenomenology and Critical Theory: Adorno." *Cultural Hermeneutics* 3, no. 4 (1976): 367–405.

Danto, Arthur C. *The Transfiguration of the Commonplace: A Philosophy of Art*. Cambridge: Harvard University Press, 1981.

Davis, Angela Y. "Marcuse's Legacies." In *Herbert Marcuse*, edited by John Abromeit and W. Mark Cobb, 43–50. London: Routledge, 2014.

De Vries, Hent. *Minimal Theologies: Critiques of Secular Reason in Adorno and Levinas*. JHU Press, 2019.

Dostoyevsky, Fyodor. *The Brothers Karamazov*. Translated by David McDuff. London: Penguin, 2003.

Douglas, Kelly Brown. *The Black Christ*. Ossing: Orbis Books, 2019.

Fanon, Frantz. *Black Skin, White Masks*. Translated by Richard Philcox. New York: Grove Press, 2016.

———. *The Wretched of the Earth*. Translated by Richard Philcox. New York: Grove Press, 2004.

Feenberg, Andrew. "Lukács's Theory of Reification and Contemporary Social Movements." *Rethinking Marxism* 27, no. 4 (2015): 490–507.

———. *The Philosophy of Praxis: Marx, Lukács and the Frankfurt School*. London: Verso, 2014.

———. "Realizing Philosophy: Marx, Lukács and the Frankfurt School." In *Critical Theory and the Challenge of Praxis*, edited by Stefano Giacchetti Ludovisi, 117–30. London: Routledge, 2016.

———. *The Ruthless Critique of Everything Existing: Nature and Revolution in Marcuse's Philosophy of Praxis*. Verso Books, 2023.

Finlayson, Gordon. "Adorno: Modern Art, Metaphysics and Radical Evil." *Modernism/modernity* 10, no. 1 (2003): 71–95.

Finlayson, James Gordon. "Adorno on the Ethical and the Ineffable." *European Journal of Philosophy* 10, no. 1 (2002): 1–25.

Ford, Simon. *Wreckers of Civilization*. London: Black Dog Publishing, 1999.

Forst, Rainer. *Contexts of Justice: Political Philosophy Beyond Liberalism and Communitarianism*. Vol. 9. Berkeley: University of California Press, 2002.

———. *Normativity and Power: Analyzing Social Orders of Justification*. New York: Oxford University Press, 2017.

———. *The Right to Justification: Elements of a Constructivist Theory of Justice*. Vol. 46. New York: Columbia University Press, 2011.

———. *Toleration in Conflict: Past and Present*. Cambridge: Cambridge University Press, 2013.

Foster, Roger. "Adorno on Kafka: Interpreting the Grimace on the Face of Truth." *New German Critique* 40, no. 1 (2013): 175–98.

Foucault, Michel. *The Foucault Reader*. Edited by Paul Rabinow. New York: Pantheon, 1984.

———. *The History of Sexuality*. Vol. 1. New York: Vintage, 1978.

———. "What Is Enlightenment?" In *The Foucault Reader*, edited by Paul Rabinow. New York: Pantheon, 1984.

Franks, Paul W. *All or Nothing: Systematicity, Transcendental Arguments, and Skepticism in German Idealism*. Cambridge: Harvard University Press, 2005.

Fraser, Nancy. *Cannibal Capitalism*. London: Verso, 2022.

Frazier, Demita. "Rethinking Identity Politics: An Interview with Demita Frazier." *Sojourner: The Women's Forum* 21, no. 1 (1995): 12–13.

Freire, Paulo. *Pedagogy of the Oppressed*. London: Penguin, 2017.

Freud, Sigmund. *The Standard Edition of the Complete Psychological Works*. Edited by James Strachey, Anna Freud, Alix Strachey and Alan Tyson. 24 vols. London: Hogarth Press, 1974.

————. *The Basic Writings of Sigmund Freud (Psychopathology of Everyday Life, the Interpretation of Dreams, and Three Contributions to the Theory of Sex)*. New York: Random House, 1938.

————. *Civilization and Its Discontents*. The Standard Edition of the Complete Psychological Works of Sigmund Freud. New York: WW Norton & Company, 1989.

————. *The Ego and the Id*. The Standard Edition of the Complete Psychological Works of Sigmund Freud. New York: WW Norton & Company, 1960.

————. *Group Psychology and the Analysis of the Ego*. The Standard Edition of the Complete Psychological Works of Sigmund Freud. New York: WW Norton & Company, 1959.

————. *Inhibitions, Symptoms and Anxiety*. The Standard Edition of the Complete Psychological Works of Sigmund Freud. New York: WW Norton & Company, 1959.

————. *Introductory Lectures on Psychoanalysis*. The Standard Edition of the Complete Psychological Works of Sigmund Freud. New York: WW Norton & Company, 1960.

————. *Moses and Monotheism*. The Standard Edition of the Complete Psychological Works of Sigmund Freud. New York: WW Norton & Company, 1964.

————. *New Introductory Lectures on Psychoanalysis*. The Standard Edition of the Complete Psychological Works of Sigmund Freud. New York: WW Norton & Company, 1965.

————. "On Narcissism." In *The Standard Edition of the Complete Psychological Works*, edited by James Strachey, Anna Freud, Alix Strachey, and Alan Tyson, 14, 67–102. London: Hogarth Press, 1974.

————. "Repression." In *The Standard Edition of the Complete Psychological Works*, edited by James Strachey, Anna Freud, Alix Strachey, and Alan Tyson, 14, 146–58. London: Hogarth Press, 1974.

Freyenhagen, Fabian. *Adorno's Practical Philosophy: Living Less Wrongly*. Cambridge: Cambridge University Press, 2013.

Fromm, Erich. *The Crisis of Psychoanalysis: Essays on Freud, Marx and Social Psychology*. New York: Holt, Rinehart, and Winston, 2014.

————. *The Dogma of Christ; and Other Essays on Religion, Psychology and Culture*. New York: Holt, Rinehart, and Winston, 1964.

————. *Man for Himself: An Inquiry into the Psychology of Ethics*. London: Routledge, 2013.

————. "The Method and Function of an Analytic Social Psychology." In *The Crisis of Psychoanalysis*, 110–35. New York: Holt, Rinehart, and Winston, 2014.

————. "Politics and Psychoanalysis." In *Critical Theory and Society*, edited by Stephen Eric Bronner and Douglas Kellner, 213–18. London: Routledge, 1989.

———. "Politik und Psychoanalyse." In *Psychoanalytische Bewegung*, 3, 440–47. Wien: Internationaler Psychoanalytischer Verlag, 1931.

———. "Psychoanalysis and Sociology." In *Critical Theory and Society*, edited by Stephen Eric Bronner and Douglas Kellner, 37–39. London: Routledge, 1989.

———. *To Have or to Be?* London: Continuum, 1997.

Gandesha, Samir. "Adorno, Ferenczi, and a New 'Categorical Imperative after Auschwitz.'" *International Forum of Psychoanalysis* 28, no. 4 (2019): 222–30.

———. "Adorno, Ferenczi, and a New 'Categorical Imperative after Auschwitz.'" Paper presented at the International Forum of Psychoanalysis, 2019.

———. "'Identifying with the Aggressor': From the Authoritarian to Neo-Liberal Personality." *Der aufrechte Gang im windschiefen Kapitalismus: Modelle kritischen Denkens* (2018): 273–97.

———. "Punk Multiculturalism." In *Poetics/Politics: Radical Aesthetics for the Classroom*, edited by Amitava Kumar, 245–61. New York: St. Martin's Press, 1999.

Gandesha, Samir, and Johan F. Hartle. *Aesthetic Marx.* London: Bloomsbury, 2017.

Gangl, Manfred. "The Controversy over Friedrich Pollock's State Capitalism." *History of the Human Sciences* 29, no. 2 (2016): 23–41.

Geuss, Raymond. *The Idea of a Critical Theory: Habermas and the Frankfurt School.* Cambridge: Cambridge University Press, 1981.

Gilmore, Ruth Wilson. "Public Enemies and Private Intellectuals: Apartheid USA." *Race & Class* 35, no. 1 (1993): 69–78.

Ginzburg, Carlo. *Clues, Myths, and the Historical Method.* Baltimore: The Johns Hopkins University Press, 2013.

Gordon, Peter E. *Adorno and Existence.* Cambridge: Harvard University Press, 2016.

———. "The Authoritarian Personality Revisited: Reading Adorno in the Age of Trump." *boundary 2* 44, no. 2 (2017): 31–56.

———. *Migrants in the Profane: Critical Theory and the Question of Secularization.* New Haven: Yale University Press, 2020.

———. "Social Suffering and the Autonomy of Art." *New German Critique* 48, no. 2 (2021): 125–46.

Gordon, Peter, Max Pensky, Espen Hammer, and Axel Honneth, eds. *The Routledge Companion to the Frankfurt School.* London: Routledge, 2018.

Grant, Madison. *The Passing of the Great Race.* New York: C. Scribner's sons, 1916.

Grossman, Henryk. *Henryk Grossman Works, Volume 3: The Law of Accumulation and Breakdown of the Capitalist System, Being Also a Theory of Crises.* Translated by Rick Kuhn and Jairus Banaji. Chicago: Haymarket Books, 2022.

Gur-Ze'ev, Ilan. "Adorno and Horkheimer: Diasporic Philosophy, Negative Theology, and Counter-Education." *Educational Theory* 55, no. 3 (2005): 343–65.

Habermas, Jürgen. *Auch Eine Geschichte Der Philosophie: Band 1: Die Okzidentale Konstellation Von Glauben Und Wissen. Band 2: Vernünftige Freiheit. Spuren Des Diskurses Über Glauben Und Wissen.* Frankfurt am Main: Suhrkamp Verlag, 2019.

———. *Between Facts and Norms: Contributions to a Discourse Theory of Law and Democracy.* New York: John Wiley & Sons, 2015.

———. *Between Naturalism and Religion: Philosophical Essays.* London: Polity, 2008.

———. *The Future of Human Nature.* London: Polity, 2003.

———. *Inclusion of the Other: Studies in Political Theory.* New York: John Wiley & Sons, 2015.

———. *Knowledge and Human Interests.* Translated by Jeremy J. Shapiro. London: Polity, 2015.

———. *Legitimation Crisis.* Boston: Beacon Press, 1975.

———. *Moral Consciousness and Communicative Action.* Translated by Christian Lenhard and Shierry Weber Nicholsen. Cambridge: MIT Press, 1992.

———. *The New Conservatism: Cultural Criticism and the Historians' Debate.* Translated by Shierry Weber Nicholson. Cambridge: MIT Press, 1989.

———. *The Philosophical Discourse of Modernity: Twelve Lectures.* Cambridge: MIT Press, 1990.

———. *Philosophical Political Profiles.* [Philosophisch-politische Profile]. Translated by Frederick G. Lawrence. Cambridge: MIT Press, 1983.

———. *Philosophical-Political Profiles.* New York: John Wiley & Sons, 2018.

———. "'The Political': The Rational Meaning of a Questionable Inheritance of Political Theology." In *The Power of Religion in the Public Sphere*, edited by Eduardo Mendieta and Jonathan Vanantwerpen, 15–34. New York: Columbia University Press, 2011.

———. *Postmetaphysical Thinking II.* London: Polity, 2017.

———. *Postmetaphysical Thinking: Philosophical Essays.* Cambridge: MIT Press, 1992.

———. *The Structural Transformation of the Public Sphere: An Inquiry into a Category of Bourgeois Society.* Cambridge: MIT Press, 1991.

———. "Technology and Science as 'Ideology.'" Translated by Jeremy J. Shapiro. In *Toward a Rational Society.* Boston: Beacon Press, 1970.

———. *Theory and Practice.* Boston: Beacon Press, 1988.

———. *The Theory of Communicative Action: Volume 1: Reason and the Rationalization of Society.* Boston: Beacon Press, 1985.

———. *The Theory of Communicative Action: Volume 2: Lifeword and System: A Critique of Functionalist Reason.* Boston: Beacon Press, 1985.

Hadot, Pierre, ed. *Philosophy as a Way of Life: Spiritual Exercises from Socrates to Foucault.* Edited by Arnold I. Davidson. Oxford: Wiley-Blackwell, 1995.

Hammer, Espen. *Adorno's Modernism: Art, Experience, and Catastrophe.* Cambridge: Cambridge University Press, 2015.

———. *Kafka's The Trial: Philosophical Perspectives.* Oxford: Oxford University Press, 2018.

Harper, Paul. *Rehearsal for Destruction: A Study of Political Anti-Semitism in Imperial Germany.* New York: Harper and Brothers, 1949.

Haskins, Casey. "Kant and the Autonomy of Art." *The Journal of Aesthetics and Art Criticism* 47, no. 1 (1989): 43–54.

Hegel, G.W.F. *Elements of the Philosophy of Right.* Cambridge: Cambridge University Press, 1991.

———. *Gesammelte Werke.* Edited by Rheinisch-Westfälischen Akademie der Wissenschaften. Hamburg: Felix Meiner, 1968.

———. *Hegel's Aesthetics: Lectures on Fine Art.* Translated by T.M. Knox. Oxford: Oxford University Press, 1975.

———. *Phenomenology of Spirit.* Translated by A.V. Miller. Oxford: Oxford University Press, 1977.

———. *Werke.* Frankfurt am Main: Suhrkamp, 1970.

Heil, John. *Philosophy of Mind: A Contemporary Introduction.* London: Routledge, 2019.

Held, David. *Introduction to Critical Theory: Horkheimer to Habermas.* Berkeley: University of California Press, 1980.

Henrich, Dieter. *The Unity of Reason: Essays on Kant's Philosophy.* Cambridge: Harvard University Press, 1994.

Heschel, Abraham Joshua. *The Prophets.* New York: Harper & Row, 1962.

Hodge, Joanna. "Adorno and Phenomenology: Between Hegel and Husserl." *Philosophy Today* 63, no. 2 (2019): 403–25.

Hohendahl, Peter Uwe. "Autonomy of Art: Looking Back at Adorno's Ästhetische Theorie." *German Quarterly* (1981): 133–48.

———. *The Fleeting Promise of Art: Adorno's Aesthetic Theory Revisited.* Ithaca: Cornell University Press, 2013.

Honneth, Axel. *The Critique of Power: Reflective Stages in a Critical Social Theory.* [Kritik der Macht. Reflexions-stufen einer kritischen Gesellschaftstheorie]. Translated by Kenneth Baynes. Cambridge: MIT Press, 1991.

———, ed. *Dialektik Der Freiheit: Frankfurter Adorno-Konferenz 2003.* Frankfurt am Main: Suhrkamp Verlag, 2005.

———. *Disrespect: The Normative Foundations of Critical Theory.* New York: John Wiley & Sons, 2014.

———. *Freedom's Right: The Social Foundations of Democratic Life.* New York: Columbia University Press, 2014.

———. "Is There an Emancipatory Interest? An Attempt to Answer Critical Theory's Most Fundamental Question." *European Journal of Philosophy* 25, no. 4 (2017): 908–20.

———. *Pathologies of Reason: On the Legacy of Critical Theory*. New York: Columbia University Press, 2009.

———. "A Physiognomy of the Capitalist Form of Life: A Sketch of Adorno's Social Theory." *Constellations* 12, no. 1 (2005): 50–64.

———. *Reification: A New Look at an Old Idea*. Oxford: Oxford University Press, 2008.

———. *The Struggle for Recognition: The Moral Grammar of Social Conflicts*. Cambridge: MIT Press, 1996.

Horkheimer, Max. "Authority and the Family." In *Critical Theory: Selected Essays*, 47–128. New York: Seabury, 1972.

———. "Theism and Atheism." *Diogenes* 12, no. 48 (1964): 39–52.

———. *Between Philosophy and Social Science*. Translated by G. Frederick Hunter, Matthew S. Kramer, and John Torpey. Cambridge: MIT Press, 1993.

———. *Critical Theory: Selected Essays*. New York: Seabury, 1972.

———. *Eclipse of Reason*. New York: Oxford University Press, 1947.

———. "Egoism and Freedom Movements: On the Anthropology of the Bourgeios Era." Translated by G. Frederick Hunter, Matthew S. Kramer, and John Torpey. In *Between Philosophy and Social Science*, 49–111. Cambridge: MIT Press, 1993.

———. *Gesammelte Schriften*. 19 vols. Frankfurt am Main: S. Fischer, 1987.

———. "Materialism and Metaphysics." In *Critical Theory: Selected Essays*, 10–47. New York: Seabury, 1972.

———. "Materialism and Morality." Translated by G. Frederick Hunter, Matthew S. Kramer, and John Torpey. In *Between Philosophy and Social Science*, 15–49. Cambridge: MIT Press, 1993.

———. "The Present Situation of Social Philosophy and the Tasks of the Institute for Social Research." Translated by G. Frederick Hunter, Matthew S. Kramer, and John Torpey. In *Between Philosophy and Social Science*, 1–15. Cambridge: MIT Press, 1993.

———. "Traditional and Critical Theory." In *Critical Theory: Selected Essays*, 188–253. New York: Seabury, 1972.

Horkheimer, Max, and Theodor W. Adorno. *Dialectic of Enlightenment, Philosophical Fragments*. Translated by Edmund Jephcott. Cultural Memory in the Present. Edited by Mieke Bal and Hent de Vries. Palo Alto: Stanford University Press, 2002.

———. "Elements of Anti-Semitism: The Limits of Enlightenment." Translated by Edmund Jephcott. In *Dialectic of Enlightenment, Philosophical Fragments*, 137–73. Palo Alto: Stanford University Press, 2002.

Howard, Thomas Albert. *Religion and the Rise of Historicism: Wml De Wette, Jacob Burckhardt, and the Theological Origins of Nineteenth-Century Historical Consciousness*. Cambridge: Cambridge University Press, 2000.

Huhn, Tom, and Lambert Zuidervaart. *The Semblance of Subjectivity: Essays in Adorno's Aesthetic Theory*. Cambridge: MIT Press, 1997.

Hulatt, Owen. *Aesthetic and Artistic Autonomy*. London: Bloomsbury, 2013.

———. "The Place of Mimesis in the Dialectic of Enlightenment." In *The Routledge Companion to the Frankfurt School*, 351–64: Routledge, 2018.

———. "Reason, Mimesis, and Self-Preservation in Adorno." *Journal of the History of Philosophy* 54, no. 1 (2016): 135–51.

Hullot-Kentor, Robert. "The Idea of Natural History." *Telos* 60 (1984): 111–24.

———. "The Problem of Natural History in the Philosophy of Theodor W. Adorno." Dissertation, University of Massachusetts, 1985.

———. *Things Beyond Resemblance: Collected Essays on Theodor W. Adorno*. New York: Columbia University Press, 2006.

Hume, David. *An Enquiry Concerning Human Understanding*. Edited by Eric Steinberg. Indianapolis: Hackett Publishing Company, 1993.

Husserl, Edmund. *The Crisis of European Sciences and Transcendental Phenomenology: An Introduction to Phenomenological Philosophy*. Translated by David Carr. Evanston: Northwestern University Press, 1970.

———. *Ideas Pertaining to a Pure Phenomenology and to a Phenomenological Philosophy: First Book: General Introduction to a Pure Phenomenology*. Translated by F. Kersten. Dordrecht: Kluwer, 1983.

———. *Ideas Pertaining to a Pure Phenomenology and to a Phenomenological Philosophy: Second Book Studies in the Phenomenology of Constitution*. Translated by Richard Rojcewicz and André Schuwer. Dordrecht: Kluwer, 1989.

———. "Static and Genetic Phenomenological Method." *Continental Philosophy Review* 31 (1998): 135–42.

Ibsen, Henrik. *A Doll's House and Other Plays*. London: Penguin, 2016.

Jackson, George L. *Blood in My Eye*. Baltimore: Black Classic Press, 1990.

Jacobs, Jack. *The Frankfurt School, Jewish Lives, and Antisemitism*. Cambridge: Cambridge University Press, 2015.

Jacobson, Eric. *Metaphysics of the Profane: The Political Theology of Walter Benjamin and Gershom Scholem*. New York: Columbia University Press, 2003.

James, Selma. *Sex, Race, and Class—the Perspective of Winning: A Selection of Writings, 1952–2011*. Oakland: Pm Press, 2012.

Jameson, Fredric. "Future City." *New Left Review* 21 (2003): 65.

Jay, Martin. "Introduction to Horkheimer." *Telos* 1982, no. 54 (1982): 5–9.

———. "The Jews and the Frankfurt School: Critical Theory's Analysis of Anti-Semitism." *New German Critique*, no. 19 (1980): 137–49.

———. *The Dialectical Imagination: A History of the Frankfurt School and the Institute of Social Research, 1923–1950*. Berkeley: University of California Press, 1996.

Jenemann, David. "'Nothing Is True except the Exaggerations' the Legacy of the Authoritarian Personality." In *A Companion to Adorno*, edited by Peter

Gordon, Espen Hammer, and Max Pensky, 271–86. London: Blackwell, 2020.

Kafka, Franz. *The Complete Stories*. New York: Schocken, 2012.

Kamau, Caroline. "On Erich Fromm: Why He Left the Frankfurt School." In *Revisiting the Frankfurt School*, edited by David Berry, 185–206. London: Routledge, 2016.

Kant, Immanuel. *Critique of Pure Reason*. Translated by Paul Guyer and Allen W. Wood. Cambridge: Cambridge University Press, 1998.

———. *Critique of the Power of Judgment*. Translated by Paul Guyer and Eric Matthews. Cambridge: Cambridge University Press, 2000.

———. *Foundations of the Metaphysics of Morals and What Is Enlightenment?* Translated by Lewis White Beck. 2nd ed. Upper Saddle River: Prentice-Hall, 1997.

———. *Gesammelte Schriften*. Edited by Preußischen Akademie der Wissenschaften. 29 vols. Berlin: Walter de Gruyter, 1912.

Kaufmann, David. "Beyond Use, within Reason: Adorno, Benjamin and the Question of Theology." *New German Critique*, no. 83 (2001): 151–73.

Kaushall, Justin Neville. "Natural Spontaneity, or Adorno's Aesthetic Category of the Shudder." *Telos* 2020, no. 192 (2020): 125–44.

Kavoulakos, Konstantinos. "What Is Reification in Georg Lukács's Early Marxist Work?" *Thesis Eleven* 157, no. 1 (2020): 41–59.

Kellner, Douglas. "Herbert Marcuse and the Art of Liberation." *Telos* 1983, no. 56 (1983): 223–29.

———. "Marcuse." In *A Companion to Continental Philosophy*, edited by Simon Critchley and William R. Schroeder, 389–96. London: Blackwell, 2017.

Kiloh, Kathy. "Towards an Ethical Politics: T.W. Adorno and Aesthetic Self-Relinquishment." *Philosophy & Social Criticism* 43, no. 6 (2017): 571–98.

Kirchheimer, Otto, and George Rusche. *Punishment and Social Structure*. London: Routledge, 2017.

Klein, Melanie. "On the Theory of Anxiety and Guilt." In *Developments in Psychoanalysis*, edited by Susan Isaacs Paula Heimann, Melanie Klein, and Joan Riviere, 271–91. London: Routledge, 2018.

Kleinberg, Ethan. "One-Dimensional Man, One-Dimensional History: Re-Reading Herbert Marcuse." *Journal of the Philosophy of History* 15, no. 3 (2021): 340–60.

Kohlenbach, Margarete, and Raymond Geuss. *The Early Frankfurt School and Religion*. London: Palgrave-Macmillan, 2004.

Koopman, Colin. *Genealogy as Critique: Foucault and the Problems of Modernity*. Bloomington: Indiana University Press, 2013.

Korsch, Karl. *Marxism and Philosophy*. London: Verso Books, 2013.

Kupferberg, Yael. *Zum Bilderverbot: Studien Zum Judentum Im Späten Werk Max Horkheimers*. Göttingen: Wallstein Verlag, 2022.

Lask, Emil. *Die Logik Der Philosophie Und Die Kategorienlehre/Die Lehre Vom Urteil: Sámtliche Werke Band 2*. Vol. 2, Jena: Schleglmann, 2022.

Lear, Jonathan. *Radical Hope: Ethics in the Face of Cultural Devastation*. Boston: Harvard University Press, 2006.

Leeder, Natalie. *Freedom and Negativity in Beckett and Adorno: Something or Nothing*. Lanham: Rowman & Littlefield, 2017.

Leibniz, Gottfried Wilhelm. *Theodicy: Essays on the Goodness of God, the Freedom of Man, and the Origin of Evil*. Translated by F.M. Huggard. Chicago: Open Court Publishing, 1985.

Leonard, Craig. *Uncommon Sense: Aesthetics after Marcuse*. Cambridge: MIT Press, 2022.

Levene, Mark. *The Crisis of Genocide*. 2 vols. Oxford: Oxford University Press, 2013.

———. *Genocide in the Age of the Nation State*. 4 vols. London: I.B. Tauris, 2005.

———. "Why Is the Twentieth Century the Century of Genocide?". *Journal of World History* 11, no. 2 (2000): 305–36.

Levin, Mark R. *American Marxism*. New York: Simon and Schuster, 2021.

Lichtenberg, Judith. "Negative Duties, Positive Duties, and the 'New Harms.'" *Ethics* 120, no. 3 (2010): 557–78.

Loewald, Hans. *Papers on Psychoanalysis*. New Haven: Yale University Press, 1989.

Lotz, Christian. "Categorial Forms as Intelligibility of Social Objects: Reification and Objectivity in Lukács." In *Confronting Reification: Revitalizing Georg Lukács's Thought in Late Capitalism*, edited by Gregory R. Smulewicz-Zucker, 25–47. Chicago: Haymarket, 2020.

Lovibond, Sabina. *Ethical Formation*. Cambridge: Harvard University Press, 2002.

———. *Realism and Imagination in Ethics*. Minneapolis: University of Minnesota Press, 1983.

Lowenthal, Leo. *An Unmastered Past: The Autobiographical Reflections of Leo Lowenthal*. Berkeley: University of California Press, 1987.

Lowenthal, Leo, and Jamie Owen Daniel. "Address Upon Accepting the Theodor W. Adorno Prize on 1 October 1989." *New German Critique*, no. 54 (1991): 179–82.

Lowenthal, Leo, and Norbert Guterman. *Prophets of Deceit: A Study of the Techniques of the American Agitator*. London: Verso Books, 2021.

Lukács, Georg. *History and Class Consciousness: Studies in Marxist Dialectics*. Cambridge: MIT Press, 1972.

Lukács, György. *Record of a Life an Autobiographical Sketch*. Translated by Rodney Livingstone. London: Verso, 1983.

Luxemburg, Rosa. *The Accumulation of Capital*. Translated by Agnes Schwarzschild. London: Routledge, 2003.

Lyotard, Jean-Fraçois. *The Differend: Phrases in Dispute*. Translated by Georges Van Den Abbeele. Minneapolis: University of Minnesota Press, 1988.

Maimonides, Moses. *The Guide of the Perplexed*. Translated by Shlomo Pines. Chicago: University of Chicago Press, 1963.

Marasco, Robyn, Christina Gerhardt, and Kirk Wetters. "The Authoritarian Personality." *Polity* 54, no. 1 (2022): 1–7.

Marcuse, Herbert. *The Aesthetic Dimension: Toward a Critique of Marxist Aesthetics*. Boston: Beacon Press, 1979.

———. "The Affirmative Character of Culture." In *Negations*, 65–99. New York: MayFly, 2009.

———. *Art and Liberation: Collected Papers of Herbert Marcuse*. Vol. 4, London: Routledge, 2007.

———. "Art in the One-Dimensional Society." In *Art and Liberation: Collected Papers of Herbert Marcuse*, edited by Douglas Kellner, 113–23. London: Routledge, 2007.

———. *Counterrevolution and Revolt*. Boston: Beacon Press, 1972.

———. "Cultural Revolution." In *Towards a Critical Theory of Society: Collected Papers of Herbert Marcuse*, edited by Douglas Kellner, 121–62. London: Routledge, 2013.

———. "The End of Utopia." *Five Lectures: Psychoanalysis, Politics, and Utopia*, 62–82, 1970.

———. *Eros and Civilization: A Philosophical Inquiry into Freud*. Boston: Beacon Press, 1974.

———. *An Essay on Liberation*. Beacon Press, 1971.

———. "The Foundation of Historical Materialism." Translated by Joris de Bres. In *Studies in Critical Philosophy*, 1–49. Boston: Beacon Press, 1972.

———. *Hegel's Ontology and the Theory of Historicity*. Translated by Seyla Benhabib. Cambridge: MIT Press, 1987.

———. "Industrialization and Capitalism in the Work of Max Weber." In *Negations*, 151–71. New York: MayFly, 2009.

———. *Marxism, Revolution and Utopia: Collected Papers of Herbert Marcuse*. Vol. 6, London: Routledge, 2014.

———. "Nature and Revolution." In *Counterrevolution and Revolt*, 59–79. Boston: Beacon Press, 1972.

———. *Negations*. New York: MayFly, 2009.

———. *The New Left and the 1960s: Collected Papers of Herbert Marcuse*. Vol. 3, London: Routledge, 2004.

———. *One-Dimensional Man: Studies in the Ideology of Advanced Industrial Society*. Boston: Beacon Press, 1964.

———. *Philosophy, Psychoanalysis and Emancipation: Collected Papers of Herbert Marcuse*. Vol. 5, London: Routledge, 2010.

————. *Reason and Revolution: Hegel and the Rise of Social Theory*. London: Routledge, 1986.

————. "Repressive Tolerance." In *A Critique of Pure Tolerance*, edited by Robert Paul Wolff, Barrington Moore and Herbert Marcuse, 95–137. Boston: Beacon Press, 1969.

————. "The Role of Religion in a Changing Society." In *Philosophy, Psychoanalysis and Emancipation: Collected Papers of Herbert Marcuse*, edited by Douglas Kellner, 182–89. London: Routledge, 2010.

————. "Society as a Work of Art." In *Art and Liberation: Collected Papers of Herbert Marcuse*, edited by Douglas Kellner, 123–30. London: Routledge, 2007.

————. "Some Social Implications of Technology." In *Technology, War and Fascism: Collected Papers of Herbert Marcuse*, edited by Douglas Kellner, 39–67. London: Routledge, 2004.

————. *Soviet Marxism: A Critical Analysis*. New York: Columbia University Press, 1985.

————. *A Study on Authority*. London: Verso Books, 2020.

————. *Technology, War and Fascism: Collected Papers of Herbert Marcuse*. Vol. 1, London: Routledge, 2004.

————. *Towards a Critical Theory of Society: Collected Papers of Herbert Marcuse*. Vol. 2, London: Routledge, 2013.

Mariotti, Shannon L. *Adorno and Democracy: The American Years*. Lexington: University Press of Kentucky, 2016.

Martin Luther King, Jr. *A Testament of Hope: The Essential Writings of Martin Luther King, Jr.* New York: Harper & Row, 1986.

Martins, Ansgar. *The Migration of Metaphysics into the Realm of the Profane*. Translated by Lars Fisher. Leiden: Brill, 2020.

Marx, Karl. *Capital: Volume I*. Translated by Ben Fowkes. London: Penguin, 2004.

————. *The Economic and Philosophical Manuscripts of 1844 and the Communist Manifesto*. Translated by Martin Milligan. New York: Prometheus Books, 1988.

————. *The Marx-Engels Reader*. 2nd ed. New York: Norton, 1978.

Marx, Karl, and Frederick Engels. *Marx & Engels Collected Works*. London: Lawrence & Wishart, 1975.

Mauss, Marcel. *The Gift: Forms and Functions of Exchange in Archaic Societies*. Translated by W.D. Halls. London: Routledge, 1990.

McAfee, Noëlle. *Democracy and the Political Unconscious*. New York: Columbia University Press, 2008.

————. *Fear of Breakdown: Politics and Psychoanalysis*. New York: Columbia University Press, 2019.

McDowell, John. *Mind and World*. Cambridge: Harvard University Press, 1996.

———. "Might There Be External Reasons?" In *Mind, Value, and Reality*, 95–111. Cambridge: Harvard University Press, 1998.

———. *Mind, Value, and Reality*. Cambridge: Harvard University Press, 1998.

McKown, Delos B. *The Classical Marxist Critiques of Religion: Marx, Engels, Lenin, Kautsky*. The Hague: Martinus Nijhoff, 1975.

McLaughlin, Neil. "Origin Myths in the Social Sciences: Fromm, the Frankfurt School and the Emergence of Critical Theory." *Canadian Journal of Sociology/Cahiers canadiens de sociologie* (1999): 109–39.

Memmi, Albert. *The Colonizer and the Colonized*. Translated by Howard Greenfeld. Boston: Beacon Press, 2013.

Mendieta, Eduardo. *The Frankfurt School on Religion: Key Writings by the Major Thinkers*. London: Routledge, 2005.

———. "The Prison Contract and Surplus Punishment: On Angela Y. Davis's Abolitionism." *Human Studies* 30, no. 4 (2007): 291–309.

Menke, Christoph. *The Sovereignty of Art: Aesthetic Negativity in Adorno and Derrida*. Cambridge: MIT Press, 1998.

Miller, Tyrus. *Modernism and the Frankfurt School*. Edinburgh: Edinburgh University Press, 2014.

Mitchell, Juliet. *Psychoanalysis and Feminism: A Radical Reassessment of Freudian Psychoanalysis*. New York: Basic Books, 2000.

Moses, A. Dirk. "An Antipodean Genocide? The Origins of the Genocidal Moment in the Colonization of Australia." *Journal of Genocide Research* 2, no. 1 (2000): 89–106.

———. "Conceptual Blockages and Definitional Dilemmas in The 'Racial Century': Genocides of Indigenous Peoples and the Holocaust." *Patterns of Prejudice* 36, no. 4 (2002): 7–36.

———, ed. *Empire, Colony, Genocide: Conquest, Occupation, and Subaltern Resistance in World History*. London: Berghahn Books, 2008.

———. "Genocide and Modernity." In *The Historiography of Genocide*, edited by Dan Stone, 156–93. Houndmills: Palgrave Macmillan, 2008.

———. "Lemkin, Culture, and the Concept of Genocide." In *The Oxford Handbook of Genocide Studies*, edited by Donald Bloxham and A. Dirk Moses, 19–41. Oxford: Oxford University Press, 2010.

Moses, Stéphane. *The Angel of History: Rosenzweig, Benjamin, Scholem*. Translated by Barbara Harshav. Palo Alto: Stanford University Press, 2008.

———. "Gershom Scholem's Reading of Kafka: Literary Criticism and Kabbalah." *New German Critique*, no. 77 (1999): 149–67.

Muller, Jerry Z. *Professor of Apocalypse: The Many Lives of Jacob Taubes*. Princeton: Princeton University Press, 2022.

Müller-Doohm, Stefan. "Adorno and Habermas: Two Varieties of Post-Metaphysical Thinking." *European Journal of Social Theory* (2023).

Neiman, Susan. *Evil in Modern Thought: An Alternative History of Philosophy.* Princeton: Princeton University Press, 2002.

Neuhouser, Frederick. *Diagnosing Social Pathology: Rousseau, Hegel, Marx, and Durkheim.* Cambridge: Cambridge University Press, 2022.

Neumann, Franz L. "Anxiety and Politics." *tripleC: Communication, Capitalism & Critique. Open Access Journal for a Global Sustainable Information Society* 15, no. 2 (2017): 612–36.

———. *Behemoth: The Structure and Practice of National Socialism, 1933–1944.* Chicago: Ivan R. Dee, 2009.

Nietzsche, Friedrich W. *Beyond Good and Evil.* Translated by Judith Norman. Cambridge: Cambridge University Press, 2002.

———. *"On the Genealogy of Morality" and Other Writings.* Translated by Carole Diethe. Cambridge: Cambridge University Press, 2017.

———. *Thus Spoke Zarathustra.* Translated by Adrian Del Caro. Cambridge: Cambridge University Press, 2006.

Noppen, Pierre-François. "The Anthropology in Dialectic of Enlightenment." In *A Companion to Adorno,* edited by Peter Gordon, Espen Hammer, and Max Pensky, 207–20. London: Blackwell, 2020.

Nussbaum, Martha C. "Capabilities as Fundamental Entitlements: Sen and Social Justice." In *Capabilities Equality,* edited by Alexander Kaufman, 54–80. London: Routledge, 2007.

Offe, Claus. *Reflections on America: Tocqueville, Weber and Adorno in the United States.* London: Polity, 2005.

Okiji, Fumi. *Jazz as Critique: Adorno and Black Expression Revisited.* Palo Alto: Stanford University Press, 2018.

Paddison, Max. *Adorno's Aesthetics of Music.* Cambridge: Cambridge University Press, 1997.

Pensky, Max. "Third Generation Critical Theory." In *A Companion to Continental Philosophy,* edited by Simon Critchley and William R. Schroeder, 407–16. London: Blackwell, 2017.

Pinker, Steven. *The Better Angels of Our Nature: Why Violence Has Declined.* New York: Viking Press, 2011.

Pippin, Robert B. *After the Beautiful: Hegel and the Philosophy of Pictorial Modernism.* University of Chicago Press, 2013.

———. "Natural and Normative." *Daedalus* 138, no. 3 (2009): 35–43.

Pollock, Frederick. "State Capitalism: Its Possibilities and Limitations." In *Critical Theory and Society,* edited by Stephen Eric Bronner and Douglas MacKay Kellner, 95–118. London: Routledge, 2020.

———. "State Capitalism: Its Possibilities and Limitations." *Zeitschrift für Sozialforschung* 9, no. 2 (1941): 200–25.

Polyani, Karl. *The Great Transformation.* New York: Farrar & Rhinehart, 1944.

Portier, Philippe. "Religion and Democracy in the Thought of Jürgen Habermas." *Society* 48, no. 5 (2011): 426–32.

Postone, Moishe. *Time, Labor, and Social Domination: A Reinterpretation of Marx's Critical Theory.* Cambridge: Cambridge University Press, 1995.

Prigogine, Ilya, and Isabelle Stengers. *The End of Certainty.* New York: Simon and Schuster, 1997.

Pritchard, Elizabeth A. "Bilderverbot Meets Body in Theodor W. Adorno's Inverse Theology." *Harvard Theological Review* 95, no. 3 (2002): 291–318.

Raines, John. *Marx on Religion.* Philadelphia: Temple University Press, 2011.

Rebentisch, Juliane, and Felix Trautman. "The Idea of the Culture Industry." In *A Companion to Adorno,* edited by Peter Gordon, Espen Hammer, and Max Pensky, 19–32. London: Blackwell, 2020.

Reitz, Charles. *Art, Alienation, and the Humanities: A Critical Engagement with Herbert Marcuse.* Buffalo: State University of New York Press, 2000.

Rensmann, Lars. *The Politics of Unreason: The Frankfurt School and the Origins of Modern Antisemitism.* Buffalo: SUNY Press, 2017.

Roberto, Michael. *The Coming of the American Behemoth: The Origins of Fascism in the United States, 1920–1940.* New York: Monthly Review Press, 2018.

Roberts, David. *Art and Enlightenment: Aesthetic Theory after Adorno.* Lincoln: University of Nebraska Press, 2006.

Robinson, Cedric J. *An Anthropology of Marxism.* Chapel Hill: UNC Press, 2019.

———. *Black Marxism, Revised and Updated Third Edition: The Making of the Black Radical Tradition.* Chapel Hill: UNC Press, 2020.

Rosen, Michael. *Hegel's Dialectic and Its Criticism.* Cambridge: Cambridge University Press, 1984.

Ross, Nathan. *The Aesthetic Ground of Critical Theory: New Readings of Benjamin and Adorno.* Lanham: Rowman & Littlefield, 2015.

Rousseau, Jean-Jacques. "Discourse on the Origin of Inequality." Translated by Donald A. Cress. In *Basic Political Writings,* edited by Donald A. Cress, 25–81. Indianapolis: Hackett, 1987.

Schimmel, Noam. "Judaism and the Origins of Erich Fromm's Humanistic Psychology: The Religious Reverence of a Heretic." *Journal of Humanistic Psychology* 49, no. 1 (2009): 9–45.

Schlipphacke, Heidi. "A Hidden Agenda: Gender in Selected Writings by Theodor Adorno and Max Horkheimer." *Orbis Litterarum* 56, no. 4 (2001): 294–313.

Schmidt, James. "Language, Mythology, and Enlightenment: Historical Notes on Horkheimer and Adorno's 'Dialectic of Enlightenment.'" *Social Research* (1998): 807–38.

———. "Mephistopheles in Hollywood: Adorno, Mann, and Schoenberg." In *Cambridge Companion to Adorno,* edited by Tom Huhn, 148–81. Cambridge: Cambridge University Press, 2004.

Schoenberg, Arnold. *Composition with Twelve Tones*. Translated by Dika Newlin. Style and Idea: Selected Writings of Arnold Schoenberg. Edited by Leonard Stein. London: Faber & Faber, 1975.

Scholem, Gershom. *Jewish Gnosticism, Merkabah Mysticism, and Talmudic Tradition*. New York: Jewish Theological Seminary of America, 1960.

———. *Major Trends in Jewish Mysticism*. New York: Schocken, 1995.

———. *The Messianic Idea in Judaism: And Other Essays on Jewish Spirituality*. New York: Schocken, 2011.

———. "The Messianic Idea in Kabbalism." In *The Messianic Idea in Judaism: And Other Essays on Jewish Spirituality*, 37–49. New York: Schocken, 2011.

———. *On the Kabbalah and Its Symbolism*. Translated by Ralph Manheim. New York: Schoken, 1965.

———. *Origins of the Kabbalah*. Princeton: Princeton University Press, 2019.

———. "Redemption through Sin." In *The Messianic Idea in Judaism: And Other Essays on Jewish Spirituality*, 78–132. New York: Schocken, 2011.

———. *Sabbatai Ṣevi: The Mystical Messiah, 1626–1676*. Vol. 208. Princeton: Princeton University Press, 2016.

———. "Toward an Understanding of the Messianic Idea in Judaism." In *The Messianic Idea in Judaism: And Other Essays on Jewish Spirituality*, 1–37. New York: Schocken, 2011.

———. *Walter Benjamin: The Story of a Friendship*. New York: New York Review of Books, 2003.

Schopenhauer, Arthur. *Arthur Schopenhauer: The World as Will and Presentation*. Translated by E.F.J. Payne. 2 vols. New York: Dover, 1969.

Sekyi-Otu, Ato. *Left Universalism, Africacentric Essays*. London: Routledge, 2018.

Sellars, Wilfrid. "Truth and 'Correspondence.'" *The Journal of Philosophy* 59, no. 2 (1962): 29–56.

Shaw, Tamsin. "The Psychologists Take Power." *The New York Review of Books*, 2016.

Shuster, Martin. "Adorno and Negative Theology." *Graduate Faculty Philosophy Journal* 37, no. 1 (2016): 97–130.

———. *Autonomy after Auschwitz: Adorno, German Idealism, and Modernity*. Chicago: University of Chicago Press, 2014.

———. "The Critique of the Enlightenment." In *A Companion to Adorno*, edited by Peter Gordon, Espen Hammer, and Max Pensky, 251–69. London: Blackwell, 2020.

———. "La Monetización Del Masoquismo." *Constelaciones. Revista de Teoría Crítica*, no. 14 (2022): 420–25.

———. "The Monetization of Masochism." *The Philosophical Salon* (2021). Published electronically October 11, 2021.

Siebert, Rudolf J. *The Critical Theory of Religion. The Frankfurt School: From Universal Pragmatic to Political Theology*. Berlin: Walter de Gruyter, 1985.

————. "Fromm's Theory of Religion." *Telos* 1977, no. 34 (1977): 111–20.

Singh, Surti. "The Aesthetic Experience of Shudder: Adorno and the Kantian Sublime." In *The Aesthetic Ground of Critical Theory: New Readings in Benjamin and Adorno*, edited by Nathan Ross, 129–45. Lanham: Rowman & Littlefield, 2015.

Skees, Murray W. "Kant, Adorno and the Work of Art." *Philosophy & Social Criticism* 37, no. 8 (2011): 915–33.

Smith, Adam. *The Wealth of Nations*. New York: Bantam Books, 2003.

Smulewicz-Zucker, Gregory R., ed. *Confronting Reification: Revitalizing Georg Lukács's Thought in Late Capitalism*. Chicago: Haymarket, 2020.

Solzhenitsyn, Aleksandr I. *The Gulag Archipelago: An Experiment in Literary Investigation*. Translated by Thomas P. Whitney. New York: Westview Press, 1973.

Stauffer, Jill. "Law and Oral History: Hearing the Claims of Indigenous Peoples." In *Logics of Genocide: The Structures of Violence and the Contemporary World*, edited by Anne O'Byrne and Martin Shuster, 208–25. London: Routledge, 2020.

Thiem, Yannik. "Beyond Bad Conscience: Marcuse and Affects of Religion after Secularism." *Telos* 2013, no. 165 (2013): 23–48.

Thompson, Michael J. *The Domestication of Critical Theory*. London: Rowman & Littlefield, 2016.

Thoreau, Henry D. *Walden*. Princeton: Princeton University Press, 1971.

Tocqueville, Alexis. *Democracy in America: And Two Essays on America*. Translated by Gerald Bevin. London: Penguin, 2003.

Truskolaski, Sebastian. *Adorno and the Ban on Images*. London: Bloomsbury, 2022.

Veidlinger, Jeffrey. *In the Midst of Civilized Europe: The 1918–1921 Pogroms in Ukraine and the Onset of the Holocaust*. New York: Metropolitan Books, 2022.

Voltaire. *Candide, or Optimism*. London: Penguin, 2013.

Ward, Eric. "Skin in the Game." *Political Research Associates*, June 29 (2017).

Weber, Max. *Charisma and Disenchantment: The Vocation Lectures*. New York: New York Review of Books, 2020.

————. "Politics as Vocation." Translated by H.H. Gerth and C. Wright Mills. In *From Max Weber: Essays in Sociology*, edited by H.H. Gerth and C. Wright Mills, 77–129. London: Routledge, 1948.

————. *The Protestant Ethic and the Spirit of Capitalism: And Other Writings*. Translated by Peter Baehr and Gordon C. Wells. New York: Penguin, 2002.

————. "Science as Vocation." Translated by H.H. Gerth and C. Wright Mills. In *From Max Weber: Essays in Sociology*, edited by H.H. Gerth and C. Wright Mills, 129–59. London: Routledge, 1948.

Westerman, Richard. "Lukács in the 1920s and the 2020s: The Practice and Praxis of Intellectual History." *Thesis Eleven* 157, no. 1 (2020): 24–40.

————. *Lukács's Phenomenology of Capitalism: Reification Revalued*. London: Palgrave-Macmillan, 2018.

————. "The Reification of Consciousness: Husserl's Phenomenology in Lukács's Identical Subject-Object." *New German Critique* 37, no. 3 (2010): 97–130.

Wheatland, Thomas. *The Frankfurt School in Exile*. Wheatland: University of Minnesota Press, 2009.

White, Hayden. *Metahistory: The Historical Imagination in Nineteenth-Century Europe*. Baltimore: Johns Hopkins University Press, 2014.

Whitebook, Joel. *Perversion and Utopia: A Study in Psychoanalysis and Critical Theory*. Cambridge: MIT Press, 1996.

Whitman, James Q. *Hitler's American Model: The United States and the Making of Nazi Race Law*. Princeton: Princeton University Press, 2017.

Wiggershaus, Rolf. *The Frankfurt School: Its History, Theories, and Political Significance*. Translated by Michael Robertson. Cambridge: MIT Press, 1994.

Wiggins, David. "A Sensible Subjectivism?" In *Foundations of Ethics: An Anthology*, edited by Russ Shafer-Landau and Terence Cuneo, 145–57. Oxford: Wiley-Blackwell, 2007.

Williams, Robert R. *Recognition: Fichte and Hegel on the Other*. Buffalo: State University of New York Press, 1992.

Wolff, Ernst. "From Phenomenology to Critical Theory: The Genesis of Adorno's Critical Theory from His Reading of Husserl." *Philosophy & Social Criticism* 32, no. 5 (2006): 555–72.

Wolff, Robert Paul, Barrington Moore, and Herbert Marcuse. *A Critique of Pure Tolerance*. Boston: Beacon Press, 1969.

Worrell, Mark. *Dialectic of Solidarity: Labor, Antisemitism, and the Frankfurt School*. Leiden: Brill, 2008.

Yates, Melissa. "Rawls and Habermas on Religion in the Public Sphere." *Philosophy & Social Criticism* 33, no. 7 (2007): 880–91.

Zahavi, Dan. *Husserl's Phenomenology*. Palo Alto: Stanford University Press, 2003.

Zammito, John H. *The Genesis of Kant's Critique of Judgment*. Chicago: University of Chicago Press, 1992.

Zuboff, Shoshana. *The Age of Surveillance Capitalism*. New York: Profile Books, 2018.

Zuckert, Rachel. *Kant on Beauty and Biology: An Interpretation of the "Critique of Judgment."* Cambridge: Cambridge University Press, 2007.

Zuidervaart, Lambert. *Adorno's Aesthetic Theory: The Redemption of Illusion*. Cambridge: MIT Press, 1993.

————. "The Social Significance of Autonomous Art: Adorno and Bürger." *Journal of Aesthetics and Art Criticism* (1990): 61–77.

INDEX